Capitalism

The Age of Unmasked Gods and Naked Kings

Abdullah Öcalan

Capitalism

The Age of Unmasked Gods and Naked Kings

Manifesto for a Democratic Civilization

Volume II

International Initiative Edition

new-compass.net

Capitalism: The Age of Unmasked Gods and Naked Kings
Manifesto for a Democratic Civilization: Volume II
2017 © International Initiative Edition

ISBN 978-82-93064-46-6
ISBN 978-82-93064-47-3 (ebook)
ISBN 978-82-93064-48-0 (hardcover)

Original title: *Kapitalist Uygarlık: Maskesiz Tanrılar ve Çıplak Krallar Çağı*
Demokratik Uygarlık Manifestosu, İkinci Kitap
Published in 2009 by Mezopotamien
Translation: Havin Guneser
Edited by: Riekie Harm and Arjen Harm

Published by New Compass Press
Grenmarsvegen 12
N–3912 Porsgrunn
Norway
new-compass.net

And:
International Initiative Edition
"Freedom for Abdullah Öcalan—Peace in Kurdistan"
P.O.Box 100 511
D-50445 Cologne
Germany
freedom-for-ocalan.com
info@freedom-for-ocalan.com

Design and layout by Eirik Eiglad
Cover Artwork: Shireen R. Moustafa, "Unnamed," detail.

Note: The juridical team of the Asrın Law Office compiled a
list of the books sent to Abdullah Öcalan during his captivity.
A complete list of books available to Öcalan can be found at
www.ocalan-books.com.

Contents

Volume II

Publications by Abdullah Öcalan in English

Manifesto for a Democratic Civilization
II: *Capitalism: The Age of Unmasked Gods and Naked Kings* (New Compass, 2017)
I: *Civilization: The Age of Masked Gods and Disguised Kings* (New Compass, 2015)

Prison Writings:
III: *The Road Map to Negotiations* (Mesopotamien, 2011)
II: *The PKK and the Kurdish Question in the 21st Century* (Pluto Press and Transmedia, 2011)
I: *The Roots of Civilisation* (Pluto Press, 2007)

The Political Thought of Abdullah Öcalan (Pluto Press, 2017)
Declaration on the Democratic Solution of the Kurdish Question (Mesopotamien, 1999)

Pamphlets:
Democratic Nation (2016)
Liberating Life: Woman's Revolution (2013)
Democratic Confederalism (2011)
War and Peace in Kurdistan (2008)
The Third Domain: Reconstructing Liberation (2003)

All of Abdullah Öcalan's English-language books are published with the cooperation of International Initiative Edition. Further information about Öcalan's books can be found at www.ocalan-books.com.

Editorial Note

By International Initiative

The extraordinary conditions under which this book was written must be understood well. The author of the book was abducted from Kenya in a NATO operation and handed over to the Turkish state. Since his capture in 1999, Abdullah Öcalan has been kept under solitary confinement on İmralı Island prison, a military zone guarded by more than a thousand soldiers.

For more than 10 years, Öcalan was the only prisoner on the island. After 2009, other political prisoners have been brought to the İmralı prison, but this has not changed the regime of solitary confinement, a regime that keeps getting worse. During Öcalan's incarceration, there has been an attempt to poison him, and he has been subjected to ill-treatment by prison personnel. The author does not have the means to communicate with the outside world, let alone the proper conditions to write a book. On the contrary: before 2009, he was often given cell-confinement penalties, which meant that his books, pen and paper would be taken away from him for long periods of time.

What you now hold in your hands is therefore not an ordinary book. Rather, it is part of Abdullah Öcalan's hand-written submissions to the European Court of Human Rights. His latest set of submissions, called *The Manifesto for a Democratic Civilization*, was written between 2008 and 2011, and the original Turkish edition of this volume was first published in July 2009. On several occasions, Öcalan insists that these defenses to the Court are not strictly related to the violations against his person or, in fact, not even limited to the Kurdish question: they address humanity at large, in defense of peoples, nature, and women.

We have tried to preserve the author's style and use of language while at the same time making it a text that is easy to follow. Above all, however, we have tried to convey the meaning the author wishes to communicate. The original manuscript was hand-written in one go, and the author did not have a chance to re-read or edit the computer-written text. In presenting this volume to an English-speaking audience, we also want to draw attention to some additions we have made to this edition. The author did not use footnotes; they have all been added by the translator and the editors. Occasionally, bracketed remarks have been turned into footnotes, and are marked by the author's initials [A.Ö.]. An index of names, places and certain terms has also been included at the end of the book. We must thank the editors, Riekie Harm and Arjen Harm; without their hard work, this edition would not have been possible.

The author has often stated his intense desire for discussing his writings with thinkers and activists from all over the world. Unfortunately, this is next to impossible. There is still no way of contacting Öcalan, and since July 2011, his right to defense has been completely ignored: although there are ongoing cases at several courts, he has not even had a single consultation with his lawyers. Still, despite the ever-worsening situation in Turkey, we continue the campaign for Öcalan's freedom—not the least to make these discussions possible.

International Initiative
"Freedom for Abdullah Öcalan—Peace in Kurdistan"
Cologne, November 2016

Preface

By Radha D'Souza

As I write this preface, I cannot help feeling how much more exciting my engagement with Öcalan's text will be if I could sit face to face with him and discuss, over cups of *chai* as is common in the Eastern social settings, the issues he raises in this volume. Hopefully Öcalan will be released from prison and it will be possible to hear him speak to the text directly. Öcalan wrote this text as a "defense statement" in a submission to the European Court of Human Rights in 2008. That a court appearance was the only opportunity that Öcalan could avail of to communicate his thoughts to the wider world is testimony to the state of affairs in the world we live in, a world where "democracy" imprisons freedoms, where the thoughts of one man become a "security threat" to states with stockpiles of the most lethal weapons the world has ever produced. Yet, in a strange way, amidst dystopic visions and cognitive dissonance that envelops us today, it is reassuring that the age-old adage, "the pen is mightier than the sword" still rings true.

I cannot read Öcalan's text in any other way except as a South Asian woman. The text is permeated with words, concepts, historical references, events, modes of reasoning, allegories, analogies and much else that connect to the wellsprings of shared intercultural meanings. The Middle East sits in the middle of the Occident and the Orient geographically and culturally. South Asia and the Middle East have close historical, cultural, intellectual and political ties with the Middle East that go back to the first river valley civilizations on the Euphrates and Tigris (Mesopotamia), the Nile (Egypt) and the Indus (India). Nothing demonstrates the closeness of our civilizations better than the Urdu language. Born from communications between Arabs, Persians, Turks and Indians, Urdu is the embodiment of the coming together of Middle Eastern, Persian and Indian civilizations. Before European colonization of our lands, our people, and our minds, the great philosophical and political debates and cultural exchanges of the time occurred between Middle Eastern, Persian and South Asian intellectuals. The confluence of Greek and Indian thought on the banks of the Tigris under the Abbasid caliphate in 8-9 centuries CE resulted in the flowering of philosophy and poetry, science and music in the centers of Baghdad, Kufa and Sinjar. Today, these sites are engulfed by destruction and unsurpassed human tragedy. The emotive meanings of those place names handed down to South Asian children through stories and folk-tales, the antics of Nasruddin Hodja for example, or Rumi's story of the parrot and the merchant on a trip to Hindustan, infuse subconscious elements into our understandings of contemporary geopolitical events in the region. For many young Europeans and North Americans Kufa and Sinjar may be just place names that they hear from sound bites on TV news channels, but these place names have historical resonances in South Asia. As I read the text, I wondered whether Euro-American and Middle Eastern-Asian readers today will take away very different things from the text.

The intellectual exchanges that enriched our pasts in the Middle East and in South Asia are consigned to the dustbins of history remembered, if at all, by exclusive circles of academic experts hidden in the concrete basements of distant universities. Öcalan must write, and so must I, about our histories and cultures, our pain and our suffering as nations and peoples through the conceptual vocabularies of Bookchin and Braudel, Foucault and Hegel, Marx and Weber, even to speak to people of the Middle East or South Asia. Who would understand it if I referred to Shah Walliullah's (1703-1762) work on rise and decline of Empires and his theories of state? Yet many educated Indian, Turkish and Middle Eastern people will know Shah Walliullah's European contemporaries Montesquieu or Vico or Gibbon, who also wrote about rise and decline of empires and the state. How many Middle Eastern people know about Indian freedom struggles or vice versa, yet even school children in both regions will know about the French, Russian and American revolutions? Those who control our minds rule over us. Those who rule over us control what we know, how we know, and how much we know. Öcalan's concern in this text is the "mentality" that enslaves us, willingly even, to the destructive power of capitalism. This "mentality" makes us complicit in the destruction of society. His concern is to find ways to re-establish "the mental structures" that are needed to bring social life to the center-stage of our deliberations.

Öcalan begins this volume by interrogating the "self," a tradition that has deep roots in the East. He locates himself in the longue durée of Middle Eastern history and its tryst with capitalism. Öcalan ends this book with his attempts to "overcome the subject-object dichotomy without denying it," a non-dualist approach with deep roots in Eastern intellectual traditions. The thread that runs through the book is the antagonistic relations between states and communities but it ends with a call to put "the World Democratic Confederacy, and regional democratic confederacies for Asia, Africa, Europe and Australia" on the agenda for political change. These ideas resonate with Ubaiydullah Sindhi's call for a confederation of Indian, Asian, and world nations written in the context of the Indian freedom struggle in 1922. In between, in four short chapters, Öcalan condenses histories of human civilizations from primitive communitarian stateless societies to Sumerian, Babylonian, Egyptian, Indian, Chinese, Phoenician, Median, Persian, Greek, Roman, Islamic, Christian and modern civilizations. What is common to these civilizations as opposed to the primitive communitarian societies is the rise of the state as a repressive apparatus that centralizes power and appropriates wealth. Öcalan sees the institution of the state as the millstone around people that is grinding down their capacities to live as human beings.

States have always oppressed people but the capitalist state is the most advanced in techniques of repression. The capitalist state destroys the very conditions needed for the existence of society. Science and technology has aided and abetted the extraordinary concentration of power over the lives of people and the destiny of humanity. People have always rebelled against state oppression. In the histories of their rebellions lies the secrets of constructive knowledge to re-build society and the possibilities of different modes of being in the world. Therefore "resistance, rebellion and constructing the new must become our way of life," a lesson that the poet-saints of the East, wrongly labelled "mystics" by the West, have repeated over and over again for centuries. There is no point in seeking power when we know it corrupts, or capture state power when we know it has always become oppressive. Yet we have a duty to struggle when the powers that be destroy the conditions necessary for life. Rebellion should accompany the equally important duty to re-build the conditions of life. Rebuilding the conditions for human life is possible only in communitarian social orders. Öcalan's concern is that denial of social life, "has rendered life meaningless and has led to the degeneration and decomposition of the society." Öcalan juxtaposes two parallel social orders which have always co-existed which he calls *state civilization* versus *democratic civilization*. It is possible for the two civilizations to coexist if they recognize and respect each other's identities. As a South Asian reading the text, Öcalan's engagement with power is infused with an approach that resonates with Sufi, Bhakti, Sikh and Buddhist traditions. I am reminded of a verse by Hazrat Nizamuddin Aulia (d. 1325 AD):

You are not my fellow traveler.
Tread your own path
May you be affluent.
And I downtrodden.

Öcalan, echoing Eastern poet-saint traditions, writes "military victories cannot bring freedom; they bring slavery." Rejection of worldly power and wealth calls for a different type of power (resilience) and wealth (human bonds) to realize the universal meanings of Life and human destiny. The source of this later type of power and wealth can only be found in human communities. Capitalism pollutes the wellsprings of the latter type of power and wealth that has sustained the resilience of communities throughout history.

For Marx, the point of departure for inquiries into capitalism was the emergence of commodity production as the general mode of social production. Commodity production spearheaded by European merchants and elites displaced rural populations, created an urban working class mired in poverty and the squalor of urbanization, state repression of the poor, and the disintegration of social order. A political exile from the Prussian state, Marx's inquiry turns to European social history for answers. From European history, Marx drew the conclusion that classes and class-struggle was the primary driver of history and that the state is, as Marx described it, "the executive committee of the bourgeoisie." For Öcalan, the point of departure is the displacement and disintegration of cohesive historically constituted communities, in particular rural communities, dispersed from their homelands, their identity, culture and history by empires of West and East. Öcalan too turns to history for answers, but for him that history is the larger history of empires, colonialism and imperialism. The history of the institution of the state is deeply entwined with the rise of empires. Communities preexisted states, indeed their labor and natural endowments have sustained states and empires in different civilizations.

Öcalan's starting point is what latter-day Marxists problematized as the "national question," a question that arose after Marx's lifetime in the course of the Russian revolution. Confronted with external aggression by the Great Powers (Great Britain, France, Austria), and internal rebellions in the Russian colonies, Russian revolution's solutions to the colonial question was very different from the Ottoman Empire's which was also confronted with external aggression by Great Britain, France and Italy, and rebellions in the Ottoman colonies. The revolutionary Russian state offered its colonies a "new deal," that is to say, a repudiation of unequal treaties with Tsarist Russia and a new constitutional basis for renewed alliances of the colonies to the Russian state. In contrast, the Ottoman colonies, European and Middle Eastern, were dismembered from the Ottoman state and forcibly allied to the Great Powers. In the end both suppressed rural communities and privileged urban industrialism. The World Wars transformed the problem of colonialism into a problem of cultural identity and put the "national question" on the agenda of global politics. Throughout the post-World War II period, national oppression and conflicts have preoccupied the hyphenated nation-state. The Kurdish struggle is one of those with a history going back to World War I. These conflicts are frequently manipulated by the big powers empowered and enriched by big capital. Nationality conflicts are typically fought around claims of independent statehood. Öcalan takes a new approach to the old "national question." Contemporary history shows, he argues, that competing claims for statehood has only brought destruction of the very same communities in whose names the struggles are waged. His point of departure is the post-World War II era when global capitalism "reached its peak" in the "fertile plains of Mesopotamia" that is home to one of the oldest river-valley civilizations, and home to Öcalan.

In Europe, nationality and modern statehood were co-terminus and hence the hyphenated nation-state. In the colonies nationality and modern statehood were never co-terminus. Instead, they were shaped by colonial wars and interimperialist rivalries. Modern political ideologies, including liberalism, Marxism, socialism and anarchism, tend to conflate nationality with essentialist ethnocentrism or religious fundamentalism on the one hand and with statehood on the other. Communities and society as the point of departure for understanding capitalism puts Öcalan on a different track of enquiry. For Öcalan, the driver of history is the conflict between a repressive state which concentrates political and economic power and the struggles of communities to survive. This formulation takes the "national question" out of essentialist versus statist formulations and puts it on renewed historical footing. The conflict between communities and states is common to all civilizations. History cannot be reduced to class and class-struggles which is but one aspect of the struggle between state and communities. The genesis of capitalist exploitation and state power have deep roots in all human civilizations. Where there is a state, there are merchant financiers and property owners who keep the political class in power. In the East, the power of merchants and financiers were never legitimized. "Throughout the history of civilization, and especially in the Middle East, these usurers and profiteers have always existed at the margins of society. [...] Not even the most despotic administrators dared to legitimize them." While it is important to recover lost cultural and philosophical resources from the intellectual histories of the Middle East, it is important to recognize that Orientalism has distorted those traditions and there is no going back to a non-existent pristine past. The struggle of diverse communities to survive has reached a crisis point in contemporary capitalism which destroys the very fabric of sociality. The conflict between powerful states and resilient communities—that shapes and drives all other conflicts—has acquired a renewed urgency at present.

If I were to assume that liberalism, socialism, Marxism, and anarchism are the only possible political theories and that Greco-Roman philosophical schools are the only schools of philosophy that we have as sources for our conceptual repertoire, then, undoubtedly, I would conclude from the above that Öcalan opposes liberalism, the ideology of capitalism, and comes close to a synthesis of Marxism and anarchism, the two consistently anti-liberal political ideologies to challenge capitalism and modernity. Öcalan does not permit *me,* the South Asian woman, such a rough and ready conclusion. For he writes quite explicitly in his critique of Western philosophy that "Eastern thought seems to have grasped this reality" [the unity of body and mind] expressing it in the saying "all can be found in the human being." The way Indians greet each other by saying "namaste" expresses in everyday life the reality that Öcalan alludes to. For, namaste— from the Sanskrit root words "namaha" and "as té" means "I salute (namaha) that (as té)," or more simply, "I salute that universe that is embodied in you." By saluting each other we acknowledge the universe that exists within each one of us. These are deeply philosophical concepts that permeates our cultural vocabularies.

Besides, how can I skip Öcalan's references to the martyrdom of Husayn ibn Ali and Mansur Al-Hallaj? How can I brush aside the profound influence of thinkers like Shahab al-Din Suhrawardi on South Asian thought? These references to Eastern philosophy, history and metaphors means it is necessary to grasp the philosophical orientation that informs the text in order to appreciate Öcalan's political conclusions. In the sections that follow I attempt, very briefly, to throw light on two concepts that inform Öcalan's analysis of modernity, state, and community. One is philosophical dualism/non-dualism and the other is the interrelated concepts of nation and state. The two concepts, one in philosophy and the other in political theory, I wish to argue, are understood and addressed in markedly different ways in Western and Eastern intellectual traditions, used here in the broadest possible sense. I hope that making these latent ideas explicit will assist readers to appreciate Öcalan's arguments. This is a text about philosophical musings. As Öcalan writes, "without philosophy, history cannot be written."

Marx traces the emergence of all sorts of dualisms and binaries in analysis of society to the emergence of capitalism. In *Grundrisse,* Marx argues that in pre-capitalist societies communities were founded on the organic unity of nature and people. Capitalism forcibly tore apart organic communities by severing the ties of people to land and nature. Commodification transformed people's relations with nature into private property relations, and relations between people into labor (class) relations. The forcible vivisection of nature from people by commodity production, argues Marx" introduces all sorts of dualisms in society such as the dualism between nature/culture, capital/labor, state/citizen, public/ private, economy/politics, public law/contract law, economics/ethics, and so forth. Öcalan's starting point is the "scientific method," which is founded on the subject/object dualism. The subject/object, the body/ mind, material/spiritual, mind/matter dualisms have deeper roots, long before the rise of capitalism in Greco-Roman philosophical traditions. Indeed, the categories and concepts in Greco-Roman intellectual traditions provided the conceptual repertoire for capitalism, and the legal and ideological resources for positivist science.

If we turn to philosophy instead of sociology or political economy, it is possible to see that the dominant mode of reasoning in Western philosophy is dualism. As early as Thales of Miletus (d. 547 BCE)" we begin to see mind/matter dualism. The British philosopher Roy Bhaskar argued that one can go as far back as Plato and we will find that certain problems in philosophy keep returning again and again in the West. Dualisms are sustained by antagonisms (thesis versus antithesis), which in turn produces more antagonisms. An endless cycle of thesis-antithesis conflicts follows as each synthesis generates a new conflictual thesis and antithesis. In this mode of dualist thinking, conflicts are perpetual and endless, indeed conflicts are the drivers of life itself. Philosophy of science straddles the dualisms, but does not help to transcend them. Öcalan's critique of scientific method is that it is founded on philosophical dualism. He writes, "the distinction between subject and object has roots that can be taken back all the way to Plato. Plato's famous theory of the duality of Forms (ideas) and their simple observable reflections is the basis of all subsequently postulated dualisms." Philosophical dualism focuses on identifying difference, oppositions, confrontations and acts as the source of conflicts. Western philosophy and positivist science argue that struggles and conflicts are necessary for motion, movement, evolution, progress and history. In this tradition, facts, empirical phenomenon and the material world have primacy over ontology or cosmology. Positivist science, Öcalan writes, founded on "the subject-object dichotomy is nothing but the legitimization of slavery."

In the Eastern intellectual traditions, by contrast, the dominant mode of reasoning is non-dualism. Concepts of unity in diversity, unity in duality, and the oneness of life-forms, led Eastern philosophers to uncover the underlying unity that holds apparently opposing phenomena together. Conflicts and struggles are not to be denied, but the underlying unity of the world should also be acknowledged. Is it not a miracle that in spite of all our differences, conflicts, antagonisms, the world has continued for as long as it has? That the universe "acts in unity"? And, that for all capitalism's "scientific" efforts over five hundred years, we are unable to say we have "conquered" nature? If anything, we are only now finding out that nature "fights back" to reclaim itself, and more and more we are seeing that nature "fights back" with ecological vengeance. Eastern philosophers asked questions about the continuities in life, the miracle of cosmological unity that sustains so much diversity and difference. Human beings are unique because they have instincts, intelligence, and intuition to grasp empirical, rational, and ontological realities. The questions for philosophy in the East were about the eternal nature of Life with a capital "L," that continues in spite of the regularity of death and destruction; the cohesion of society and history persists despite the diversity, difference and discord in social life. As Öcalan writes, "it seems that the sole purpose of life is to find the mystery of the universe in the resolution of this dual antagonism, life and death."

Eastern philosophers sought answers for their questions in ontology and cosmology. They treated perception and empirical phenomenon as secondary to ontological truths about Life which were, in their view eternal truths. These philosophical ideas gave rise to "non-dualist" science, a science that recognized the contingency of human life on nature, the contingency of individual life on communitarian collective lives, and the inner lives of individuals, call it whatever: aesthetic, ethical, emotional, psychological, or spiritual. These ontological truths meant Eastern science saw the role of science not as an endless frontier open to human conquest but as an endowment, a gift from nature, God, or whatever, which may be used to sustain life, which may be enriched, but it must always be held in trust for future generations. Individual lives were transient, whereas Life was eternal. Individuals were trustees of nature's endowment and science must take account of the place of human beings in the universe when they investigate nature. As an endowment, nature's gift cannot be appropriated and owned as private property. The opening lines of the Rig Veda, "life lives on life" for example sets up a deep ecological principle: that is to say, if we want Life to continue, we must make sure we conserve it. Jainism since 7 BCE has advocated the methodology of "anekantavada" or the philosophy of many-sidedness. Anekantavada invites us to move away from dualist arguments like "A is right and B is wrong" or the reverse and ask instead: "if A is right and B is also right what is the nature of reality that makes A see what A sees and B see what B sees." Mind and matter, economic and political, material and spiritual lives are not antithetical relations in Eastern intellectual traditions. Earning a living is necessary condition for life, but at the same time earning an honest living requires deep spiritual commitment, just as spiritual life requires fulfilling biological needs (food, clothing shelter and such).

20

Non-dualist thought produced a very different type of political philosophy. Politics is ethical action. When discord, disunity and divisions occur, when states and kings become tyrannical, when reproduction of the conditions for human life become impossible, then, human beings must rebel, indeed it is their duty to rebel. The purpose of rebellion is to restore society and regenerate the conditions needed for human life to continue. The Sufi pirs, the bhakti saints, the sikh gurus, insisted on the unity of "this worldly" life constituted by communities (civil society) and states (political power) and "other worldly" life which is concerned about the human purpose, human destiny, human conditions and humanity's place in the universe. Politics as ethical actions must bring the two dimensions of life and Life, the empirical life and the cosmic life, together here and now in what we do and how we do it. The present is the site where the past and the future co-exist.

The East never developed a theory of "divine rights" of kings as ideological justification for power. The first principle of Islam, "there is no God but Allah," insures against despotism of kings and subjects them to a higher law. Throughout history, popular rebellions have overthrown kings and reduced mighty states and empires to dust. Nor did the East develop laws of inheritance like primogeniture that allows land to be inherited by the oldest male to the exclusion of other sons and daughters. The oldest male is undoubtedly privileged, but equally he has additional responsibilities that requires him to hold land in trust for the extended family, take responsibility of the elderly, the sick, destitute relatives, and less able members of the community. Consequently, the institution of private property never acquired the kind of historical stability and continuity that it did in European societies. Depending on how we see these histories, we could argue that power and wealth created stable states and empires and landed aristocracies in the West. The political stability came at the cost of internal cohesion of communities. The East was colonized, subjugated, and frequently appeared chaotic. But communities remained resilient amidst the political chaos. Their inner resilience continues to challenge powers of states and empires to this day.

Öcalan is worried that the spread of modernity may lead to disintegration of society that have remained resilient so far. Modernity, "by denying the social life, has rendered life meaningless and has led to the degeneration and decomposition of the society." It is therefore important to overcome Orientalist approaches to Middle Eastern culture and thought, and instead recover from it philosophical and conceptual resources necessary to address the disintegration of society and community which disorganizes the conditions necessary for human life. Seen as a whole, this text seeks to transcend dualist approaches by moving away from adversarial conceptualizations of nature versus human beings as in liberal science, or communities against states as in anarchist thought, or politics versus economics as in socialist thought, and seeks to synthesize different approaches to modernity by adopting non-dualist approaches to diverse oppositional ideologies. These philosophical differences need to be borne in mind to avoid confusions in the readers" minds about Öcalan's evaluations with reservations and qualifications of different modernist solutions offered by Western political theories to the problems of modernity.

Öcalan is satirical when he writes, "I am thankful for Hegel's insightful description of state as *God descending to earth* and Napoleon as *God's march on earth.* [...] I read the Hegelian philosophy and saw how the new god came down to earth as the nation-state and began its walk in the shape of Napoleon." Critique of the nation-state is a central thread in the text. Unfortunately, I must rely on a translation of the text, an English translation at that, because of my ignorance of Turkish language. With these limitations, I would like to alert readers to two words that are central to ideas constitutive of the European nation-state. Hegel more than any other European philosopher provides the hyphen to concepts of nation and state. The word "quom" in Arabic, Turkish, Persian and Urdu is often translated as "nation" and the word "watan" is translated as "homeland." The words "quom" and "watan" do not have identical conceptual content in Middle Eastern/South Asian languages as in English.

The hyphenation of nation and state in European modernity follows a particular understanding of nation and statehood. The Oxford English dictionary defines "homeland" as "a person's or a people's native land." This dictionary also defines nation as a "large body of people united by common descent, history, culture, or language, inhabiting a particular state or territory." A state is defined as a "sovereign state of which most of the citizens or subjects are united also by factors which define a nation, such as language or common descent." And, the nation-state is a "sovereign state of which most of the citizens or subjects are united also by factors which define a nation, such as language or common descent." It is important to note that territoriality is common to all the four words in the English language. There is a historical sequencing in the definitions, with homeland being primal nativist identity with land and the nation-state as the coalescence of family, civil society, citizenship and statehood at the pinnacle of historical development. The idea of nation-state conjoins concept of historically constituted communities and historically evolved institution of the state occupying defined territories. In Europe, nations and states were coterminous and coevolved. This is not the conceptual content of the words "quom" and "watan."

In the East, territoriality and historically constituted communities are not necessarily coterminous. It is possible to have "quoms," that is to say, historically constituted communities without territory. Equally it is possible for several "quoms" to belong to the same "watan," which means that several historically constituted communities can have a shared homeland. These significant differences in the meanings are lost in transliteration. Modernity brought with it real difficulties of translating concepts of quom and watan into modern political vocabulary of the hyphenated nation-state. Depending on the nature and type of anti-colonial nationalism in different parts of the Islamic world in Arabia, Maghreb, Turkey, Persia and South Asia, the evolution of the word quom to the modern day "quomiya" translated as nationalism and "watan" to "wataniya" translated as patriotism or citizenship, evolved along very different trajectories and acquired different modern meanings in different regions. In South Asia, a diverse continent where many quoms have shared a common watan for a long period in history, the leaders of the radical anti-colonial Ghadar movement called for a radically different constitutional model for *azad Hindustan* (free India) after the end of British colonialism. Their vision of a free Hindustan consisted of establishing a confederation of quoms with a shared watan. They called for "a federation of the republics of India," where each quom of Hindustan would form a confederation and Hindustan would be home to all those who live there and made it their home. Unfortunately, the liberal, modernist meanings of nation and state prevailed and the struggles for control of nation-states and bloody partitions continue. The very fact that common words with shared meanings acquired diverse meanings under specific contexts of anti-colonial movements suggests the need for caution in the way ideas about nation, nation-state and communities are understood in English and Eastern languages. Equally, it should alert us to the way we read Öcalan's juxtaposition of community and state in the text. If we understand community as quom and state as the territorial authority, the arguments about reconciliation between state and community in the text becomes easier to grasp.

The conditions under which the text was written and smuggled out as "defense statement" in the European Court means that it would be unfair to read the text as if it were written by an erudite philosopher writing in the comfortable environment of a university. For that very reason, the value of this text lies in the fact that it comes from a person who has engaged in real struggles in the real world and continues to do so under conditions of solitary confinement for over seventeen years. It is refreshing to see philosophy return to politics.

Introduction

As I pursue my defense against the capitalist system, I know that I have to start by breaking loose from its system of mental chains.[1] If we want to free ourselves from capitalism, we must reject worshiping it like the golden calf, because, make no mistake, just as a Muslim should call out *Bismillah!* ("In the name of God") before undertaking a new venture, capitalism imposes its own sacred dictates upon us.

The first of the capitalist dictates that we must reject is its so-called "scientific method." This method is not the *ethics* and *morality of freedom* that have passed through the filter of social life and that will exist as long as human society exists. On the contrary, I am talking about a most advanced, servile attitude to life, which, precisely by denying social life, has rendered life meaningless and has led to the degeneration and decomposition of society; I am talking about the material and immaterial culture that has spawned this attitude.

My fundamental argument for attempting this break can be nothing but *myself.* Descartes was not even aware that his philosophy provided the basis for capitalism.[2] While he doubted everything, should he not have suspected himself as well? More importantly, how did he end up in such a situation? There are other examples of such stages of doubt in history: the construction of god by the Sumerian priests, the deep theistic doubts of Prophet Abraham—last of its example being Prophet Muhammad's venture—and the Ionian skepticism. At such historical stages, both the new mentality that has been entered into and the previous mentalities that need to be rejected have the characteristics that radically re-mold the society or, at the very least, provide the fundamental paradigm for this remolding. The real reason behind the doubt is the failure of the deep-rooted mentality (or ideological structure) to respond to the newly emerging lifestyle. The mental structures needed for the new life are quite difficult to develop, requiring a profound progress of one's personality. No matter what one might call such doubting—whether a prophetic action, a philosophical phase or a scientific discovery—in essence they all pursue the answer to the same need: *How will the mental structures of the new social life be established?* The terrible skepticism is characteristic of this intermediate stage. The splendid lives of Descartes, Spinoza and Erasmus bear the traces of such a historical phase in a location that became the cradle of capitalism's permanent rise in the sixteenth century, that is, the modern-day Netherlands.

My life story coincides with the beginning of the 1950's when the drive of global capitalism of the era reached its peak. On the other hand, my place of birth is the most fertile land in the upper part of Mesopotamia— the Fertile Crescent enveloped by the Taurus-Zagros mountains— the location where the remnants of the oldest and most deep-rooted mentalities can still be found, and where the Neolithic age and the initial urban civilizations existed for very long periods: These are the mountain skirts that bore the civilization.[3]

My imprisonment on İmralı Island and being condemned to live in a single person dungeon by the wardens of the capitalist system (a punishment exceeding that allotted by Zeus by binding Prometheus to a rock in the Caucasus) compelled me to come to understand the antagonism between their system and myself. I remind myself of these historical facts and analyze them over and over again in order to understand what really is afoot, so as not to stare myself blind on the role of the Republic of Turkey. If I were to fall into this trap, I would have become nothing more than the bull that keeps on attacking the red cape; the Republic of Turkey has no doubt been reduced to the bullfighter. These are the predetermined roles we are required to play continuously and efficiently. However, what is necessary is for us—*for me*—to define the true masters of this savage game—a king's game—by taking into account all relevant facts.

To prevent delusions that affect the society as a whole, we need to reconsider the example of Karl Marx. No one can doubt the seriousness with which Marx endeavored to analyze capitalism and to break its stranglehold on society. However, it is also generally accepted that the enormous movements for social change inspired by him could not overcome being capitalism's best servants.[4] In this sense, it is clear that I shall not be a mere Marxist disciple.

While trying to define my identity, I think it is worthwhile to understand my desire to start with the fundamental parameters. What are these parameters, the boundaries that have determined what I am? The transition to the Neolithic, the remnants of its mindset and customs, as well as power hierarchies and the state cults based on city-based civilization and, finally, the incomparable facts of the games of capitalism. Perhaps a sub-layer should also be mentioned: The distinct features of the human species—the risks they create and the ease they offer to living.

As I pen these lines, I am aware of the location in which I am held and how this location falls within the boundaries of legitimacy determined by capitalism. I am not about to deny that my continued existence—nor my Prometheanization—depends on these boundaries. I am continuously developing a sense of awareness of my strength and the meaning it contains.

If we are to give some known examples like Mani who was put to death by the Sassanid Empire; Husayn ibn Ali, Mansur Al-Hallaj, and Shahab al-Din Suhrawardi who were executed by the Islamic rulers; hundreds of followers of Jesus who became martyrs, and followers of the Buddha who fled the horror of the rulers; those who were burnt on the stakes of the Inquisition of the Christian Church; and those who died in the genocides of capitalism. What all these people have in common is that they persisted in being aware of life. They refused to be content with the curtain pulled between themselves and life—this was their crime.

If the life-death dilemma has been turned into a devastating deadlock, the reason is no doubt societal. Fundamentally, there is no death such as the one presented to us nor a life advertised as such. For that which is presented to us as life is not real; it is a simulation that we have come to perceive as reality; it is a mechanical imitation of life. Respect for life, even mediocre respect, demands the end of this wretched, vicious deception.

I am nearly sixty years old but I have not yet lost my childhood curiosity about life. I still wonder about the frontiers of life. I could not grow up within the boundaries of what is acceptable in the capitalist system; to me it seems inevitable that a life determined by these boundaries would be either dishonest or insignificant—or perhaps both! We must value life above all else. Our main task is to understand what life is! Indeed, to understand is to live, to live is to be able to understand. I do not believe that the cosmos could be interpreted in any other way. Although absolute meaning is nearly impossible to realize, I insist that this is the truth that drives life. Nothing can be stronger than the power of meaning: all others cannot evade being displays of pseudo-power compared with the power of meaning.

Thus, coming back to my own reality, these parameters cannot provide an answer to my interest in life. Worse, they are the essential reason for my profound skepticism. I am more than skeptical—I am disgusted. As I started writing this text the highest executive body of the Republic of Turkey and the United States of America, as the highest executive body of the capitalist system, declared the PKK "the mutual enemy of the governments of USA, Turkey and Iraq." Experience has brought me to a profound understanding of the meaning behind my being in this location and this situation!

In short, the capitalist way of life is not for me. I cannot say that I never aspired to it. But I am totally aware that I have no talent for success. I am also aware that I can never be a "husband-man," neither in the precapitalist nor later meaning attached to them. I may be ridiculous in the eyes of the system, but I regard this system as dreadfully bloody, suppressive and exploitative; life within it is nothing but a disgusting, terrible existence. Life determined by the parameters of the capitalist system constitutes the opposite of what I believe life should be.

Nevertheless, I have to defend myself. And defending myself as a human being is not only the most basic sign of life, it is also my fundamental duty towards those who have any claim to a communal life. Furthermore, if I want to take my responsibilities of citizenship seriously—even though I don't share the rulers' idea of what citizenship entails—then to be aware of our duties too is a requirement of this morality.

Thus, the problem is not whether one lives or not but to know how to live life truly. What is even more important than immediate achievement is to not give up the quest. The capitalist system has developed a betrayal unmatched in history, where actions belie words and words are used to justify actions. Hence, in servitude of the hegemonic system of capitalism, action has been reduced to a mere mechanical tool. Capitalism has been a global hegemonic system for at least the last four hundred years. Consequently, if we do not come to understand the true nature of capitalism, any attempt to establish a form of free life and the development of a program for ensuring it will be hampered by all sorts of diversion—as many historical examples illustrate. We will have to learn to look at the concepts and implementations of capitalist modernity and the implementations thereof with the attitude of a dervish, a prophet, the Buddha; if not, all our attempts to fight it will simply benefit the system. Much has been said and done to counter capitalism, but we must now admit that the majority of these attempts could not escape ending up in servitude to it.

I do not believe that capitalism, although at the phase of being a global empire, is really that powerful. In fact, I think it may be at its weakest stage: it is constantly inapt and prone to breakdown. What has not happened is the correct and competent defense of society against capitalism. Capitalist hegemony is cancerous (and I don't mean it metaphorically) but we cannot view this system as an inevitable fate. We have to realize that it is the weakest of all hegemonic systems. What is needed is to live communalism correctly and competently. Throughout history we have tried to fight the "strong man" or hegemon by using its own weapons. Replicating its perceptions and actions—similarity in method—has only bred the very image of the system we have tried to overcome. In the process of fighting Rome, many Romes were born. The original Uruk cities still continue to breed themselves in such forms as the "New Iraq." Little has changed and much has been repeated.

It is important not to exaggerate the power of the hegemony. While no society has ever readily accepted rulers, exploitation, and coercion, neither have they ever assumed that they can't live without the presence of power. We must rid ourselves of slogans such as "brand new society" and "social forms that differ from all others." Such empty concepts will not result in anything worthwhile. All societies develop as an existential form of the human species, but in a similar manner. Love that is blind leads to the worst ignorance—whether love for power or sexual love. But when love is charged with meaning it is like Nirvana or *fenafillâh* ("To vanish in God"), like being fused in truth. It is *Ana 'l-Haqq:* it is the state of a just and free society becoming sovereign, or the state of full democracy.[5]

Karl Marx's mostly positivist approach to the analysis of capitalism is incomplete and he did not even attempt an analysis of the concepts *power* and *state.* I have never found this approach deep enough. While I do understand the concept of exploitation, I have always thought of exploitation as an outcome. To take an outcome as a starting point seems an inadequate approach and, furthermore, politically it implies a state of complete defenselessness. Marx's work was done during the revolutionary period of 1848 in which, besides the seigneur's fall and transformation, he observed the bourgeoisie's walk to power quite well. His work was in the field of political economy, philosophy, and socialism. However, not only did he not grasp the phenomenon of power—which reorganizes itself and, like an octopus, wraps itself around the poor and proletarian majority of society—he could not even avert his own system from becoming its instrument. He was not aware that his own proposed theoretical and practical model has helped to maintain capitalist hegemony. The latest example—where China's practice has become the strongest pillar of the USA's hegemonic capitalism—has a lot do to with this unawareness. The strength of capitalist hegemony is due to the race in voluntary slavery it has given rise to. Today, will we find a single worker that would refuse working for wages if higher wages are offered? The situation is truly sad.

The struggle of the worker against capitalism can be likened to the relationship between a husband and wife. If the husband is able to provide his wife with the necessities for daily life, it is really difficult to convince her to struggle against her husband. If the worker is given good wages, it is really difficult to convince him to struggle against his master, the capitalist. Far from being free the worker who jumps for joy when receiving the minimum wage becomes the servant of his master's system to be used against the societal multitudes. This is especially so when the number of unemployed grows; then a worker with a steady job feels secure—more secure even than a public servant. Just as there is proletarianization of the state bureaucrats, there is bureaucratization of the proletarians. In a way, the mixture of feudal noble-bourgeoisie at the top occurs in a similar manner between the worker-public servant at the bottom.

I am quite certain that I was right not to give in to the village society. But I was wrong in believing that capitalist modernity could offer an alternative to this way of life. Earlier in my life I made the huge mistake of radically breaking with the village society; even though it had not been democratized, it was far removed from fundamental stages such as nation-state and industrialization. A source of my profound sadness sits here. My father, whom I rarely mention, not only saw the life energy in me, he also saw the bitter truth when he told me, "When I die you won't even cry." He was almost as sagely as my mother. He was a believer of the old world. He truly belonged to the world of labor and was a democrat in essence. I still wonder how the capitalist deity could hold such a wretched and deceitful attraction for me.

I think city society, which, like a magnet pulled me away from village society, is the main locus of our social problems. The city-state-classed civilization and the societal form it has caused are the main culprits of not only society's internal decay but also its detachment from nature. Even the most primitive clan society is not as ignorant about life as the city civilization. In fact, if civilized city society has, during the phase of capitalism, become a total murderer of the environment, this must be due to the systematic ignorance within its own structure.

Rationalism, which has become detached from emotional intelligence, and sexuality, which has long lost its meaning, are the fundamental indicators of the carcinogenic face of capitalism. In order to hold on to power, the system will rely on the nuclear horror; to have cheap labor it will incite a population growth that cannot be borne by our world. All this is related to the essence of the system and especially the way power is shaped. All the world wars, colonial wars and the wars for political power against the entire society, affecting it at all levels, mean nothing but the failure of the system. Liberalism and individualism are often seen as the main ideological axes of capitalism. But I claim that no other system but the ideological hegemony of capitalism has ever had the power to hold the individual prisoner.

Contentwise, it could be argued that the language I continue to use does not differ much from the legitimacy of the system, and that I too am a product of the system. But the place I find myself in is worthy of an opponent of the system. I cannot but profoundly be aware that a committed anticapitalist is on trial; in turn, the system is also tried, although of course it involves much more than simple case law. During the past four hundred years of capitalist hegemony numerous cultures have been wiped out—the area I grew up in is like a graveyard for ancient cultures. I should be considered to belong to the Kurds, who have not yet conceptualized themselves and who have witnessed all these cultures with a graveyard stillness. It hurts to see that even the graves of the cultures who gave most of the early inventions to the world now face being wiped off the face of the earth. The recent savagery in Iraq is, in a way, the revenge of the cultures.

It is essential that we defend Middle Eastern culture against the capitalist system. This, however, cannot be achieved without surpassing orientalism. Reemploying Islamism will mean falling back on the most ineffective derivative of orientalism. You may wonder what is left once we have surpassed orientalism, as well as the leftwing and the rightwing interpretations of Islamism. This is exactly what must be the starting point for my defense. If not, I shall be no more than a mere mouthpiece for the system.

From its first victory on the shores of North Western Europe and the island of Great Britain, capitalism has continued its victorious march as world-system for the past four hundred years. It has stumbled onto the Middle East's most ancient cultural centers. In fact, capitalism itself is the latest offspring of this ancient culture—although an unworthy one that denies its parentage. The conflict between the two runs much deeper than we think. (The war currently waged is really a war between amateurs—a copy of the wars between Alexander and Darius III, with G. W. Bush as Alexander and Mahmoud Ahmadinejad as Darius.) The dialectical paradox continues intensely and in multiple forms. And not only in dominant circles—the anti-power opposition of society has also extensively stepped in.

I am trying to voice forms of complete opposition to power. Being against capitalism's extraction of profit is only one of the forms. Being against this is not sufficient to qualify as a socialist. Moreover, it alone cannot constitute a promise of triumph. Failure to carry out resistance and accomplish forms of free life, both theoretically and in practice, with a conductor's mastery, will result in a fate no better than what is described in the "Curse of Akkad" and the "Nippur Lament."

My comrades and friends see what I have been through as a grave tragedy. But let them all rest assured that if not for this tragedy, I would not have known free life. While all is worthless how can we look into each other's eyes! What kind of honor of life can I talk about when I am a son who could not even cry at his father's death? Don't get me wrong. At the time of his death in 1976, I had just started on my first visit to Kurdistan at the foot of Mount Ararat, spreading the ideal of a free identity. (I hear that the Kurds from that region, Serhat, still talk about those days with much reverence!) Our reality still stands as it is. It was exactly 35 years ago that I began this march—indeed, this marathon—to freedom. How shall this marathon (where each breath taken, each location visited, each individual taking part can be called a legend in its own right) end? Even if we could win multiple victories with armies as mighty as those of Alexander, it would most certainly not be the victory of freedom. Military victories cannot bring freedom; they bring slavery; they can only be valued when won in defense of self, friends, and comrades. On the contrary, I find defending myself against such victories as necessary as defending myself against power itself. If I had my own armies, I would consider defending myself against their victories as the greatest struggle.

Far from being honorable and free, life has become a misery. It has lost all meaning. We live in a world of lies, self-deception, and an ugliness that has permeated everything. The fact that I have endured being alone in a small cell for the past nine years has much to do with the outside world being far worse than the İmralı dungeon. And this will form the essence of my defense: although it will be based on exposing civilization in general, the exposing of capitalist hegemony will be conducted in much more depth. There are many indications that signal the end of the system as well as many true sagas that agree with this—but the real problem lies in deciding which sound, free, equal, and democratic values should be communalized out of this chaos.

When we consider that even the capitalist system is trying to rescue itself from itself, it becomes evident how careful we must be in building communality. If socialism, which has a history of two hundred years, has been assimilated by capitalism, then we need to be very careful not to end up with the same fate. Moreover, we cannot regard Socrates, Buddha, and Zoroaster as silent and having uttered their last words. If we understand anything of the philosophy of freedom, then we must eagerly strive to implement their ideas. On the other hand, humanity is in pain. If we cannot respond to this pain, if we cannot stop the depletion of nature, if we cannot reply to the love that has been betrayed, then what kind of life are we talking about?

When asked whether my defense is scientific, I have a question in reply: *What kind of scientism?* If the essence of science is to "know thyself," then contrary to widespread belief, positivism, which forms the basis of the system's official ideology, inhibits this truth. Religion and metaphysics, so severely criticized by positivism, are perhaps much closer to science than positivism. This is especially true for the humanities but also for natural sciences. In my opinion the shallowest metaphysics and religion is positivism itself. At no other time in human history was there an attempt to construct such a profound command over nature and society. This was possible only through a positivist religion and metaphysics.

If we do not achieve "knowing thyself," even the simplest of scientific efforts will inevitably result in being a dangerous dogmatic religion or philosophy. I am not referring to human-centered ideologies when I talk about "knowing thyself." I am saying that the cosmos and chaos can only be grasped through introspection and intuitions that do not exclude profound experiences. In due course, I will show that science based on the subject-object dichotomy is nothing but the legitimization of slavery. I will also show that subjectivism is at the same time equal to overestimating and belittling one's self. I will demonstrate that scientific objectivism is a horrific means of advocating capitalism and its hegemony. Our philosophy perceives life as a whole—attributing meaning to everything from the look of a horse to the singing of a bird; from being respectful to an old sage, to responding to the quest in the eyes of a shy young woman. There is a huge ignorance in the mass production of children and this is the result of an understanding of sexuality that is worse than a genocide. Thus, such a philosophy bases itself on a science that tries to expose the reasons for this in humans and in hegemonic systems as well as a science that tries to analyze the links of life's evolution.

Capitalism does not advance science, it only makes use of it. Taking advantage of science in such a way not only leads to questions about morals, it also helps to spread Hiroshimas: it ends meaningful life. Can such a life be the victory of science? I don't deny the technological inventions and scientific discoveries, but I am trying to show that positivism, the religion of scientism, is not science. Unless we rid science of the dominance of positivism, we will not succeed in breaking the domination of any ruler, let alone that of a nation-state. Positivism is the religion of paganism of our times.

After leaving my village I was infected by a skepticism like that of Descartes. I ended in a state where I found nothing to believe in or to devote myself to. This was due, on the one hand, to the tragic loss of the old culture within me and, on the other hand, my fear of never reaching capitalist modernity which was growing to gigantic proportions like a Leviathan before my eyes. I barely believed in myself but I tried to stand on my own two feet. This was no doubt a strange situation. Societies usually find a way to suppress the minds and hearts of its members. Strangely though, I could not see myself as belonging to any society. Under those conditions I lost my belief in family and village. Enrolling at university, becoming a revolutionary, and my then religiousness were all just for show—ironically enough, my teachers and companions thought I was really clever and a true believer. But I was not a thorough nihilist either: there was just nothing I understood well enough to want to do something radical about. In retrospect, I realize that this was, in fact, a beneficial period. The fact that I was not committed to any course helped me to break away and start anew in my quest for truth.

This aspect of my personality contributed to a better understanding of the hegemonic system's structural crisis. I had gained the strength to interpret history, too. All this enabled me to not be afraid of chaotic situations but to restore meaning to them and find a way out. When I finally realized that dogmatic beliefs, linear development, scientific certainty and strict laws all have their origins in the very same dominant mentality, I felt immensely at peace. When I intuitively understood the dimensions the function of nature had attained within the human being, I felt my consciousness had burst through. As I overcame my self-estrangement, the source of all fear and doubt, I developed the necessary power of perception and the ability of interpretation that give me the necessary insight and courage to face all situations engineered by humans.

The capitalist stage of city, classed, and state-based civilization is not the final phase of human reason. Furthermore, it is the exhaustion of the traditional reason that capitalism rests on and the emergence of freedom-loving reason with all its richness. In this sense, the age of capitalist modernity can be interpreted as the age of hope.

Factors that Gave Rise to Capitalism

The Thief in The House

Often capitalism is defined as an economic system, but viewing capitalism as a religion may lead to a better understanding of this system. Its first major victory was the European ethos, and although Europe has said and done much about capitalism, it has not refrained from mystifying it—as any religion mystifies its own existence. Even the Christians, socialist, and anarchists who are considered to be its opponents have contributed to this mystification. Eurocentric thought and reason is a school of thought in its own right, to which the "scientific method" has played a fundamental role. Its hegemony as a world-system began in the sixteenth century. In fact, the propagators of Eurocentric thought are more masterful in mystifying social reality than the Sumerian priests were in constructing gods.

I am not talking about a science that is cognizant of nature—including the human being. Science, as the common treasure of humanity, is so anonymous that it cannot be attributed to a single person, community, institution, or nation. If one must talk about divine sanctity at all, it may be the best to bestow the title of divine sanctity in this sense upon science. However, *scientific method* means something else in European terminology. It is the prototype, or rather the embryo, of the contemporary dictator in whichever totalitarian or authoritarian form. The term *method* means "procedure," "path," and "order." Initially, it was a positive development and contributed to the ability of perception. However, it carries the risk of acquiring the role of a mental dictatorship if adhered to for too long. Persistence with method in the name of science may lead to the most dangerous dictatorships—as was the case with the fascism that resulted from the adherence to the scientific method by the advocates of German nation-statism. The true intellectual revolution that undoubtedly *did* take place in Western Europe cannot be blamed for Eurocentrism. Besides, this revolution took all its precursors from intellectual developments outside Europe.

The sociology developed by Max Weber in his monumental work *The Protestant Ethics and the Spirit of Capitalism* played an important role in linking the development of capitalism to European rationalism. Although rationalism may have been one of the determining factors in the formation of capitalism, a reductionist explanation contributing its existence solely to rationality and laws is inadequate.

In the sociology of Karl Marx, the victory of capitalism as a system is attributed to its economic productivity: the fact that it has been more productive than any other modes of production, the development of surplus-value, and the ability to transform this into profit and capital, ensured its victory. However, this explanation does not sufficiently take into account other fundamental factors such as history, politics, ideology, law, geography, and civilization-culture. The danger of this fundamental shortcoming is that this school of thought can easily be transformed into economic reductionism. Of course, the analytical value of socio-economic explanations cannot be denied, but if their roles relative to the other fundamental factors are not sufficiently clarified, then there will always be the danger of sliding into dogmatism despite claims of being scientific. This has often been the case.

Others link capitalist development directly to power relations and its most visible judicial expression, the modern state. The roots of power hierarchy are ingrained in our past, mainly due to its role in the administration of material life. But coercion alone cannot generate material life, economy, and its extreme derivation, capitalism. It has always had the roles of organization, development, and prevention intertwined. The fact that capitalism won its victory in North Western Europe illustrates the importance of geographical factors and location. Although Amsterdam is often pinpointed as the cradle of capitalism, the role of geography is limited, as is the role of any other factor. Thus, its role should not be overemphasized but should be sufficiently taken into account so that the value of its meaning becomes more visible.

The interpretive power of explanations based on civilizational and cultural factors are indisputable. For instance, I find the thesis that capitalism coincides with the decaying stage of civilizational development very valuable. In fact, the geographic location where the main civilizational river pours into the ocean (symbolically enough the Atlantic Ocean at the shores of Amsterdam!) is also the temporal end of this system. Of course, the system has been carried over to the other side of the ocean and has successfully climbed to the peak of globalization under the leadership of the new hegemonic power, the nation-state of the USA. However, life has acquired a quality of excessive artificiality and pretentiousness. The "society of the spectacle" and consumption has become dominant. Instead of an economy that satisfies needs, it is an economy that inflames desires. In addition, power relations have seeped into all societal relations. All these factors, including the fact that ideologues of the system talk about the end of history, evidently express the present level of decay and chaos of the system.

Realities cannot be conceptually divorced from history and time. Development, evolution, and the formation of diversity and differences can only manifest themselves within history. The "final word" can only be said in relation to a specific form—no single form has the privilege of becoming *the* eternal form. In the formation of societies, concepts such as *eternity, till doomsday comes, the final prophet, permanent rules, continuous* and *eternal improvement* develop due to the dogmatization of thoughts and beliefs, as efforts to become permanent rulers and the efforts of the privileged to perpetuate their advantages. For them such concepts are essential to win confidence and maintain their interests. Now liberalism, the central ideology of capitalism, claims to be the final word. It is the same old game in modern guise.

We should not define capitalism as a way of acting and thinking which has been created at a certain time, with a certain center, and is unchanging. Intrinsically, it should be understood as the action of opportunistic individuals and groups who, when they see the potential for the development of surplus goods, have established themselves in the fissures of society; their nibbling away of the social surplus becomes systemic. They never number more than one or two percent of a society. Their strength is in their opportunism and organizational skills. Their victory relies on their controlling the goods that are in demand and fluctuating prices at the point where supply and demand intersect. If they are not suppressed by the official forces of the society but instead the official forces of the society have become indebted to them and in return the profiteers are continuously supported through rendered favors, then these groups may legitimize themselves as the new masters of that society. Throughout the history of civilization, and especially in the Middle East, these usurers and profiteers have always existed at the margins of society. In the past, society's hatred prevented them from coming out of the fissures they hid in. Not even the most despotic administrators dared to legitimize them. They were not only scorned but were seen as dangerously corruptive powers, the seed of malice. Their rise in Western Europe is unique in the history of humanity, as is the unrivaled number of wars, plunder, massacres, and exploitation that centered on this area over the last four hundred years—clearly a legacy of the hegemonic system.

But we should not forget that the fiercest counter-struggle has also been staged in this geographic area; thus, this area cannot be seen as a total loss to humanity. What I hope to do is to synthesize the gains made by humanity in the West with the ancient, positive values of the East in order to allow for a meaningful way out.

Rationalism

In the historical rise of capitalism, a leading role is given to rationalism, a branch of Western thinking that emerged concurrently with capitalism. Rational thinking is presented as a distinguishing characteristic of Western society, implying that no other society in history has been able to effectively use its reasoning powers. It is said that the West created science through use of reason; once it was clear that science was power, the system inevitably became hegemonic.

In order to define the type of reason that enables the system to sustain itself, we first need to define reason itself and, thus, the human being as a biological species with its distinguishing features. We can look at the human from two perspectives: as a biological species and as a social development. I will attempt to arrive at a clear definition by investigating both the biological and the social sides of the human being.

Mental aspects of the human as biological species

I will begin my analysis of the mental aspects of human beings as a biological species by attempting to determine the role of reason in the system of living beings in general, as well as in the micro- and macro-dimensions of the universe.

On the level of the subatomic particle, postulating a form of intelligence is inevitable if we want to explain diversity, distinction, and development. All development in the universe happens in an incredibly small area, the particle; the extremely high speed of particle and wave movement causes them to transform into one another, leading to the development of great diversity. Not only development—in terms of diversity—in the subatomic world but also in the physical and biological worlds occurs in this way. Let's be careful, we are really wandering at the boundaries of metaphysics here. And while the question of why the universe exists may sound like a metaphysical one, it is not an inappropriate one. Let us not forget that the one posing the question is a human being and thus a social entity as well as a material body. The distinction between mind and body is a heinous philosophical and religious diversion that has led to the denial of life. The universe itself does not make such a distinction. Phenomenology is the study of subjective experience and does not believe in an existence beyond that. We are what we sense, feel, and think. Metaphysics, on the other hand, is the reflection of entities on feelings and thoughts.

Moving to the level of the macrocosm, we should view the universe itself as the fundamental, categorical existences such as animate-inanimate, finite-infinite, similar-different, matter-energy, time-space, and action-reaction; in other words, the universe is an integral whole. Subatomic-macrocosmic is the fundamental, dialectical dual antagonism of the same integral whole. Time and space materialize as the unity of depth and width; that is, they become tangible or apprehensible.

If we look at how even a primitive life-form is organized, we can catch a glimpse of a marvelous element of intelligence. The earliest manifestation of this intelligence is its striving to become eternal by dividing itself at instantaneous intervals. And these primitive beings have not died out. Their resistance to annihilation has led to the development of the intelligence found in the human species. How did the potential for being alive in a single cell develop and diversify itself into the human being with its astounding intelligence? It just may be that for the animate cell it was sufficient to multiply itself, and in order to do that it started to feed and protect itself. It just may be that the subatomic particles resolve their problems of reproduction, nutrition, and protection so as not to vanish only by way of such micro-universes. In other words, there could have been reasoning behind these developments: it might have been a manifestation of universal intelligence. Let us not exclude ourselves from this universe of the microcosms—we are very much part of it. It just may be that our quest for reproduction, nutrition, and security is an expression of the combined reflection of this micro-universe. Could it be that the macro-universe has the same form of existence? It is determined to grow to the boundaries of eternity, manifesting its intelligence by pushing the limits of space and time. It is a possibility that the macro-universe too reverberates in the human intelligence.

I know that my conjecturing is becoming extreme, but you will concede that the intelligence of the human being could not just have fallen from the sky. Can we really think of intelligence in the absence of existence and evolution? How realistic is it to think that intelligence is unique to humans? Even death seems to be necessary so that life, and therefore existence, can be understood. We can assume that without death life would not have been noticed. In fact, eternal living—in the absence of change—is essentially *not* living. This is because an environment where there is no discernment is an environment where nothing happens. If that is the case, then, for life to materialize, death seems inevitable and we should not fear it so. A more appropriate way of participating in universal life would be to understand the life that is made possible by it. Just as we can't escape death, we can't escape life either. In fact, it seems that the sole purpose of life is to find the mystery of the universe in the resolution of this dual antagonism, of life and death.

Consider a scenario where we arrived at the most competent meaning of life by resolving this dual antagonism. What would we have achieved? This question seems to be simultaneously immaterial and essential. Complete knowledge of the mystery of the universe may be called the final victory of life. It would bring us to the Sacred Books' heaven, to Buddhism's Nirvana, and Sufism's state of entrancement—that is, it can be interpreted to be the sanctification and never-ending celebration of life.

Some Western intellectuals proclaim that the emergence of life was completely incidental and restricted to our planet and that when the solar system is exhausted all shall vanish in a meaningless cosmogony. This, on the other hand, is a state similar to the concept of hell. Of course, there are arguments underlying this concept, but the rationale behind this understanding of life is most barren and not very strong. We know neither the universe fully nor the competent meaning of life. It is almost as if our world is so alive and fair that it does not give way to a life that does not have a sufficient environment to be realized. But, at the same time, it offers the habitation required for each living being's potential.

Although we should not look at the history of humans coming into being in a human-centric way, viewing it as an ordinary event is disrespectful to the marvelous evolution of the universe. The worst metaphysical approach is positivism with its attempt to explain the phenomenon of the human being by separating and detaching it from the universe. When we unmask the relationship between positivism—the crudest form of materialism—and capitalism, we will not only understand the meaning of life but approach it with much more respect.

In conclusion, it seems that we have the chance to discern the universe in the most competent way through the observation of human beings as a biological species. But it is one thing to be aware of this potential and another to realize it. Eastern thought seems to have grasped this reality, expressing it in the saying "all that can be, is found in the human being."

I must reiterate that from a human-centric perspective, we will see all of the other parts of nature—animate or inanimate—as at the disposal of the human being. It is the philosophical pillar on which hierarchical, authoritarian, and totalitarian perceptions of power are built. It leads to an abstract intelligence, detached from life, and at the same time it is the result of such intelligence. Ecologic philosophies that view the human being as disastrous for nature amount to the same thing. Such thinking stems from an unproductive philosophy that has only fragile bonds with life. Anyone unappreciative of the true nature of the evolution that led to the existence of the human being either has a tenuous link to life, or is linked to systems of extreme exploitation. But, this evolution lays before us serious moral questions as well. Before we proceed, let us define the relationship between intelligence and society.

Mental aspects of the human being as social entity
Socialization activates latent intelligence

As the socialization of its intelligence potential increases, the human species' intelligence increases. Moreover, its anatomical structure necessitates socialization; the human is compelled to a degree of socialization not found in any other species. Unlike the young of other animals, the human childhood continues beyond the age of fifteen: in the absence of society, the human child would not survive. The human child is very weak at birth. All other animal offspring can survive on their own in a much shorter time. All living beings, both as species and as part of the totality of living beings, require a coexistence specific to their sort. The society specific to the human species has an existential quality which is more than just coexistence. The result is that human sociality is very complex and it needs to be understood in depth. Thus, if the human species lost its sociality, it shall either go back to an apelike existence or it shall perish. Conceptualizing society as second nature will allow a more in-depth approach.[1]

Socialization itself is the intelligence that is no longer latent as it efficiently enters a process of activation. Existence in a community not only necessitates thought; social development is indeed a sine qua non for the development of thought. The development of nutrition, reproduction, and security increases as well with increased socialization. On the other hand, nutrition, reproduction, and security, factors common to all living beings, are also indicators of intelligence and of a most stringent instinctive way of learning. If we go one step further, we can extrapolate that the development of the universe as a whole can be associated with intelligence and learning. In a way, society, as second nature, is a higher level, a reflection of the first nature.

There is the danger of aberration in the structure of thought and action that gives priority to first nature without understanding second nature, the society. If indeed the human being is the product of this second nature then, in order to understand the human being, we must give priority to understanding the nature that has formed him. Hence, I am not convinced that a science exclusively focusing on first nature can be objective nor that it can at all be independent of second nature. I feel that the aberration is located here. I believe that physics, chemistry, and even biology cannot be studied independently of second nature and human sciences.

I am aware that I am touching the borders of religious law. However, the fundamental question that needs to be clarified is whether the distinction between subject and object is in any way meaningful, especially seeing that all laws relating to first nature are expressed in the human being via second nature. How far can we separate knowing and being known? An even more critical question is whether it is not a fundamental deviation to turn knowing and being known into a subject-object dual antagonism. In my opinion, the postulation of first and second nature as being subject and object has formed the basis for all of the mistakes made by human beings and the painful social processes that we have encountered. This system of logic has imprisoned and exploited the entire society since the onset of the capitalist system. What is worse is that the system unscrupulously applies this logic of coercion and exploitation to the elements constituting first nature. Sociality, which developed as a solution to the human species' tragic situation, however, has become problematic (factors that form these problems include economy) at certain stages of its development, both within the texture of society itself and within the natural environment. But let us now analyze the development of intelligence.

Development of emotional intelligence

Sociality awakens and enables a constantly working mind. This continuous state of operation, in accordance with evolution, has led to the development of the brain. Although it required a long period, an active social life had been the fundamental factor in the development of human intelligence. I don't find explanations based on individuals' being geniuses very convincing. The social uniqueness thus forms the basis of each individual's intelligence.

According to available anthropological data, social life of pre-sapiens hominids centered largely on the activities of hunting and gathering, during which sign language was used. During these stages, serious problems of social origin were paltry: natural evolution still dominated and was able to stabilize itself. The emotional aspects of intelligence were dominant. The fundamental characteristic of emotional intelligence—including instincts— is its reflexive operation. But it is the most ancient form of intelligence, deriving from the first animate cell. It manifests as instantaneous reaction to warnings, which is the best way to fulfill its function to secure its own protection. Through such behavior this type of intelligence can be observed in all living species, even plants. Its most advanced form has been attained in humans: intelligence with five senses operating in complete coordination has not developed in any other being but the human.

The outstanding characteristic of emotional intelligence is its commitment to life. Its basic function is protecting life and it accomplishes this without room for error, that is, through instantaneous reaction. It guards the balance within nature and thus can be called the intelligence that makes possible the continued existence of natural life. Deficiency of this intelligence leaves life susceptible to all possible dangers. Respecting and valuing life thus is related to the development of emotional intelligence. We owe our feelings completely to this type of intelligence.

Development of analytical intelligence and a system of ethics

Once emotional intelligence was fully developed, the probability of establishing links between senses increased. This developed intelligent actions by establishing associations between all the senses, especially between that of sound, sight, and taste. Sign language was replaced with symbolic language after the necessary physiological development had taken place. The shift from communication through signs to communication through words—thus abstract thought that represent concepts—constitutes one of the most important revolutions in human history. Now to refer to objects and events that fulfilled their needs all that was needed was to name them. This was a monumental phase. Then, with the development of verbs and conjunctions, it became possible to express the various relationships between the objects and their functions. The transition to the use of sentences was made and the language revolution completed.

This was a new form of intelligence. Even in the absence of objects and events, thinking about them was now possible due to the mastery of words: conceptual or theoretical intelligence had arrived. This incredible development produced an intelligence capable of producing uncountable benefits, and yet it can lead to the gravest harm. Its fundamental characteristic is the ability to operate detached from the emotions. This type of intelligence has made conceptual—analytical—thought possible, bringing the major advantage that humans can now imagine endlessly and think about the entire universe without becoming exhausted. It has enabled humans to create the incredible world of symbols, to imitate nature and develop astounding inventions. It has given them the ability to plan, to ambush, and to attempt conspiracies, thereby enabling them to obtain anything they desire. And thus the fundamental source of problems within and outside of society.

The interconnectedness of the analytical and emotional dimensions of intelligence is an important asset and is seemingly unique to humans. But this ability can be used either to the benefit or detriment of society. Since its onset, society's response to this double-edged gift has been to base itself on morals as its fundamental organizational principle. Without social morality, humans cannot cope with analytical intelligence. Every community has seen the raising of its members as morally upright to be its fundamental task. The concepts of *good* and *evil*, the fundamental dual antagonism of morals, are thus related to the function of analytical intelligence: that which attempts to benefit society is seen as morally good and rewarded, and that which attempts to harm society is condemned as morally bad. In fact, all moral traditions condemn evil as something that should not occur and thus it is suppressed and, if it does occur, it is punished. Until, of course, the morals of goodness guide society.

Enslavement of society through analytical intelligence

Development of patriarchal society and a patriarchal mythology

The remedy of morals has never obtained an absolute preventative power. The societal fissures will always be home to the crafty, schemers, and entrappers. In fact, there is an ancient culture underlying this, namely hunting. The basis of hunting is the setting of traps and the scheming against other living beings—the roots of this culture go back further than the animal kingdom to that of the plant. (Thus, these roots are also the biological roots of analytical intelligence.) But in human society the synthesis of hunting culture and analytical intelligence enabled individuals early on to develop the ability or power to form hierarchies within social structures and upon nature. This was the start of the catastrophe. The distinction between heaven and hell developed parallel with the ability of analytical intelligence to establish a social hierarchy: in hierarchical societies, a handful of "strong men" holding the strings of society evoked the imagination of a heaven-like life. Alas, for the society at the bottom, the path to hell—continuously worsening, although its emergence was never understood—had been paved.

The strong man's first victim was the woman. Due to the female's stronger bonds with life, her natural emotional intelligence is better developed than that of the male. She is not only the mother of the children, that of labor blended with much pain, she is also the one primarily responsible for social life. She is not only aware of life; she also has more knowledge to sustain it. She is a gatherer, equipped for this by both her emotional intelligence and what she has learned from nature. Anthropological data indicates that for the greatest part of history social accumulation centered on the mother-woman, making her the center of the society's prosperity and values. It can be surmised that she was also the mother—the creator—of surplus-value. The strong man, whose primary task was hunting, realized the advantages that controlling the accumulated goods would give to him. Lowering the woman's position to that of sexual object while raising his own to that of father—or rather, master—of the children, with the right to control all the material and immaterial cultural accumulation, whetted the strong man's appetite. The organization of his power, acquired through hunting, enabled him to establish the initial social hierarchy. This was the first instance of analytical intelligence used for malicious purposes within the social structure: it became systemic.

From the available archaeological records, we can deduce that the matriarchal society based on crop yield was the dominant culture throughout the Mesolithic and Neolithic in Upper Mesopotamia. Traces of this can be seen in the written history. In Neolithic society, religion and language based on the woman was well developed. The transition from the sacred matriarchal cult to the patriarchal cult ensured that analytical intelligence was wrapped in the armor of sacredness. This may be a strong postulate to put forth as to why the patriarchal system has become so deeply rooted. We are able to determine that the physical location where the patriarchal mentality originated is the Tigris-Euphrates basin. It spread all over Mesopotamia from its starting point in Lower Mesopotamia around 5,500 to 4,000 BCE and became the dominant social culture. The societal problem emerged for the first time in serious dimensions within the patriarchal societies that became cult-like centered around the strong man. The onset of woman's enslavement first prepared the ground for the enslavement of her children, and then the enslavement of men.

The domination and control over female and male slaves intensified as their experience in accumulation of value, and especially that of surplus-product, increased. Power and authority increasingly gained importance, and the collaboration between the strong man, the wise old man, and the shaman grew into a center of power not easily confronted. At this center the speculative intelligence developed an extraordinary mythological narration in order to achieve its intellectual domination over society. In this mythological world, historically known to us from the Sumerian society, the strong man is exalted to the point of divinity, the creator of heaven and earth. Whilst the woman's divinity and sacredness is first demeaned and then obliterated, the dominant male is presented as the absolute power. Thus, through extensive use of mythology, everything is turned into the relationship between ruler and ruled, creator and created. This mythological world, as a result of making the entire society assimilate, becomes the fundamental narrative and gradually becomes religionized. We now face a speculative and institutionalized form of intelligence that recognizes no boundary.

The emergent hierarchical order of relations is the initial exploitative, oppressive, and institutionalized authoritarian system materialized and legitimized by the mythological intelligence and its mental forms with its origins in patriarchy. This process has occurred in different phases of many societies, albeit in different forms and with differing intensity. The intelligence rendering possible the oppression and exploitation cannot possibly be emotional. One cannot think of a mindset that can cause the societal problem unless it reaches the level of analytical intelligence and becomes integrated with the games of entrapping that exist within the hunting culture. This mindset needs to generate fake myths in order to disguise its true function.

However, attributing the entire intellectual world to hierarchical powers would be a mistake. Positive traditions of thought and institutions have also been created through the synergy of analytical and emotional intelligence. This is why we can observe during such times not only physical wars but also ruthless wars of different mindsets and ideas. We can thus retrace and find the source of what we call ideological war as expressed in religion, philosophy, ethics, and arts. Conflicts that we come across abundantly in mythology and religions are in essence nothing but the expression of economic and political struggle. Until the era of the capitalist ethos all economic and political wars for power were disguised behind mythology and religion.

Development of the marketplace, classed- and urban society

The state is the representative of permanently institutionalized hierarchical structures. The transformation of power structures from individual representation to institutional representation is related to the development of class society in parallel with urbanization.

More often than not, we see the phenomena of city and class as related to the capitalist system. But it is of crucial importance that we understand their origins—if the onset and origin of a social phenomenon cannot be clarified, the phenomenon itself will not be adequately understood. The establishment of the city has not yet been explained sufficiently and it is at least as important as the onset of capitalism. It thus requires re-evaluation. In my opinion, it is not wrong to see the city as having proto-capitalistic characteristics. Just as the market is a sphere of relations where capitalism has been nourished and came into existence, the city can be described as the place where the market has developed and became permanent. This is important for the subject under discussion as this was also the most advanced location of speculative intelligence. The city, due to its feature of being a market, not only demands an abstract and analytical intelligence but also conceives it—an establishment that is an acute tool for socialization. It is the environment of relations where not only historical developments like the rationalization of the mythological and religious world, and the speeding up of scientific developments and their distortion occur, but it also results in philosophy. Work done is mainly based on analytical intelligence.

The abstract world of concepts and their manifestation in art has enhanced the magnificence of the city. Amidst this speculative environment of relations isolated from emotional intelligence and knowing no boundaries, a tremendous world of images is injected into the mentality of the society through all different sorts of entrapping and scheming. It is true that reason develops in the city environment, but what attributes does such reason have? Does it bring about enlightenment or ignorance? As yet, these questions have not been answered satisfactorily. The city society is the primary web of relations that generate war and exploitation, power, and class. At the same time, the city results in the willing embrace of class by the majority of the society, and is a set-up that totally destroys the environment. Although the mythological and religious expressions of rural communities are linked to analytical intelligence too, they primarily play a positive role. Not only their gods but also their forms of belief reflect their sincere worlds full of emotions. The deities are good friends, compassionate, forgiving, and merciful: they lessen sorrow and ease hardship. However, as the mythological and religious forms become urbanized, the gods, too, become abstract, scrutinizing, punitive, and always have to be pleaded with. They inflict pain and relish their rule. This is a reflection of what happens when a commodity enters into circulation: the gods of the market and the city are entwined.

The concept of *class* developed in the aftermath of the disintegration of—not only, but especially—blood based hierarchic groups such as family, clan, and tribe. As the upper groups started to become the state, those at the bottom turned into groups that became the ruled. This was a merciless and alienating process, linked to the decline in emotional intelligence. The more the oppressed classes became dependent on the ruling class, the more they legitimized the ruling class' intellectual domination, thus endorsing their own state of decay. This is the epitome of damnation for the oppressed: it is the lowest pit of being impoverished from both types of intelligence and the validation of despotic exploitation of oneself. Such a deprivation of intelligence is in the worst situation of becoming déclassé within society. The more the abstract analytical intelligence at the top victimizes and enslaves, the more slaves and beggars destitute of reason—the more dim-wits—are being created.

Protestantism paves the way for capitalism

If history is divided into several periods by mindset, then the mythological and religious phase can be said to weigh more in the early ages (from 5,000 BCE to 500 CE), the synthesis of religion and philosophy during the theological medieval age (from 500 to 1500), and the separation of philosophy and science during the modern age (from 1500 to the present). As mythology becomes dogmatized, religion is formed. Mythology cannot exactly be called religion. Religion requires forms of unchanging belief and worship. It is totally fictive. Believing these fictions is the basis of religion. The only positive aspect of religion is that as the transition to abstract thought was made, it gave rise to a profound cleavage. It has thus reluctantly prepared the ground for scientific and philosophical thought, compelling their onset.

Philosophical and scientific thought develop in a dialectical link with religious thought. Philosophy and science bear profound traces of religion. Although the source of philosophy is mostly this fictive intelligence, it continuously links the concrete with observation. It does not entirely detach itself from emotional intelligence. It has the highest abstraction power of all forms of thought. Its contribution to science is bigger than that of religion.

Science is actually not that different from philosophy; it can be seen as philosophy with a more advanced experimental base. Both try to render meaning to both natures through observation and experiment. This is the right way to go about it. But their most significant deficiency is the lack of an answer to the question religions asks: Why? It is not a sufficient response to life to only answer the *how* of nature. To assume the huge universe is motiveless, purposeless, and without a reason as to why it exists cannot really be a desirable approach. A science which has no answer to the question of *why* there is life cannot escape being the tool of the enslaving rulers.

The separation of science from philosophy and religion (in relation to the questions of reason and purpose) is closely linked to capitalistic mentality. I strongly put this forth as a thesis. I can make my case accordingly: Religion, philosophy, and even mythology constitute the memory, identity, and mental protection of society. Despite their huge distortions and that they are shown to be in opposition to sociology, they constitute a sociological reality. Without them, society's ties with history and memory are cut off; the science resulting from such a society can't help but be of service to the present ruler, which is what capitalism does. Why have mythology, religion, and philosophy been reduced to worthlessness in the capitalist system? The answer is quite clear: religion, philosophy, and mythology have continuously excluded and refused to legitimize capitalistic elements such as the usurers and the speculators lurking in the fissures of society. As long as religion, philosophy, and mythology hold their position within a society's thought system and emotional intelligence continues to have influence on the society, capitalism will not be able to establish itself as the leading system. This is because amidst the ambiance of such a mentality—and morality—no ruler will be able to legitimize capitalism nor defend it as a socio-economical system to base itself upon.

But, as the sociologist Max Weber argued, the mental world of the Protestant denomination of Christianity prepared the mental grounds for capitalism and morally gave free passage to it. It is possible to criticize this evaluation, although it bears some truth. Firstly, Protestantism is itself a very weak religion and is quite close to the capitalist form of science. More importantly though, Protestantism marked the start of the era of national religions. It was like a precursor for nationalism and nationalism itself is nothing but an ideology of capitalism. It may help us to understand the major religious wars in Europe when looked at from this perspective.

Capitalists succeeded in being victorious in places either where religion had a light impact or where—for instance in the Netherlands, England, and the USA—Protestantism was newly adopted. These countries were also the places where different sects found shelter. I am not defending the orthodoxies of religion here. What I am saying is that, because Protestantism had the least strict morals in Christianity, it became the gateway for capitalism. (This is where I deviate from Weber: he sees this tolerance as a positive characteristic, while I see it as a negative characteristic.) It may sound paradoxical, but the capitalist mindset has gained legitimacy only at the weakest or last phase of the very long historical walk of the religious mindset.

The capitalist mentality

When defining the mentality of capitalism, one can focus on several of its characteristics but the one aspect that has to be taken into account is that it is an extremely eclectic system. Although it can be defined as being more dogmatic than the strictest religious dogma, it is also speculative and more far-fetched than the most abstract philosophy.

I do not believe that science is the product of capitalist development. What happened is that the capitalist economic revolution and the scientific revolution coincided at a very unfortunate stage of development in Western Europe. The constructors of the capitalist mindset used this to spread the falsehood that capitalism generated science. The fact that some individuals who contributed to science lived in societies where rapid capitalist development took place does not necessarily mean that capitalism spawned these scientists. Although it is true that these scientists were in conflict with religious thought, most of them did not demean themselves by accepting the capitalist mindset.

The truth is that capitalism utilizes all the different forms of thought in the same way that it secures profit and capital from speculating with commodities and money. Thus, it evaluated the different forms of thought, taking from each the elements that suited it, combined them and reintroduced them to the market in the form of new philosophical or religious schools, promoting them as liberalism and positivism. Alas, it has succeeded, or displayed its craftiness, in making these two forms of thought the dominant mentality of modernity.

Indeed, positivism and liberalism which constitute the capitalist mentality are more pagan than paganism itself. While on the one hand science has been castrated by positivism and molded to oppose the world of belief and morals, on the other hand through liberalism it has transformed an individualism that destroys society into a nation-statist god capable of augmenting individualism to the point of committing genocides. No religious ethos has ever generated the amount of wars, oppression, and torture like the capitalist ethos. The mindset of no other society's individual has been so irresponsible and had such a passion for profit making as the individual of the society where capitalism is victorious. No other society has generated so many ruthless, genocidal, assimilationist, and dictatorial individuals.

Capitalism is a system of monopoly built upon the world of commodities and money. In constructing the present-day financial ethos, it has bound human society with mental forms unheard-of in history. It has made humanity prostrate itself before its contemptible idols. In other words, it has only brought intellectual failure and decay. It is therefore vital that we know what the capitalist mindset entails.

Firstly, I must point out that one-dimensional definitions of capitalism result from works that are under grave influence of the intellectual work of the system itself. Such interpretations can be seen even in the analyses of Marxists and anarchists who claim that they work within the parameters of scientific sociology and that they are extreme anti-capitalists.

In Marx's own evaluations, the economic infrastructure plays a central role in explaining all the legal, political, and ideological forms. Perhaps this is one of the principal reasons for the failure of socialism, although many major struggles have been waged for it. Without a long-term knowledge and trial of any given form of mindset, no human society can build and subsequently institutionalize its material (economic) way of life. No system analysis that ignores the development of the mindset can escape serving the hegemony of these very systems, even if they form their mindset in total opposition. The dominant systems guarantee their own hegemony through intellectual and political institutionalization. The new material life can only be arranged within this framework. Marx claimed he provided a corrective to Hegel's dialectics, but he was gravely mistaken. It is now far better understood that Hegelian idealism—which was the height of metaphysical thought, building on Luther (who constructed the ideology of Protestantism) and Kant (against strict objectivity he takes into consideration subjectivity and partially morals)—was in fact one of the fundamental pillars paving the way for the German nation-state. Paradoxical as it may seem, Karl Marx continued building on this line of thought in the name of the proletariat and the anti-capitalist system. The end result was that the German ideology caused fascism and Hitler-like leaderships. The danger present in this line of thought was best detected by the German philosopher Nietzsche.

Intellectual works by the Nietzschean school of thought are true opponents of capitalist modernity. It is a grave shortcoming that his work has not been developed into a political philosophy and implementation. The efforts of later French philosophers such as Deleuze, Guattari and Foucault and those of the Italian Gramsci were inadequate and have not been transformed into political institutionalization. What came to light in the practice of real socialism was its objective complicity with capitalist modernity in the name of the left for at least the past 150 years. The Soviet Russia and Chinese experiences confirm our evaluation conspicuously. (I shall return to this in the relative sections.) Generally, I find the critique on the birth of capitalism by the early leading anarchists—especially Proudhon, Bakunin and Kropotkin—much more enlightening. Although these anarchists saw the ideological and political dimensions far clearer, they lacked a correct political philosophy and failed to institutionalize their thoughts, combined with being unaware of morals and historiography, and this reduced them, in the final analysis, to an ideological commodity for capitalism. I must yet again point out that, if work on a particular mindset is not combined with a competent politics, moral, and historical work and implementation, then it will not escape being used by its opponents, and hence being counteracted either through annihilation or assimilation. Unfortunately, anti-capitalist works on creating a new mindset have shared the same fate as works and movements trying to establish a different mindset throughout history; Christianity, Buddhism, Zoroastrianism and Manichaeism are just a few examples. I am not suggesting that these teachings were in vain or that we are fated to live with the capitalist mentality—if I thought this, I would see no need for this book nor would I render meaning to freedom morals. I am merely making a criticism. Attaining a successful alternative system to capitalism and its historical building blocks can only be achieved if political philosophy, political institutionalization, and actions regarding the material life are passionately furnished under the guide of works for a mindset that is in complete integrity.

The role of political and military force is critical for maintaining the capitalist system's hegemony. But what really maintains the hegemony is the possession of society through the cultural industry and society's subsequent paralysis. The mindsets of communities under the influence of the system have become increasingly backward and pliable. Many philosophers have suggested that society has come to belong to the order of the zoos: just as a zoo, society has been turned into a spectacle. The sport, art, and culture industries, and especially the sex industry, bombard the emotional and analytical intelligence intensely and continuously through widespread advertisement campaigns. The total dysfunction of both types of intelligence completes the mental conquest of the society of the spectacle.

This society is worse off than a possessed society; it can be administered as the system desires. In fact, the initial experimental society of the spectacle of fascism has not failed—the ringleaders have been eliminated. But during and after the Cold War, the system made the society of the spectacle dominant over all societies via nation-states and global financial firms. The current material and immaterial conquest of societies by capitalism far exceeds that of mighty empires such as those of the Sumerians, Egyptians, Indians, Chinese, and Romans. Clearly, the empire phase of capitalism (previous phases being colonialism and imperialism) is the height of its hegemony. Although this phase objectively carries chaotic aspects and show signs that it experiences intense decay, the capitalist system aims to compensate for the effects of decay by deepening the hegemony of the mind.

A major factor in arriving at this level of control is the industrialization of sex. People have been made to seek success in sexual power. Sex was meant to have the function of being an instructive activity to create awareness and eternality of life in all human beings; thus, it is not only meaningful, it is sacred. Human societies throughout history held this basic belief, as all anthropological studies confirm. If there is any relationship that should not be commodified—industrialized—then, above all, it is the sexual relationship, because it is linked to the sacredness, supremacy, and continuance of life. Moreover, it has the responsibility not to endanger other lives.

Sexual abuse is one of the most fundamental hegemonic tools of the system. Therefore, it has not only been turned into a huge industry, it has corrupted sexuality within the society and turned it into the religion of dominant male sexism far worse than the ancient concept of phallus divinity. This new religious indicator has taken effect especially in each male and has had the seat of honor especially in literature and the arts, thereby transforming these fields into a terrible tool for brainwashing. Chemical drugs are nothing next to this new sexual religion. All individuals of society have almost been turned into perverted sexuality through mass media advertisement campaigns. It does not really matter whether you are young or old, everyone is used, even children. Woman has been turned into the most advanced sexual object, condemned to believing that she is worth nothing if she does not continuously evoke sexual desire. The sacred hearth and home has been turned into the location of sex. All that is left of the sacred mother and goddesses are "old wives" seen as worthless and disregarded; a very sad and painful situation.

The process of turning women into a sex tool has reached its peak in the use of artificial insemination. If she is unable to have children, that too is at excruciating levels due to pressure of the system. In accordance with the tradition of having as many children—especially male children—as possible, which is essentially a tradition of the patriarchal society, the role of the women from lower classes—with the help of technology—has been reduced to breeding machines. In this way, while on the one hand the difficult task of raising children has been imposed on the poor and the need for young workers has been met, on the other hand the family institution itself is being further degenerated. Thus, two birds are killed with one stone. The upper-class women and men degenerate the meaning of having a *child* through artificial insemination or adopting a child or keeping a pet in order to satisfy such a deficiency. In the meantime, this elite also strive to be eternally sexy and ritualize the new religion of sex. The end result is a meaningless increase in population, an unheard-off level of unemployment, and an environmental crisis brought on by the fact that the earth can no longer bear the human burden. I will talk about how to tackle this problem in my next book: *Sociology of Freedom*.

The second effective tool of enslavement lies in the industrialization (the widespread commodification) of culture. A society's culture, in the narrow sense of the word, defines the mental world of that society. The three fundamental elements of any society's culture are its thought system, taste and morals, and it has taken the political and economic power centuries to besiege and buy off these fundamental elements. Throughout the history of civilization, they found it essential to bind all the cultural elements to themselves in order to gain legitimacy. Those holding economic and political power have realized this since the earliest days of civilization and have swiftly taken precautions. One can date back the beginning of cultural assimilation to the establishment of hierarchies. Culture is the real tool of governance of the hegemonic power system. In the absence of cultural hegemony, economic, and political monopolies cannot rule. Systems that are based solely on coercion and exploitation can only secure their existence for a short time through plundering, and when there is nothing left to plunder they will either turn against one another or collapse.

Thus, culture is also vital in capitalist civilization. Culture, which is the combined intellectual world of all social fields, is first assimilated to align capitalist civilization with economic and political power. Then it is turned into an industry so that it can be extensively and intensively spread on the world communities—nations, peoples, nation-states, NGOs, and firms. Literature, science, philosophy, all the arts, history, religion, and law are turned into objects and commodified. Books, films, newspapers, TV, the internet, radio, etc., function as the market place where the commodities of this industry are for sale. Besides generating huge material gains, the true (and truly destructive) function of these cultural commodities is the intellectual captivity of society on a scale unmatched in history. They achieve this also through forming bovine-like class, nation, tribe, and other communities, creating a mass of people who have lost their meaning and who are, in short, impulsive and fickle. Even the most impoverished segments of society cannot think of anything else but to aim at becoming extremely rich—even if it is for a day—so that they can live as they desire. The master-builders of this system are the nation-states, global companies, and media monopolies. Aside from consumption and making more money, they have no interest in society.

Let us take heed: impoverishment is used like a cultural phenomenon. Even during the despised Middle Ages impoverishment was a reason for rebellion. Thus, if under the official cultural hegemony obtaining a salary has become a goal, this shows the cultural victory of the system.

The gravest aspect of falling victim to the hegemony of the cultural industry—which is intertwined with the sex industry—is the voluntary acceptance of this enslavement and, even worse, its perception as an act of freedom. This is capitalist rule's most powerful base and most effective tool for legitimization. The empire-stage of capitalism is only possible through the development and use of the cultural industry. And the struggle against the cultural hegemony requires the most difficult of all struggles: intellectual struggle. Until we are able to develop and organize the essence and form of a counter-struggle against the cultural war waged by the system through invasion, assimilation, and industrialization, not a single struggle for freedom, equality, and democracy has a chance to succeed. I shall open up these questions to discussion in my next book, *The Sociology of Freedom.*

Since the beginning, in various societies, sports have had the function of preparation for participation in society, in assisting with socialization. Ever since the Roman Empire's period of decay, we have seen the beginning of the industrialization of sports—the institutionalization of the gladiators being a prime example. Capitalism, from the beginning, has turned sports into a professional occupation by ruining its amateur character. Later, it imposed the industrialization of sports through which capitalism has managed to integrate sports with the economic and political power. Sports has become another important area of anesthesia that is commoditized. Instead of encouraging the participation of individuals in society based on high spirits and physical endurance, the lure of making money and, subsequently, rivalry, are frantically incited and the society is turned into a passive spectator. The culture of the arena, becoming the bait for the lions and forcing gladiators to kill one another, has spread to all types of sports. The breaking of records and applause are the two dominant images. Supporting a specific team has become more important than having a specific religion or philosophy, and so the rulers have attained another effective tool for easy rule. (Can we imagine any religion or philosophy playing the role football does for the nation-state governments?)

Thus, these three areas—sex, sports, and culture—have been transformed into industries through which the art of administration has reached its peak. Governance of global capital and the rule of the nation-state cannot be achieved without it. Let me make it clear that I am not critical of sex, culture, or sports per se. On the contrary, I am criticizing the fact that the most vital areas of social formation and sustainability are corrupted through their industrialization.

The virtual world is another important tool for domination in capitalism's intellectual hegemony, mostly enforced by the media. The virtualization of life is indeed analytical intelligence reaching the edge of its limits. Virtually presenting something as terrifying as war can, on its own, demolish morals. Any life that has not been experienced by the human body and mind has always been seen as false, a "fake" life. Calling something "virtual" does not alter what that life is: a fake. I am not criticizing the technical developments that made virtual life possible: I am criticizing its abusive aspect and thus the paralysis of the individual's mind. Unrestrained use of technology is a most dangerous weapon. The fundamental factor compelling virtual life is capitalism's domination of technology and its desire to control billions. Life is no longer lived as before; increasingly, it is becoming virtual—like being dead while standing on your feet.

The most concrete form of virtual life is the simulacrum. Simulating past events, relations or monuments does not make one more knowledgeable—to the contrary, it stupefies us. No development can be achieved by imitating the monuments of civilization. Differentiation, which is at the essence of life, is never based on repetition. (Even history does not repeat itself!) Indeed, imitation is the negation of development. But still, the imitation culture has become hegemonic. Everyone imitates everyone to the degree that they resemble each other and flocks are successfully formed. The age of finance cannot sustain itself without the presence of virtual life. It can only be sustained through unlimited stupification and that can only be possible through fake, virtual life.

Our most basic duty is to respond to this in the name of free life. The ability to define and organize free life is imperative if communities are to survive. This is essential if society is to remain standing. We must construct a sociology of freedom that can generate effective responses to the problems discussed above. Let us now interpret the success of the capitalist system in developing virtual life from several perspectives.

The first big success was to subordinate society through the loosening of the functional ties of society with morals and religion, and by making morality and religion of secondary importance while replacing it with secular law. Religion and morals are only allowed when they serve the system. Law and secularism thus are the tools used to transfer social supervision into the hands of capitalist power. The elimination of religion and morals by secularism and law does not only put the aristocracy and the slave-peasants of the old society under control, it also opens space for capital and workforce as well as creating reserves. Religion and morals are not totally eradicated. Because they are intensively used tools by the civilization, they will also be much needed by the capitalist system as the "last word of the civilization"—on the condition that they are not party to economic and political power and thus pose an obstacle. Reform of religion and the state of law have become the main indicators of capitalist modernity. They play the essential role of being the two main tools to make the transition to a capitalist economy and society. At the same time, the system uses these tools to resolve problems relating to its mindset.

The second success of the system is its use of the "scientific method," with the object-subject dual antagonism being the padlock of its intellectual hegemony. The principle of objectivity which is held to be essential for the scientific method is in reality a prerequisite for the domination of subjectivism. In order to rule one must be a subject; those who *are* ruled will then quite naturally fall into the role of being the object. To be an object is to become a *thing* and to be ruled as a *thing*. To become a *thing*, the object, is the methodological expression of the way in which the subject rules as it pleases—it is the creed of science. The distinction between subject and object has roots that can be taken back all the way to Plato. Plato's famous theory of the duality of Forms (ideas) and their simple, observable reflections is the basis of all subsequently postulated dualisms. However, its mythological basis can be seen in the Sumerian and Egyptian societies— the true roots are the rise to divinity and exaltation of the hierarchy at the top, and the turning of those at the bottom into servants. The concept of the creator-created, ruler-ruled dualisms can therefore be expressed as god-subject, word-goods. Thus, this concept developed from the duality of perfect ideas or forms and simple reflections to the point where a distinction is made between subject and object. Indeed, the soul-body distinction can be seen in this context as well. The political implication of this distinction, on the other hand, is the denial of democracy, paving the way for oligarchy and monarchy.

It must be fully understood that with the onset of capitalism, the analytical intelligence wrapped itself in the most deceitful and conspiratorial forms. The stock exchange is the most striking expression of this reality. It is one of the areas where the speculative intelligence earns most of its profit. In this system speculation and speculative intelligence become twins. This is also true for the political and military fields. War is based on deception and craftiness; it is the peak of the hunting culture. Speculative intelligence has become a tool of manipulation and conspiracy within the stock exchange, politics, and the military unmatched to date. It leaves no room for conscience and emotions. While in one part of the world people can be killed with nuclear and other bombs of terror, in another part of the world some can earn billions without any effort. It could be said that capitalism reveals its mindset most on the stock exchange and in politics and war. There is not a single human value or emotion that it would not violate for profits.

But emotional intelligence is a sine qua non for life. As we are detached from this form of intelligence, the meaning of life is gradually erased. Ecological disasters signal the dangers awaiting life. Speculative intelligence is the culprit; it has been used in such a distorted way and nourished with language, power, city, state, science, and arts that it has turned into a global Leviathan, the world empire of the global capital. In order to stop this monster a comprehensive effort full of emotional intelligence is needed. It is necessary to drive back its suppression of free life in order to render it harmless. We must stop its ability to maintain and sustain itself before it turns our planet uninhabitable. The fundamental duty of a sociology of freedom is to attain the theoretical perspective for such a vital act and to succeed in structuring it accordingly and appropriately.

Economism

All viewpoints that see the birth of capitalism as the natural result of economic development can be categorized as economism. Marxism has been especially reduced to economism, in a way, from this perspective. So much so that capitalism has been perceived as if it was an economic model. Consequently, economy and politics have become the cornerstones of the social sciences, and, when the modern state is constructed, decisions taken on its economic life are turned into disciplines of science.

Capital generates profits through the exploitation of prices that are determined in the marketplace. This may have played an important role in the development of such a misconception—as if it was possible to have a capitalist development separate and outside of a general civilizational development, outside of history, society, and power relations. Paradoxically, those who most fiercely thought themselves to be anti-capitalist and have fought against it were the ones to give it this undeserved credit.

One can understand the English political economists and might expect them to present this new economy as a model as the economists and politicians of a country where capitalism won its victory. Thus, Karl Marx's extensive study of this model has been both important and explanatory, especially his critique of the English political economists. It is extremely unfortunate that his monumental work was left unfinished and that later Marxists completely caricatured him. The fundamental flaw of this study is its failure to systematically analyze capitalism's relationship with that of power and state. He sought to determine the role of ideology. His analysis on the mindset of capitalism is at times quite powerful. But Marx's crucial mistake was to base himself on the positivist perspective, which by then had already left its mark on the intellectual environment and was the favorite ideology of the Enlightenment. Marx did not doubt the view that like the physical sciences, social sciences can be engineered as well. The result of this positivist perspective was that one of the most valuable studies of all time, *Das Kapital*, has had far less effect than it should have had. This perspective also brought about the treatment of his work as a sacred text instead of research. We know what disciples are capable of. Thus, Lenin's efforts to analyze imperialism, monopolistic capitalism, state, and revolution did not go beyond Enlightenment philosophy. Despite his many positive contributions, in my opinion the main factor underlying the collapse of the Soviet experiment was Lenin's inability to surpass capitalist modernity.

The anarchists' analysis of capitalism is also largely concerned with economics. They tend to just condemn capitalism on economic grounds, as if the mere act of condemnation on economic grounds will bring about its collapse.

The main reason for the ineffectiveness of all these schools of thought is the fact that the concepts their arguments are built upon are crippled by positivism. The typical argument runs like this: "All sciences have their own rules. Economy is a science; hence, it has its own rules. Capitalism is a system that generates crises and, in accordance with the rules of economy, capitalism is a system that cannot be maintained. What then needs to be done is to accelerate the working of these rules. As a result, capitalism shall collapse and communism shall be established." This argument is built upon misconceived notions about social reality. Society has systematic (or perhaps quite chaotic) functions that far exceedes those generally stipulated by Enlightenment ideologies. Society, together with its intellectual and institutional structures (including its economy), qualitatively differ from the definitions made by positive sciences. Furthermore, while active, it mostly has a chaotic nature. Thus, the society requires different approaches when being analyzed and in connection requires the development of different approaches.

In light of the above criticism, we can proceed to establish a more understandable relationship between economy and capital. Firstly, although it may seem paradoxical, we should not regard capitalism as an economic system. There have been many important analyses of capitalism, especially and including that of Marx, but all of them are flawed by the assumption that an economic interpretation is imperative. Even Fernand Braudel fell into this trap when he explained the birth of capitalism with its feature to establish monopoly over prices formed in the market. Had sociologist Max Weber interpreted capitalism as a religious cult in its own right instead of ascribing the *esprit* of capitalism to Protestant ethics, his analysis would have had more explanatory power. Secondly, analyzing capitalism as a political regime will bring us closer to understanding the profit that is present in its essence. But we must avoid the pitfall of power-and-state-reductionism: we must not be thrown from economism into power-ism.

For I believe that capitalism is the culmination of an old tradition which has been militarily, politically, and culturally organized to cunningly usurp social values, especially those pertaining to material accumulation. Capitalism has gradually become the dominant social format in Western Europe since the sixteenth century. This birth can be described as the modern link of the tradition whereby a band of looters gathered by and around the strong man seizes the social values generated by mother-woman. Capitalism is the act of groups with advanced speculative intelligence who would not abstain from using violence when necessary and frequently. They are the early capitalists of England, the Netherlands, and, prior to them, of Italian city-states like Genoa, Florence, and Venice; they were intertwined with the state, and, like members of a sect, had their own special lifestyles.[2]

These early capitalists were masters at accumulating incredible amounts of wealth. They accomplished this through a few innovations in the economic area, namely mastering the generation of big profits through the use of money, and by tampering with prices formed at markets around the world.[3] Depending on their time in history, these groups can be referred to as dynasties, aristocrats, or bourgeoisie. They differ from the bandits of Antiquity and the Middle Ages mainly in that they mostly established themselves in cities; they became intertwined with state authority; if needed, coercion was used in a more disguised fashion and as only a secondary tool.

If we were to believe their defenders, the early West European capitalists were able to render their first profits by using their intelligence and the amount of money they initially had within the framework of the innate economic rules. However, if the history of capital is properly examined it will be seen that this is nothing but a fairy tale: No economic rules underlay the colonial wars where the initial accumulation was extorted. Portugal, Spain, the Netherlands, England, France, and earlier on cities like Venice and Genoa, obtained colonies entirely through coercion. And it was the obtainment of the colonies that enabled the accumulation of the initial capital (as a study of the markets of the nearby countries and the colonized areas will no doubt make clear). The forty thieves have thus turned into the bourgeois masters. The greatest distortion made by speculative intelligence is in the area of economy and politics.

However, the various disciplines of economic science very successfully continue their main task of disguising the essence of capitalism. The theory that makes the most successful presentation will be rewarded. Economic science, more than any other science, has tampered with the facts and turned them inside out. Thus, the main aberration of the speculative intelligence is in the area of capitalist political economy. Capitalist modernity is the only system that has had the luxury to emerge totally from such a counterfeit science.

Participating in economic activity (that is, accessing the material objects needed to live) is the main problem of being alive. Economy is crucial for evolution to materialize. All living systems sustain their continuity through much needed objects that are suitable for their own digestive systems. This is a universal rule: evolution maintains continuity of life through differentiation. The universe has continuously striven for or enabled an equilibrium that would prevent the excessive growth of a particular species, preventing its invasion over other species. Excessive numbers of mice have been balanced with snakes; sheep, goats, and herds of cattle with beasts of prey, so that plants are not totally destroyed—thereby creating an opportunity for their continuous existence and allowing their development as a species. The question, "Why does natural evolution do this?" can only be answered by looking at its results. I believe the main reason for evolution is to ensure and develop the continuity of the living systems. Can this be called the brutality or justice of nature? Is it the result of a profound intelligence or is it linked to being primitive? Should it be included within the scope of metaphysics or not? All these questions regarding universality are meaningful and should be explored with the use of analytical intelligence. They can also be linked to existentialism.

The most significant answer that can be given to these questions is that evolution is continuously on the lookout for competency. It is as if the universe's search for perfection and competency is desired or looked for throughout the course of time. Or else, how can we explain the evolution that has ended up creating the human being as well as the development of the tight-bonded human society? This magnificent evolution has also allowed for a formation called conscience and morals. What is the meaning? Mercy and justice! The essence of this principle has been expressed as: "Sheep and wolf would wonder about if opinions did not differ so."[4] There is another universality hidden here: is it possible for the lamb and the wolf to be friends? Human action has proved that this is indeed possible. That is, to think and act that a *man is wolf to another man*— capitalism's principle of brutality—cannot be true is indispensable to being human.[5] In fact, do both the wolf and the sheep not have the same ancestry?

Capitalism tries to make the limited number of examples that may be perceived as acts of savagery throughout evolution as a pretext for its birth. More importantly, why should we not take the evolution from seaweed to moss, from moss to tremendously beautiful trees, leading to the rich system of grass eating animals (who do not eat each other) as an example for human life instead of formations that can be interpreted as evolution cancer? The only reason I am including such examples is to show that in natural evolution there is no room for developments that justify theories of capitalism's birth. Included in such examples should also be the adverse principle of continuously increasing the army of unemployed in order to compel the people to work for low wages.

While the human species developed on the basis of incorporating all of the evolutionary processes within their structure, they continued their existence on the basis of sociality. If we are to interpret science, without becoming bogged down in the religion of positivism, then we must understand well that this is another important finding. In my next book this characteristic of the human species as well as its characteristic of moral selection or judgment (or, indeed, free selection opportunity) will be discussed.[6]

I must emphasize that traces of a limited number of examples of savagery (like cannibalism) may be found in evolution and such examples may be interpreted as a disease, deviation, or a remnant of the human species' evolution. Besides, we must understand with utmost clarity that the natural rhythm of evolution does not occur in this manner. In civilization in general or, more specifically, in its capitalist phase, a social system—the second nature—cannot be generated from such a remnant characteristic. We should not just determine this (maybe a task for academics) but also adopt it as an essential principle of life. If we were to accept such a view, it would amount to the crippling of our social interpretations.

Under the profound influence of the Enlightenment, and by basing his theory on positivist science, Karl Marx was quite ambitious to turn the study of economy into a scientific discipline.[7] Thus, the idea of an evolutionary and universal societal development according to set stages became the base for economic science and for Marxism.[8]

When Marx formulated his theories, the notions of scientific certainty and linear progress were already deep-seated in people's minds, and sociology was at its infancy. Romanticism, whilst attempting to combat this approach, fell into voluntarism, thereby aggravating the intellectual problems. Nietzsche's approach was based mainly on relativist, cyclic, and emotional intelligence and was never developed any further. Within this intellectual turmoil liberalism took over and did as it pleased. On the one hand, capitalism philosophizes, or indeed religionizes, physical sciences (including chemistry, mathematics and biology) with positivism; on the other hand, it philosophizes or religionizes social reality with liberalism in the same way. This is how capitalism attained its ideological victory and with the onset of the nineteenth century, the system's globalization can almost be seen to take place. The economic war, on the other hand, had been won earlier.

I will thus summarize the *rhythmic development* of the societal progress which is indeed not adverse to natural evolution. While doing this, I will attempt to substantiate my belief that a civilization based on excessive urbanization and the centers of state and power that grow with hierarchy and class distinction, force all life into either the category of "excessive lionization" or its reverse, "excessive cattlization."

Let me expand: Since the earliest times, depending on their intellectual development, communities have searched for and developed the necessary material objects; their main concerns being food, shelter, protection, and reproduction. In accordance with these fundamental needs, they were satisfied with what they found to eat, took shelter in caves, defended themselves at riverbanks and the edge of forests, and gave priority to the fertile mother. Gradually, a hunting culture developed. This culture developed because it offered protection and nutrition. But at a certain stage of sociality there was tension between the women who were prevalent in gathering and (mainly) men who specialized in hunting, resulting in different cultural evolutions (a growing dichotomy that eventually gave shape to the "lionization of man" and the "cattlization of woman"). This, I believe, is how the two differing initial economies came into being. The woman's culture reached its peak during the Neolithic period when, in the aftermath of the last glacial period (which ended around 15,000 BCE), the abundance of flora and fauna enabled a paradisiacal life. Since the period, the main stream of social development has become more differentiated in the times of written history and civilization and has left its mark on globalization. The extant developments based on language groups are also the product of this period.

The only important remark one could make about capitalism during this, the longest period of humanity's history, is that the hunting culture gradually gave rise to the dominance of the man.

As far as can be discerned, the Neolithic culture that became permanent at around 10,000 BCE, was still predominantly woman-centered. The transition from caves to tent-like huts and the sowing of seeds, gradually led to the agricultural and village revolution.[9] Now the surplus product, however limited, could be stored.

Economy, not as an intellectual construct but in terms of its essence, can be traced back to this kind of accumulation. The roots of the term *economy*, "oikos and nomos," are the Greek words for *house* and *law/ custom*; thus, its original meaning was "household management." The birth of the initial sedentary agricultural family groups, centered on the woman and based on the (albeit limited) ability to save and store durable food, led to the birth of economy. However, this was not an accumulation for the merchant or the market but accumulation for the family. This must be the true human economy. The development of a widespread gift culture prevented this accumulation, which would raise wrongful desires, from constituting any *danger* to society. (Quite possibly, the saying *possessions bring greed* is an insight stemming from the period of the gift culture.) Gift culture is an important economic system and is compatible with the rhythmic development of the human being's social evolution.

Most probably, this period was also the beginning of the culture of sacrifice and the concept of sacredness. It is quite plausible that the notion of gods resulted from the community's respect for its own identity due to, and the initial expression of, this increased yield. This increased yield brings praising with itself. Its roots rest on evolution as a community. To give one's self an identity, to exalt one's self, to pray, to worship, to present one's self as the increased progress of the intellectual world, are cultural elements closely associated with the agricultural revolution. Archaeological findings strikingly confirm this point of view. More concretely, the concepts of mother-goddess and sacred mother as well as the vast number of female figures can be seen as supporting evidence for this view.[10]

The *danger* feared would indeed eventually arrive: growing experience and intellectual development brought an increase in residual product accumulations. When these could not be depleted through gifting, the hunter-man, waiting on alertly, started to contemplate trading this surplus in addition to his profession and placed it in his culture. The accumulation of different surplus products in different areas put into motion what we call trade. The fact that these products satisfied reciprocal needs caused trade, as well as the merchant as the second big societal division of labor. Albeit with reluctance, trade and the merchant were legitimized because the products brought in further developed the division of labor and that in return made possible a more productive production and life. Trade became more meaningful when, on the one hand, there were food and weaving and, on the other hand, mineral deposits.

We know from history that trade was widespread after 4,000 BCE. For instance, the original city-state civilization called Uruk (4,000-3,000 BCE) in Lower Mesopotamia had trade colonies in Elam, the southwest of present-day Iran and Upper Mesopotamia, to the areas of present-day Elazığ and Malatya. The first gateway to colonialism was thus formed. (Trade and colonization go hand in hand! Prior to Uruk, the dominant culture during 5,000-4,000 BCE is the Ubaid period. It is the first observed initial patriarchal culture prior to state formation and its colonies have been observed.) In return for pottery and textile products, (mostly) metal ware and wood products were transported. As the merchant and trade take shape, so does the market: The old centers for presenting gifts and performing sacrifices slowly turned into market places. The merchant, who attained the privilege to price the different products of the different regions, accumulated property on a scale not possible before: the primitive capitalist was born.

At the start of the trade era, the transition from a gift economy to exchange value had not yet been made.

At this point, I think it is necessary to rethink Marx's treatment of the labor theory of value. Indeed, trade paves the way for commodification (that is to say, turning a product or a good into a commodity, into merchandise) because goods are exchanged. To society, the importance of a good is its use value and the use value is how well the good satisfies a need. This is of importance to the human being.

Exchange value, on the other hand, is a highly contentious concept. It is, thus, of vital importance that it be correctly defined. The view that human labor is the basis of exchange value is highly disputable; this is true also for Marx's analyses. Whether defined in terms of concrete or abstract labor, exchange value always has a speculative aspect. To illustrate, let us presume that the first merchant from Uruk, in one of his colonies along the Euphrates, tried to exchange stones and metal compounds in return for pottery. What would have determined the exchange value? In the first place, it would have been the degree of mutual need, and, secondly, the merchant's initiative. If the need for his merchandise was great, the merchant would have been able to price it as he pleased; there was nothing that could have prevented him from doing so apart from his own conscience or whether he had the necessary power. What happened then to the role of the labor?

I am not arguing for the complete exclusion of the labor factor, but I do insist that it is not the main determinant of exchange value. This can be seen in all exchanges of goods throughout history. At times, there may be exchange of goods with equal value, but this will be more of a theoretical labor-value exchange. In practice, the decisive factor is speculation. In some cases, there may be an excessive accumulation of goods, leading to situations where they are abundant and not really needed or wanted and must be eliminated. In order to eliminate the goods there may be a need for additional labor. In such situations, the value of labor is not lost, but, once again, labor is not the decisive factor: it is the merchant who has the power to create shortages or redundancy, thereby determining the value of the good. Throughout history a good has always been produced as the end result of a multitude of unnamed workers. So, what is the mechanism that shall repay what owners of dead labor deserve? If we add to this the living labor of creative craftspeople and even the much-required social activity, then clearly such labor cannot in any way be meaningfully priced.

This is where the fraudulent English political economy reveals its true face. Capitalism attained its initial victory as a system in England and the Netherlands. In order for it to be legitimized, theoretical justification was crucial, in particular an acceptable theory was needed to disguise its essence of speculative acquisition. Just as with the initial Uruk merchants' religions, the construction of a new version of the mythological narrative was given to what they called the political economists, who were really the inventors of the religion of capitalism. What was being constructed was nothing but a new religion, with its own sacred book and intricate sects. Political economy is the most fraudulent and predatory monument of fictive intelligence, developed to disguise the speculative character of capitalism. The English classical school of political economy came up with just the right bait: the labor theory of value. I really do wonder why they decided on this notion. I suspect a main reason was to distract the workers. Even Karl Marx could not refrain from taking this bait. I feel great sorrow as I make this critique, but I have to lay down my doubts if I have any respect at all for science. The second big merchant rush can be seen from 2,000 BCE onwards, in the Assyrian colonies. No despotic regime—I shall explore the relationship between capitalism and power in later chapters—before them had created a civilization comparable to the one created by the despotic Assyrian regime based on trade and merchant colonies. Between 2,000 and 600 BCE, they established the most advanced global trade between a home country and its colonies the world had seen until then. The Phoenician merchants, at around the same period and with the support of the Egyptian civilization, were experts in trade and colonization as well, but not of the same magnitude as the Assyrians. An examination of the interwoven quality of Assyrian and Phoenician wealth with trade and tyranny would enable us to follow the European colonists' trail much better and deepen our understanding of how countries like

England, the Netherlands, and Portugal (as well as Spain, France, Belgium, etc.) appropriated such enormous amounts of wealth.

The morals and culture constructed on the base of this appropriation still have Lebanon and Iraq in its grasp; they are still subjected to the most sorrowful wars. The need to secure the merchant and its trade colonies (or, rather, the merchant's interests), has always been one of the main reasons for war and the establishment of states. Trade, the petrol trade, is at the heart of the wars in today's Middle East, too. We would do well to carefully analyze the merchant civilizations.

As we move towards capitalism and the center of civilization shifts to Europe, it is once again trade that leads the way. With the coming of Islam, the trade and merchant civilization, which had been born in the Middle East, took another leap forward during the Middle Ages. Khadija and her employee Muhammad, who later became her partner, laid the foundations of their own trade civilization because of contention with the merchants and usurers of Jewish background and Syriacs of Assyrian descent. Through coercion their trade civilization based itself in Mecca and Medina. Under the religious disguise of Islam, the development of trade revived the ancient Middle Eastern cities. As the Byzantine and Sassanid Empires were defeated they attained large city and market networks especially in Aleppo, Baghdad, Cairo, and Damascus. Globalization was achieved through their trade networks from China to the Atlantic Ocean, from Indonesia to inner Africa. A prevalent commodity and money market was formed. A huge amount of money was accumulated by Jews, Armenians, and Syriacs.

European civilization is wholly based on this inheritance. The trade culture that made another advance via the Muslim merchants of the Middle East was moved to Europe at the beginning of the thirteenth century via the Italian cities of Venice, Genoa, and Florence. Money and trade were the main reasons for the wealth of these cities, who led the trade between Europe and the Middle East until the sixteenth century. They achieved small victories for capitalism at city level in terms of concept as well as their implementation. Mediterranean piracy and price monopoly between the Eastern and Western sides of the Mediterranean played a major role in this achievement. Besides coercion, speculation was also used effectively. As trade expanded capital, capital led to the city, the city to the market, and the market to the expansion of speculation: capitalist civilization had dawned. (As we will discuss in the next section, an earlier European version of the capital-based city civilization occurred during the classical Athenian and Roman eras. However, at the time capitalism did not secure its victory due to agriculture still being widespread and because of their defeat in religious wars.) From around 1300 to 1600 the successful trial of capitalism in the Italian city-states enabled capitalism to expand to Northwest and Northern Europe. Spain had already been conquered. From the sixteenth century, for the first time in their long history, the merchants had exceeded their previous victories over cities— they now attempted (and obtained) victory in countries as a whole.

By the middle of seventeenth century a world-wide market had formed. Africa and the Americas had been put under colonial domination. India and China had been reached through the Atlantic Ocean, dispensing with the need for the Ottoman Empire. Europe was on its way to full urbanization. For the first time cities began to prevail over agriculture. Feudal kingdoms turned into modern monarchic states. The Ottoman Empire, which was the last Islamic empire, experienced consecutive defeats. The Renaissance that started in Italy in the fourteenth century had spread all over Europe, resulting in the Reformation in Northern European countries. It seems that, for the very first time, religious wars were petering out. More importantly though, all the Chinese, Indian, Islamic, and even African and American cultures and their civilizational values had been channeled into Europe. On the one hand, we see the birth of modern states and, on the other hand, the birth of nations.

As capitalism headed toward victory, it based itself upon this history and culture, accumulation of trade, the civilization itself, political power, and the entirety of the world which had been marketed. How can we even think that it would have been possible for the capitalist economy to leap forward without the formation of these preconditions to base itself upon? Without them capital itself can't even be envisaged. Its first step was the initial formation of cities, states, and class at Uruk in Lower Mesopotamia. The second huge step was the establishment of trade and urbanization in Phoenicia and Ionia. Its third huge step was taken in Italy, the Netherlands, and England when the capitalist economy achieved a permanent victory through huge trade, urbanization, and expansion to a world level. With this, capitalism had in fact established itself as above and anti-market, which is still the reality today under the hegemony of the USA. Here, again, Fernand Braudel is closer to the truth than Karl Marx as he insisted that capitalist economy is *anti-market* because it is based on speculative, monopolist price adjustments in big trade fields.[11]

We are witnessing a form of economy that is based on plunder. The appropriation of the accumulated commodities has indeed been most elegantly camouflaged in ideological wrapping. This is only possible under societal circumstances where devotion to religion and morals has become secondary, with the widespread development of the market within society's structure, and where there is an increasing urban control of the rural. In this new form of appropriation, the mechanism of market price formed by supply and demand, and reflected via money, was considerably more advanced than in the past. Instead of the early loan sharks and dealer's banks, there now were the highly sophisticated mechanisms of deposit slips, paper money, credit, accounting, and incorporations. These constituted the main topics of the economic contents in the modern age. But what was really missing was a scientific explanation. Providing this was taken up by the English political economists, and later, paradoxically, its opponents— especially Karl Marx and the socialists—continued this task for them.

This order of depredation called the capitalist economy has colonized all societies, all territories of the new and the old world, and re-enslaved them. It has enchained all power centers to itself, amongst others national states by means of debt (a form of appropriation). It has waged some of the bloodiest wars in history and tampered with the fabric of society in order to have its hegemony approved. Whilst this was the case, Karl Marx and his successors, as well as similar schools of thought, were *not* constructing a science when they declared capitalism as revolutionary in the face of the old society. I think *Das Kapital* is one of the most deficient books against capital and most open to wrong interpretations. Once again, I am not blaming Marx; rather, I am saying that aspects of history, state, revolution, and democracy have not been developed well. And the European intellectuals, who claim to be so scientific, based their analyses and research on *Das*

Kapital, and did *not* in fact generate—not intentionally—anti-capitalist science and ideology "on behalf of the workers."

Liberalism won the ideological war when it took advantage of the fact that the birth of capitalism was declared revolutionary by these intellectuals. It also won the class war—despite the tremendous struggles waged by its opponents—by first assimilating the German social democrats, then the real socialist system (including in Russia and China), and last but not least the national liberation systems by the powers of modernist ideology, nation-state, and industrialism. There is a clear defeat of these three currents (social democracy, real socialism, and national liberation movements) by liberalism, but unfortunately as yet there is no clear self-criticism. If their analyses of capitalism (which is nothing but a war against the working class, society, and its whole history) had been truly scientific, their opposition would not have been defeated to this degree. And, even worse, their inheritance would not have been wasted so easily.

Let us now proceed to define the reality that is called "capitalist economy" and evaluate it according to its functionality. I see no need to redefine basic economic terminology such as *surplus product, surplus value, labor value, wage, profit, price, monopoly, market,* and *money,* as there have been countless scrutinies of them. I shall thus proceed to examine the issues that I feel are lacking and at times comment on their content.

Capitalism has shattered all the historical accumulation of humanity. It is a system that assimilates this accumulation mercilessly by employing refined methods, genocides, and nuclear horror. Economic and social conceptualizations such as *profit and price,* and *bourgeois and proletariat* are the initial steps to scientize (in the positivist way) this system. Economism's basic assertion is that the proletariat alone creates *value* through their labor, the capitalists (in a way the owners of the proletariat) in return for the invested money and other tools of industry snatch the remuneration from this *value,* calling it profit. This interpretation is expounded as a scientific certainty. (This must be what is called economic determinism!) However, a value description so removed from history, society, and political power is problematic. Even an individual deified as a capitalist or worker cannot construct value as such. Economic values have clear historical and social attributes. In the beginning, exchange of goods was a shameful act and the reason why all surplus was given as gifts can be attributed to this sacred meaning given to value. Even today no farmer will claim that the crop is all *their* production; they rather will say "thank God for the blessing" or that they are "benefiting from the cultivation of their ancestors' property." By this, they show a far better understanding of the source of the value than the so-called scientists.

How shall we then define the reward for a mother's labor of carrying the proletariat for nine months and then nurturing him or her until he or she is fit to work? And how do we determine the owners and how do we reward all those who, over thousands of years, had contributed to the construction of production tools, which now have been stolen by the capitalists? Let us not forget that, in not a single case the value of the tools of production is equal to what it is sold for at the market. Even the technical inventions used in a modern factory are the products of thousands of people's collective creativity. How are we to determine the value of their labor and whom are we to pay? Unless morals are totally denied, how can we possibly not acknowledge the social share of these unknown contributors? Will it be just to distribute these historical and social values between only two people? I can continue these important questions, but these adequately illustrate the problematic nature of the profit vs. wages dilemma.

Let us now relate the owners of profit and the earners of wages to the bourgeois and the proletarian classes. Is it factually correct to claim that these two classes were revolutionary at their birth and gave rise to the new society that replaced the old one? There is no counterpart in history for an alliance like this. There are not many historic examples that show these two classes opposing each other in a deep-rooted conflict. Those that do exist, merely show the continuation of the tradition of old conflicts. But what stands out, observable from real life, is that just as the position of the slave was but that of an attachment to the Pharaoh's body, the position of the worker is but that of an attachment to the bourgeois. There is no successful act of rebellion by slaves against their masters. Even Spartacus, often held to be an antecedent of the proletariat rising against the bourgeois, was nothing but a rebel who longed to become a master. Most likely he had nothing else in mind.

It should not be forgotten that the relationship between boss and worker, based on the slave-master relationship that is thousands of years old, is in many ways an interdependent relationship. It is not one of profound rebellion against and victory over the boss—there are only a few exceptions. The relationship that has mostly been maintained over the millennia is on the level of devotion to the boss. It is also clear that events often called workers' rebellions are in fact the rebellion of semi-peasants and of people protesting against unemployment. Rebellions relate to general social influences and they reflect on the relationship between the boss and worker. What is more important, however, is that true rebellion is not a rights-struggle by the worker against the boss, but a struggle against proletarianization and being jobless. In my opinion, social struggle is more meaningful and ethical when it does not accept proletarianization and being turned into a worker as well as refusing to accept being jobless. We should not hail the slave, serf, and worker as they are oppressed. To the contrary, what should be hailed is the ability not to become a slave, serf, or worker. The common, opportunistic trend is to first acknowledge and define the masters and then to propose struggle to its servants. This is indeed the mindset that has frustrated all rights and labor struggles throughout history.

In short, it is neither possible to attempt any kind of sociology nor to develop a successful social struggle based on these early "scientific" concepts! As I point this out, I need to reiterate that I do not deny the role of labor, value, profit, and class but I do not approve of the way they are used in the construction of science and indeed of sociology.

Capitalism occurs at the higher levels of society's economic life. In its early stages, capitalism is dependent on the accumulation of capital through price monopoly by big merchants in the markets. Capital, by definition, is monetary value that continuously increases itself. Huge value accumulations are squeezed out in far-off markets with enormous price differences between them. The second way to obtain enlargement is by demanding interest and *iltizam* in return for monetary loans granted to the state.[12] Famine, war, and mining ventures are periods and areas in which capital is able to grow. Aside from trade, capitalism participates in agriculture, industry, and transport when it deems these areas to be profitable. After the Industrial Revolution, the main area for capitalist profit was the industrial sector. Demand and supply are always manipulated so that the capitalist can determine both production and consumption. Profit margins increase proportional to capitalism's ability to determine production and consumption. Big trade and industry were the profit areas during capitalism's initial and maturity phases; however, today it is mostly the financial sector. Money, deposit slips, banks, and tools of credit assist the acceleration of capitalist economy by shortening, intensifying, and expanding the profit cycles. In this way, major speculative balloons are formed in profit rates and thus periods of crisis are made intrinsic parts of the capitalist economy.

There are of course other methods to inflate profits; increasing unemployment (which causes wages to fall) and investment in countries that have cheap labor are two examples. Finally, though this form of economy that originated in the ancient hunter and trade culture has grasped the chance to advance itself (through attaining power to fluctuate prices; to escape social supervision by loosening morals and religion; to enchain the political power through debt) and has formed a monopoly over the market, it is unavoidable that such an economy is ultimately nothing but an economy of plunder. It gains a foothold in industry only for profit, basing itself on the type of production and consumption that increases profit rates and results in crisis, decay, and collapse (which have been there since its birth) as it increasingly harms the social structure and the environment.

However, *this* is not the economy in its entirety. Trade, agriculture, and industry on the one hand, and transport, technical tools, and markets on the other, are not the inventions of capitalism. On the contrary, they are the fundamental social economic institutions that have been subjected to capitalism's severe exploitation and plunder. They are determined by history and civilization and are intertwined with politics.

I have tried to show that economism is nothing but a tendency to distort the definition of capitalist economy. I have also attempted to show how capitalism *should* be interpreted in terms of history and society, politics and civilization, and its cultural ties.

Capitalism's relationship with political power and law

The nucleus of capitalism was formed in the seedbed of political power and law. Capitalism benefits from all forms of power and their legal systems.

When it suits its purpose, capitalism is the most ardent advocate of such power and legal systems; but, when its profits are under threat, it will overthrow that particular system without hesitation, using various types of conspiracies.[13] It even at times takes part in the boldest revolutionary games. It wages power struggles—especially during times of crisis and chaos—using both fascist coup d'états and bogus state communist coup d'états.[14] Indeed, it has waged the most extensive of all colonial and imperial wars.

I must emphasize that capitalism's need for the armor of power has never been equaled by that of any other economic form. Capitalism could not have come into existence without this armor. The principal assumption of the political-economy "scientists" is that profit, surplus product and value were formed outside power relations for the first time in history. They claim that this was achieved through economical methods such as the voluntary union of capital and labor. According to them, this is indeed capitalism's key characteristic. In fact, what we face here is a rhetoric as distorted as the labor theory.

Let us look at the picture they paint us: Capital was peacefully formed somewhere or other. As a result of peaceful relations, villagers, serfs, and craftsman came together, left their production tools behind and put together the new economic form right there and then—almost like a happy revolutionary marriage. This is how the story is more or less told, through the formation of a synthesis they have come up with a new economic form. In all their texts, the giants of political economy—whether left or right—have almost given this idea the status of a creed. Without it, there would be no political economy. Add competition in the market place to this credo and you have the fundamental principles of political economy—a perfect book.

I don't see the need to make any claims myself. The research by the sociologist and historian Fernand Braudel, published as *Civilization and Capitalism* (on which he worked for 30 years, producing a magnificent, three-volume monument), explicitly refutes this claim through extensive observations and by using a comparative approach. His first conclusion is that capitalism is anti-market. Secondly, that capitalism is completely in league with power and ruling. Thirdly, that capitalism has been monopolist since the beginning, before the establishment of industry, and it is still monopolist. Fourthly, it did not come about as a result of competition from below and within but rather externally and from the top through plunder and monopolistic practice. This is the main substance of his book. There are some aspects that I disagree with or that I find insufficient. But in general, and in its essence, it is the most valuable historical and sociological interpretation that I have seen. It is a good start to correcting the damage and distortions (done to social sciences) of the English political economists, French socialists, and German historians and philosophers.

Thus, there is no economic order formed between capitalist and worker through a union of their strength and labor accumulation in a voluntary and free competitive environment. No other tale is so far off the mark. None of the elements and economic power which we can regard as belonging to the capitalist class can survive without the protection of political power; indeed, without this protection the capitalists cannot maintain their rule. Moreover, without an extensive siege of the political power, there can be no market for the exchange of goods and labor through free competition in any of the city markets. Most importantly, without brutal and unfair coercion, it would not be possible to separate the serf, peasant, and urban craftsman from his land or workbench. In Europe, the land and plant workers rebelled against such coercion from the 14th to the 19th centuries.[15] Thousands were executed, millions killed in civil wars, and many more withered away in prisons and hospitals.

But this was not enough: religious and national wars, along with colonialist and imperialist wars, immersed the world in blood. The relationship between such coercion and the monopolistic and plundering character of capitalism can be clearly seen at its inception. No rhetoric by political economy can reverse this reality.

To illustrate this more concretely, we should have a closer look at the sixteenth century wars that carried the capitalists to victory. The emperors of the Habsburg dynasty's Spanish branch, the kings of the Valois dynasty in France, the Anglo-Saxon Stuarts' that usurped England's Norman kings, and, more interestingly, the House of Orange-Nassau, the heirs to the crown of the Netherlands (who have never been mentioned in this regard before), were to be the century's principal contributors to power and war.

The Habsburg kings and emperors were encouraged as the Muslims were driven from Spain at the end of the fifteenth century; they then rapidly moved towards empire. They saw themselves as the heirs of Rome. This was particularly due to the fall of Constantinople at the hands of the Ottoman dynasty in 1453 and the fact that the Austrian Habsburgs led the war against the Ottomans. The French Valois dynasty too desired an empire. They too saw themselves as the true heirs of Rome. Both the English Kingdom and the Netherlands' House of Orange waged proto-national liberation struggles to prevent being engulfed by these two empires. The Kingdom of Sweden, the Prussian Princedom, and even Muscovy's Tsardom followed a similar course. If the Habsburgs and the Valois had succeeded in engulfing the English Kingdom and the Orange Princedom at the onset of sixteenth century, then it is highly probable that the capitalist development that occurred in the cities of Northwest Europe (and especially in England and the Netherlands) would have shared the fate of the Italian cities of Venice, Genoa, and Florence.

The fundamental reason why these very strong, capitalist Italian cities were not able to declare the victory of capitalism all over Italy was because they were politically weak. Or rather, the hegemonic wars and conquests that the Spanish, French, and Austrian kings and empires waged against the Italian cities (and thus on their wealth) resulted in the surrender of these cities. They had to be content with restricted economic and political power. Therefore, not only was the union of Italy delayed until the nineteenth century, but capitalism's Italian experiment was half-baked and not able to spread across the country. Albeit temporarily, coercion played a decisive role. But (and as any capitalistic agency would do) the Italian urban capitalists enchained these states (that is, the Spanish, French and Austrian) by financial means in return for abandoning any claim they may have had to sovereignty: not hesitating to become an instrument of give and take policies. This is because capitalism—as a new religion—was being constructed around money.

There were two reasons why the Kingdom of England and the Principality of Orange were able to stay the imperial states. One was the fact that the capitalists gave credit to the English and Dutch states; the other that they constructed the maritime transport industry in cooperation with these states. (In fact, England and the Netherlands concentrated their efforts on naval forces instead of land forces.)

At the time, there were two strategic developments. First: The English Kingdom and the Principality of the Netherlands focused on a state model that reorganized itself and operated in capitalist way. They were the first states to nurture themselves with regular taxes, balance the budgets, to have rational bureaucracy, and to protect themselves with professional armies. Moreover, they defeated the naval forces of Spain and France with their superior naval forces. Their success in the Atlantic Ocean and their later hegemony in the Mediterranean determined the outcome of the colonial wars. This was the beginning of the end of the Spanish and French kingdoms. (The success that the Spanish and French kings had with their land forces cost so much that it turned into a Pyrrhic victory.) The improvements in the power structures of England and the Netherlands thus were decisive for the fate of the capitalist economy. It is once again observable that at a very critical moment political force can play a decisive role in the formation of an economic form. And so, where the Italian cities failed, London and Amsterdam succeeded.

Second: In the imperial states of Spain, France, and Austria a development different to the one in England and the Netherlands took place in the sixteenth century. These three states, who shared bonds of kinship but also severe mutual conflict, wanted to establish empires similar to that of Rome. The English Kingdom had abandoned such a desire earlier on. Instead of just a European empire, it had set its eyes on becoming a world empire. But despite the many reforms aimed at turning the Spanish, French, and Austrian state regimes into modern monarchies, they were still at heart political instruments shaped according to the old societal systems. They were far from creating a modern taxation system, bureaucracy and a professional army. They had budget deficits and as a result were constantly in debt. They were unable to resolve the perturbations caused by capitalist development. In contrast to England and the Netherlands, they had no support from the capitalists; instead, there were major internal conflicts due to debts and tax farming. The imperial states had more problems than England with the feudal aristocracy on issues such as centralization and advancement towards a monarchic kingdom. Due to the urban and rural conflicts, society as a whole was in a state of unrest—these rebellions alone would have been enough to suffocate the monarchies. The clandestine support England and the Netherlands gave the opponents of the imperial states led to the outbreak of many revolutions. (Of course, the results of a revolution may differ greatly from one's objectives with starting it, just as it was with the French Revolution.)

The very same powers that prevented the political and social victory of the capitalist economy in Italy—the French, Spanish, and Austrian monarchies—could not escape repeated defeats inflicted by the productive state models financed by England's and the Netherlands' urban capitalists. Once again, we can very clearly see the relationship between economic form and coercive systems; we also see that their relationship was decisive in the birth of strategic outcomes. Sixteenth century Europe is the perfect laboratory for observing the relationship between coercion, power, and economy. It is as if the entire civilizational history has awakened to tell its own story: "The better you understand sixteenth century Europe, the better you will understand me!" A short summary of the historic and social development of the relationship between coercion and economy may clarify the issue at hand:

In the pre-civilization period, the "strong man" of the clan used the organized forces that existed for hunting to obtain control over the initial economy of society.

In the social epochs preceding civilization, the initial organized force of the "strong man" did not only trap animals. It was this organized force, yet again, that coveted the family-clan unit that the woman had established as a product of her emotional labor. The take-over of the family-clan constituted the first serious organization of force. What were usurped in the process was woman herself, her children and kin, and all their material and moral cultural accumulation. It was the plunder of the initial economy, the home economy. The organized force of proto-priest (shaman), the *hakīm sheikh* (experienced, wise elder), and the strong man (with his organized force) allied to compose the initial and long-term patriarchal hierarchic power, that of holy governance. This can be seen in all societies that are at a similar stage: until the class, city, and state stage, this hierarchy is dominant in social and economic life.

The economic formation of the civilizational period that began with the establishment of class-city-state—the power center personified with the priest, king, and commander define the state.

The institutions of religion, politics, and military forces are all interlinked, thus forming power itself. The main characteristic of this power system is that it organizes its own economy as state communism. This economy is what I call (at the time I hadn't yet seen Max Weber use the term) *Pharaoh socialism*. Pharaoh socialism worked the people like simple slaves: their reward a bowl of soup in order to keep them alive (as can be seen from the thousands of slave bowls found in the remnants of old temples and palaces). Remnants of the matriarchal economy continued to exist within the patriarchal, feudal, and tribal economy.

Force, when institutionalized as the state, sees economic plunder as its right wherever it goes. Plunder, in a way, is thought to be the right of the one that uses force. Force is divine and sacred; everything it does is righteous and legitimate. This was especially so in the main centers of civilization (such as the ones in Middle East, China, and India) where the political superstructure or highest caste saw infrastructure as part of the economy and believed they had the power to administer them however they liked. At the time, neither market nor competition had yet developed, nor had the concept of economic sector as it exists today. However, trade did exist and was seen as one of the main functions between states. Trade was far from being privatized: state monopoly was at the same time a trade monopoly. Some market towns were established at the periphery of states; some even turned into city states. Trade was done by caravan, which meant that robbery by the strong man of the area (and much later by pirates, bandits, and the robber barons—the "forty thieves" of Scheherazade's story) was as bad as the state robbery.

Their cultural inheritance from the violent Babylonian and Assyrian empires saw to it that autonomous towns, markets, and trade became widespread and extensive in Greco-Roman civilization.

The despotic Babylonian and Assyrian states (themselves the heirs of Uruk and Ur) made a new contribution to civilization and economy by introducing trade agents, who were in fact the embodiment of the concepts of markets, trading colonies, and profit. There had already been trade colonies in the Uruk era and even earlier; increased exchange at the end of the era and the formation of the market prepared the ground for the rise of the Assyrian state as the first "magnificent" empire in history. Empires were a response to the need for economic security. In Assyria, the backbone of the economy was trade. This trade and trading colonies required a political organization in the form of an empire. History sees the Assyrian Empire as the most brutal example of empire and despotism. Here, once again, the basis is the trade monopoly—yet a draft of capitalism. The Assyrian trade and monopolist capitalism brought with it the most brutal regime.

By adding the urban trade-colonies of the Phoenicians to their Assyrian inheritance, the Greco-Roman political power was able to create an economic infrastructure with a more advanced political superstructure. Exchange had by now become widespread, and autonomous cities, markets, trade, and competition (although limited) came into play. Urbanization started to balance the role of the rural areas. The rural areas now produced more surplus product for the cities so that it could be exchanged. Textiles, food, and metal trade developed. Road networks were built from China to the Atlantic Ocean. As a result of the trade between East and West, the political power in Iran was transformed into a permanent merchant empire. This put so much pressure on the Greeks and Romans that Iran became hegemonic. They were also the main obstacle preventing the Chinese, Indian, and Central Asians from fulfilling their desire to occupy the West. At the same time, the Iranian Empire was the obstacle that prevented the West from fulfilling their desire to occupy the East. Alexander and the Diadochi were the first to destroy this obstacle and occupy enormous parts of the East, but only for a short time (330-250 BCE).[16]

The early examples of capitalist economy are seen most clearly in the Greco-Roman civilization. That these powers were on the verge of capitalism is clear from the degree of autonomy of the towns, the fact that exchange and determining of price took place at the market, and the existence of big merchants. Capitalism was not yet the dominant social system, as the rural areas were still stronger than the towns. The existence of the empires (that relied predominantly on a rural economy) did not allow capitalism to become the dominant social system. The capitalists' ability to intervene in production and industry was very limited and they were subject to strict intervention from the political powers. They mainly remained at the level of large-scale merchants. At the time, the status of the slave was still one of devotion to the master and there was little chance of a free labor force. Women were sold and bought as concubines and men as slaves. The determining factor in a slave economy is violence; the existence of slaves as an economic value alone clearly shows the relationship between violence and economy, that is, an economy based on seizure of surplus-product. Since their formation and the start of their capitalist exploitation, the political and military castes of the Chinese and Indian systems of Antiquity believed their main duty was to rule the entire society. They viewed the rest of society as a subservient, economic sector and saw it as their divine right to make them work.

As explained earlier, the term *economy* originated in the Greek world. Its original meaning of "family management" points to the connection between economy and women. But it also points to the role of traditional political power that, as political monopoly, played the same role in the economy as the monopolies in the age of capitalism. I must underline that there is a strict correlation between political monopoly and economic monopoly and, in general, one requires the other. The political powers of Athens and Rome were so huge that, paradoxically, it shut its doors to capitalism. On the other hand, urban power was so small relative to that of the rural areas, that neither Athens nor Rome could command a city-based economy. Nevertheless, in this period of civilization, capitalism was introduced into the system, even though it was not yet ready for wholesale, systemic capitalist development.

Trade and the sword played a fundamental part in the rise of Islam, thereby determining values that found their way to Europe.

In medieval Islamic civilization, trade had reached a point where it played an influential role. Economically, the Prophet Muhammad and Islam were closely connected to trade.[17] Sandwiched between the Byzantine and Sassanid Empires, an Arab aristocracy had developed, founded on trade.[18] This became the main social and economic factor in the rise of Islam. From its birth, Islam has predicated itself on the strength of the sword. The Jews' and Syriacs' (remnants of the Assyrians) domination of trade and money clearly was one reason for the conflict between them and Muhammad's followers. In fact, they as the two political monopolies did not give the Byzantine and Sassanid Empires much room to act. Again, this situation at such a turning point in history and in this ancient location clearly shows the relationship between coercion and economy.

The Middle Ages were, in a way, an Islamic era. For trade to forge ahead security was needed and thus empire was needed. But exactly because of the need for security, trade was continuously obstructed and the transformation of trade capital into capitalistic production mode continuously prevented. The social fabric of the rural areas was under the scrutiny of religion and morals, and the limited freedom this capital gained in the towns could not be transformed into political power. Although there was an extensive network of towns and markets, and the towns had grown considerably, they were not strong enough to surpass the status of the Italian cities. The problem was definitely not one of technology. It was due to religious and political monopolists. It is in accordance with Islam's religious-political system that the merchant was often subjected to confiscation of his goods.

The fact that Islam has not given way to capitalism is a positive aspect of Islam. It still is the most serious obstacle to capitalism through its conception of *ummah* and internationalism of peoples, its opposition to interest, its assistance to the poor, etc. If these are interpreted positively, they may be important contributions to projects for social freedom. However, it should be noted that the present day Islamic radicalism carries with it a right wing and economic nationalism full of neo-Islamic capitalism.

It was the Arabs and Berbers under leadership of the Andalusian Umayyads who carried the Islamic civilization culturally to Europe. It was the Italian city merchants who carried it economically, through trade. The Ottomans only carried it through political monopolies, their only influence an impetus to the growth of capitalism when the European political and religious forces utilized this system in order to keep standing against the Ottoman onslaught. Had the Ottomans not existed, it just may be that the religious and political monopolies of Europe would not have been forced to organize themselves economically, politically, and militarily according to the capitalistic method. One can see yet again that power results in power and that it accelerates the search for modes of economy.

As Max Weber demonstrated in *The Protestant Ethic and the Spirit of Capitalism*, the decisive contribution of the Middle East to the birth of capitalism in Europe is related to Christianity. I hope to go into more detail in my next book. By the tenth century its role of determining the ethics of Europe was completed; thus, the Middle East played a fundamental role in the birth of feudal Europe (both politically and religiously). Then the Middle East once again was channeled to Europe via the Crusader wars.

When this brief summary of the historic and social developments is viewed together with my evaluation of the sixteenth century, the century that birthed the capitalist system, our understanding of Middle East's influence on the birth of political power and capitalism will be enhanced—at times it inhibited and prevented, at times it accelerated and even fertilized. The dictum that state monopoly equals capitalist monopoly is demonstrated most clearly in the capitalist system. I will now briefly touch on a few aspects regarding the relationship between law and the new system.

Law as an institution imposes itself on a society as trade, market, and town relations develop. Societies where law comes into play are societies where morals are worn out, where the role force plays has increased and caused chaos, and where inequality is distinctly experienced. The problems concerning morality and inequality arise around the class divisions and markets of the cities. Thus, for states law becomes inevitable. Although it is possible to govern the state without law, it certainly is very difficult.

Law can be defined as the act of the state's political power becoming permanent, orderly, and institutionalized—in a way it is a state which has attained calmness and steadiness. No other institution has such close ties to the state as law. The relationship between trade and state has become increasingly complex and sophisticated, from the beginning to date—the phase of capitalism. Codes of law were drawn up in many states, from Ur to Babylon to Rome.[19] These codes mostly dealt with security of property and prevention of the loss of life. Usually, law tries to relieve problems caused by politics, but there are times when it aggravates these problems.

The role of law, contrary to general belief, is *not* to ensure equal treatment of all citizens but to legitimize the existent inequalities, to keep these at an acceptable level, and to render political power untouchable. In short, viewing law as the permanent regulation of political power monopoly is closer to the truth.

The relationship between law and morals is of great importance. Morals are the cement of a society. There is no society without morals. Morals are the initial organizational principle of human society; their true function to regulate the ordering and shaping of analytical and emotional intelligence into a code of principles and conduct for the good of society, a code that sees the entire society as equal, but protects the role of and right to diversity. At first, morals represented the collective conscience of society. However, moral society suffered its first blow with the institutionalization of political power and hierarchy in the form of the state when class division brought moral division.

This was the start of the morality problem. Whereas the political elite sought legal solutions to this problem, the priests responded to the morality problem through methods of religion—both law and religion claiming morality as their source. In the same way that the permanent, orderly and institutionalized mechanisms of political power constitute law and attempt to solve their problems through legal methods, the constructors of religion attempt to resolve the moral crisis with religion. The difference between them is that law has the power of implementation, whereas religion relies on the fear of god and conscience.

Because morality pertains to the human's ability to choose, it is closely connected with freedom. Morality entails freedom, society shows its level of freedom through its morals. Hence, if there is no freedom, there are no morals. The best way to bring a society down is to cut its ties with its morals. Weakening of religious influence will not lead to such a collapse. The vacuum thus created can be filled with various ideologies and political philosophies and economic lifestyles (which themselves have almost become religion). However, the vacuum left by the dissolution of morals can only be filled by being doomed, and by deprivation of freedom. It is thus of grave importance to formulate the true function of morals. It is the duty of ethics, as the theory of morals, to examine the existence of morals as a fundamental philosophical question and to restore its principal role. But its true role must be laid bare. Until morality becomes the fundamental principle of life, this will continue to be a problem of undiminishing importance within the society.

Understanding the relationship between political power, law, and morals is important for our discussion of the birth of the capitalist economy. In a society where religion and morals (or even feudal law) are not sporadically disrupted, where they are not worn out, it will be impossible for a capitalist economy to secure a place for itself. I am not advocating the approach of the former upper classes to that of religion and morals; I am saying that the ethics of major religions and major traditions and teachings of morality will find a system such as capitalism extremely difficult to be compatible with their own principles. Furthermore, whereas the influence of political power on moral and religious issues is limited, the downfall of religion and morals signals the end of a political power. Discussions of reformation, law, and moral philosophy in the sixteenth and seventeenth centuries are, clearly, closely related to the birth of capitalism.

The Protestant Reformation and the ensuing debates and wars were the main determinants of the fate of modern age Europe. In his evaluation of the role of Protestant morals, Max Weber neglected a very important point: Protestantism eased the birth of capitalism but has dealt a huge blow in general to religion and morals, especially Catholicism. Protestantism is thus also quite responsible for all the sins of capitalism. I am not defending religion and Catholicism, but I maintain that Protestantism has left society more defenseless. Wherever Protestantism took root, capitalism thrived. In a way, it has acted as Trojan Horse for capitalism.

There were philosophers that gave early warning against the problems that resulted from Protestant reformation and the new Leviathan it has created. It would be more realistic to call Friedrich Nietzsche the spearhead of taking a stance against capitalist modernity. Even today these philosophers are important for their anti-capitalist stance and their quest for a free society and a free individual.

The discussions and re-theorizing of law by jurist-philosophers such as Thomas Hobbes of England (1588–1679) and Grotius (Hugo de Groot) from the Netherlands (1583–1645) helped to pave the way for the new Leviathan, the capitalist state.[20] By handing the monopoly of violence to the state, society was disarmed.[21] The end result was the centralized nation-state that culminated in fascism, a form of state that has centralized power on a scale unknown in any other time in history. The theory of the indivisibility of sovereign rule entails that all the social forces apart from state are left with no power, leaving society destitute and without its tools of self-defense against the capitalist monster. In short, these two philosophers declared man's inhumanity to man and presented the good news, namely that the monarch's monopolist power was absolute. This paved the way to the capitalist monopoly. If I may repeat: political monopoly equals economic monopoly. The Florentine philosopher Niccolò Machiavelli (1469–1527) openly declared, without hiding behind any disguise, that for political success, when the need arises, no moral rule should be adhered to, thus uttering the principle required for fascism centuries earlier.

I do not wish to be misunderstood: I do not reject or criticize all the efforts of reformation. In my opinion, religious reformation should not happen once but as often as possible. For many years now, I have been saying that an Islamic reformation, one more profound and ongoing than that of Christianity is a necessity. Clearly, such action requires capacity and personality. But if we are to transcend Middle Eastern despotism, it is unavoidable. I plan to discuss this and related subjects in a separate work.

I will not discuss the Renaissance and Enlightenment here. Of course, it is not proper to generalize and I need to say this clearly: As much as there were those who deliberately opened the way for capitalism, there were those who tried to block it. It is understandable that capitalist elements wished to assimilate their opponents (by relying on the power of their money) as much as the political power wished to tie their opponents down. But, of course, there were the great freedom philosophers who wished to serve humanity even at the risk of being burnt: reformers like Giordano Bruno and Erasmus, as well as utopists and proponents of communes.[22]

I want to stress that during the ages of the Renaissance, Reformation, and Enlightenment all civilizations came alive; they all were revived. They expressed, pictured, and turned themselves into melodies. They became both divine and subject. They fought and made peace. They won and were beaten. However, in the end, the capitalist elements that had been lying in ambush in the marginal corners and crevices of society for countless centuries crowned their system with glory by exploiting and assimilating the *zeitgeist* through the use of violence, money, and material power, for they were the best prepared organizational and material power at the time. And their system is still continuing its victorious march.

The location of capitalism

The locality of a society is a question that is well worth our consideration as it entails an understanding of the development of human society and its relation to geography. This is a comprehensive topic, and one can add a long list of questions and answers to the topic of geography, from the formation of our solar system, to the evolution of plants and the animal world as well, approximately when the human species began to take shape. The effect of geographical conditions on the initial societal form of the human community—tribes—the *longue durée* phase is more significant. It may be more correct to view the inability of the tribal society to advance to another phase as due to unsuitability of the geographical conditions and not to insufficient internal evolution. If not, a few million years of clan existence might have been enough for internal evolution. Geographers agree that in general the geographical environment at the end of the last glacial period was similar to that of the present. At the end of the last glacial period, after different phases in Asia, Europe, and Africa, the human species began a new period with the onset of Homo Sapiens.

Thus, it is clear that there is a close correlation and dialectical relationship between humans and geography. For example, if the atmosphere, plants and animals, the soil, and freshwater resources are exhausted, the human species will not survive. It is as if all this is the result of a grand intelligence; even a temporary deterioration of such resources may bring the end of human life. Therefore, the relationship between humans and geography must always be taken into consideration. In its absence, there can be no social science. Until recently, most philosophical, scientific, and religious work has treated this relationship as beside the point. Oddly enough, mythology—considered to be farther removed from reality—was more interested in topics dealing with the relationship between geography and humans. Science's lack of interest in this issue must be the result of the separation of analytic intelligence from emotional intelligence.

Various anthropological and archaeological studies suggest that after 20,000 BCE three cultural groups became more prominent. The first group, the Semitic peoples, arrived from the African continent in the last wave of immigration. They mainly spread to North Africa and Arabia, and partly to the foothills of the Taurus-Zagros mountain system. A branch of the second group broke away from the Siberian foothills and reached the American continent over the Bering Strait, while the main branch spread to the western shores and islands of the Pacific Ocean or to the inner lands of Central Asia; a sub-branch (the Finno-Ugric branch) spread to Eastern and Northern Europe. They are today referred to as Asians and Native Americans, and the Chinese, Japanese, and Turks constitute the greater number within this group. The more prosperous and extensive area in between these two groups was where the Indo-European group was located. This is the main group that started the civilization and, before that, the Neolithic Agricultural Era. The other two groups made a delayed transition to the Neolithic and to civilization in the north and the south. Such a transition is difficult to imagine without the transfer of accumulations from the Indo-European group.

Most leading anthropologists, archaeologists, geologists, and biologists agree that the Tauros-Zagros foothills offer the most suitable conditions for the transition to the Neolithic and the Civilization Eras. Amongst the decisive factors were the available species of animals and vegetation, abundance of rain and rivers, climate, and geology. It also had the ideal location as it was the main area of transition between Africa, Asia and Europe, and the ideal place for a stopover. The leading core of the Indo-European group were called Aryan by those who first started the civilization. They played a leading role in establishing both the Neolithic-agricultural and the city-state-civilization eras and in spreading them around the world.

In the preceding volume on civilization, I have discussed in detail how different cultural groups have spread around and influenced the world. I will not repeat myself as our concern here is to determine the role of this aspect of geography in societal development, and why capitalist economy finally attained its victory in the then relatively unknown Netherlands and in English at the time.

Present day social scientists see the role of geography mainly in terms of geopolitics or geostrategy, thus not taking into consideration the essential aspect of geography. However, establishing the relationship between historical sociality and geography (in its unrestricted sense) is more fundamental and should have higher priority than the role of geopolitics or geostrategy—it is more meaningful to deal with the roots than the offshoots! Generally speaking, to attain a meaningful anthropology and knowledge of history, it is essential that we examine the different eras and civilizations with regard to their geography. We cannot reconstruct history without location. Indeed, the dual antagonism of space-time, being the main dimensions of the universe, is always on our mind. Their effect on each other, even their ability to transform and unite, is a crucial part of the sciences.

I want to return to our story of the strong and crafty man.[23] But let me first say that in order to practice meaningful science, we need to establish a relationship between narrative, knowledge, and science. In my opinion, a science without a story cannot be deemed meaningful. And, I believe, that the historical story of the strong and crafty man is a concept that should be a cornerstone of the social sciences. We need this concept for a more accurate interpretation of various social relations. In fact, in areas where there are numerous events and relations, making use of narratives render the most valuable contributions to science. Determining such numerous amounts of events and relationships is not possible under the religionism called positivism. But science may be developed far better through the use of religion, morals, and other forms of art—all are narratives of some sort.

To return to the strong and crafty man: Until he makes the transition to the position of dominant man and bases himself in the centers of super power, he has pursued a long road with many mazes and many conspiracies. Thus, it is important that we look for the locations where these men have their power centers and the locations where they hide or shelter should the need arise. We will understand them better if we conceive of these men as a strategic force that continuously designs social tactics—that is, economic, political, and military tactics.

The strong and crafty man entered the house economy of the woman like a burglar. Not content with plundering, he subjected her to constant rape in order to turn the sacred family home into a robber's nest, the den of the forty thieves. He has never moved past the mentality of a *self-conscious* traitor. His initial accumulation of capital took place in two locations: firstly, in order to get control of the house economy, he occupied the home; secondly, in reaction to the state's official and legitimized monopoly, he created a private monopoly similar to the one of the forty thieves. Because he was scared of society and of the state's surveillance, he quite early on started to move between these locations with a masked or false face. He expertly hid in the cracks and crannies of society's fabric where he lay in ambush. When the time was right, he pounced on his prey like a lion; at other times, he would camouflage himself chameleon-like by blending in with the environment he found himself in and caught his prey with the craftiness of a fox. He became the expert on trade at marginal points—towns and rural areas out of the easy reach of civilization were closely under his watch. He knew how to rob both the urban and the rural by striking a balance between them. He was astute enough to make smaller gains from short haul trade, the biggest gains from long haul. The fundamental rule of his profession was to know where the most profit was to be made and to steer towards those places. But viewing his action as the strategic piracy of these roads is quite instructive! This is probably what is meant by the saying "capital has no homeland."

If city, market, and trade are the preconditions for the existence of capitalism, why did it not declare its victory in these locations much earlier? Instead of rising to success in Amsterdam, it could just as well have happened in the city of Uruk. At this point, I have to point out that capitalism as a system has no direct relationship with the advanced science and technology. In my opinion, the reason why it couldn't succeed may have something to do with the religious, political, and military power monopolies not allowing it any space in which it could establish its own hegemony. These centers of power, previously tested and who had gained legitimacy, might have viewed a fourth pillar of power as excessive and, due to its structure, a threat to their own existence.

At times, capital did try to hijack the system by establishing itself as the fourth monopoly, but it was always defeated—this may well be one of the reasons for the ruins of so many cities that were found in unexpected locations. The reason for wealthy merchant cities' sudden disappearance from history (both in antiquity and in medieval times) may be related to political and military resistance of the fourth monopoly, primitive capitalism. A case in point is that of the city of Harappa (at its peak around

2,500 BCE). Part of the advanced Indus civilization with its sophisticated architecture, trade network, and writing system, this large and wealthy city was erased from the map quite early on, around 1,900 BCE. While the reason for the demise of Harappa is not clear, it could well have been due to Harappan competition and rebellion against the monopoly of the priest-politician-soldier triumvirate. It is highly probable that while Harappa may have been a trade colony of a Sumerian based civilization, it might later have desired independence and hence rebelled. Had the rebellion succeeded, since Harappa did not possess the same conditions as its competitors, it might have attempted establishing a system like that of Amsterdam (the initial capitalist experiment).

An even more striking example is the story of Carthage. This city, built by Phoenicians around the eighth century BCE at the far end of Mediterranean, was based mainly on trade. Because of its location both the West Mediterranean and North Africa served as its hinterland. While Carthage grew into the richest Mediterranean city of its time and clearly had an advanced society, due to the circumstances at the time it did not establish an empire. This was its weakness. And it prevented others from doing so (probably the reason behind its conflict with Rome). Due to its location, it was easier for Rome to progress beyond city-state by conquering other territories in the Italian peninsula and thus have the ability to establish a republic or an empire.[24]

The only way for Carthage to escape eventual ruin would have been to do what Amsterdam did when it was under threat by the empires of Spain and France, namely reinforcing the city's advanced trade monopoly by establishing a capitalistic state device coupled with geographical expansion (in North Africa or, as the Moroccan Umayyad dynasty did, in Spain). It had no other option if it wanted to escape the Roman Republic. But then, Rome had no option but to defeat Carthage: if it did not, a nearby competing empire that could have meant the end of Roman superiority. Quite reminiscent of the relationship between Cuba and the USA!

A similar case was the famous East Syrian city of Palmyra that fell victim to Rome in the 3rd century, during the first crisis of the Roman Empire's decline. During my stay in Syria, I often visited the ruins of Palmyra and was truly captivated by this city in the heart of the Syrian

Desert with its single spring surrounded by a forest of palm trees. It is indeed a fascinating city with its castle, high walls, agora, famous Temple of Bel, the senate building, the Valley of the Tombs, long markets, and numerous palaces. The stone carvings are extraordinary. A city that leaves one in deep reverence and horror.

Palmyra acquired its importance due to its central location on the East-West and North-South trade networks; this city-state also functioned as a buffer between the Roman and Iranian Sassanid Empires. For many centuries, it grew and grew due to its trade monopolies. The enormous wealth it acquired probably outdid that of Amsterdam in its golden age and that of present-day New York. As with Carthage, the Roman Empire grew uncomfortable with this city-state and in 44 BCE made its first attempt to occupy it. From then until 272 BCE, Palmyra was under varying forms of Roman rule and became the most important caravan city of the Roman Empire. During its final period, the city grew dissatisfied with being a kingdom dependent on Rome and desired to transform itself into an empire equal to Rome. Could Palmyra achieve what Carthage could not?

For Rome, this possibility held a dangerous threat. The Roman emperor Aurelius seized the city and left it to Zenobia with the status of province of Rome. On his return to Rome, the news reached him that the city had rebelled once again and desired its independence. In anger, he turned back to Palmyra and this time he left behind only ruins, taking Zenobia to Rome in chains after she was caught in the act of running off to the Sassanids.[25]

So, the only way out for Palmyra would have been to do what Amsterdam or London did. It put up resistance. But it was not successful.

It may also be instructive to add classical Athens to this list of victims. This city, the result of sea trade, was the star of the civilization between 500 BCE and 350 BCE. It is possible to presume that it was a city with the most developed primitive capitalism. Big and private (not state) trade monopolies did business from thousands of kilometers away. All the wealth flooded to Athens. The trade networks from the Eastern Mediterranean to Marseilles, from North Africa to Macedonia and from all of Anatolia to the Black Sea, flooded Athens with surplus product and money. It had already created philosophy and brought craftsmanship to the verge of establishing factories. The art of ship building was at its peak and money was well in circulation. It had colonies everywhere. The rich came to Athens from all over the world. It can be seen as the first cosmopolitan city. In my personal view, it's one and only shortcoming—that it could not attain unity within the Peninsula—was the only obstacle preventing a capitalist victory. There was no shortage of labor either. The slaves sold at the markets were indeed very cheap. The level it attained forced Athens to either surpass the old structures of slavery and become a nation-state within the boundaries of the Peninsula and reach the position Netherlands had attained, or to be defeated by its rivals and be left in an insignificant state. The ground forces of the Spartan Kingdom and the Persian Empire attacked this city for more than a century. Athens, however, strove to stand strong based on its democracy. The claws of the Macedonian Kings, Phillip II and his son, Alexander, resulted in a strategic defeat for Athens. Eventually, in the face of the Roman and Anatolian Hellenistic kingdoms, Athens had no chance for making the necessary advance.

I could also give examples from the medieval period—from the Islamic civilization and the Indian peninsula. But the most striking examples of this period are the famous capitalist cities of the Italian peninsula. Venice, Genoa, and Florence lost their chance of being an Amsterdam or London when Spanish, French and Austrian empires desired old style empires and, thus, broke their domination over other towns and in the peninsula. The Italian cities established everything necessary for the construction of modern capitalism.

They had the capital accumulation, banks, firms, credit system, and deposit slips as finance tools; they had short and long-haul trade; they had various types of craftsmen and artisans and could manufacture all the industrial items of the time; they had at their disposal republican and imperial practices, religion, and various denominations. In fact, the Italian Peninsula in the period 1300–1600 BCE was the laboratory for, and prototype of, the Europe that would soon arise. It was also the homeland of the Renaissance—without any doubt partly as a result of its relationship with and its historical inheritance from the East. The accumulations of the East were channeled to the Peninsula via the city trade monopolists of mainly Venice, Florence and Genoa, and a few others with big appetites. More importantly, for the first time in history a massive hinterland for the accumulation of capital was formed due to the urban movements that developed throughout Europe under the lead of the Italian cities—an Italian merchant could be seen in every European city. While the Catholic Church had already laid the foundation for the civilization, the Renaissance provided the definitive and unambiguous leadership.

The only reason why Italy did not proceed to develop into an England or another Netherlands was its geography. Paradoxically, the same geography that made Italy the leader in city capitalism also brought city capitalism to the threshold of victory within the borders of the Peninsula but could not provide the final impetus for the final victory. The reason is quite simple: For Italy to have earlier taken the place of England would have required that it demolish Spain, France, and Austria—a repeat of Rome's advancement towards empire that would have enabled Italy to become the second world empire, after Rome, on a capitalistic socio-economic base. It is clear why Spain, France, and Austria besieged the Italian cities: inevitably these cities, strengthened by a new socio-economic unity, would first have expanded inevitably into Europe then around the world; this would have meant the end of their own empires. The Italian cities had all the prerequisites— foremost of which was capital—to do just that. Their failure to accomplish this victory was a great misfortune for them and nationally it meant a setback for Italy of three hundred years or more.

In my opinion, the fact that they just missed becoming a second Rome is due to geographic reasons. The first Rome also narrowly escaped Hannibal's assault after the Carthaginians' long march from the north. Now, the attackers from the north had the resources of forty Hannibals and the cities had no chance. Their only chance of success would have been through a religion of swords, the method used by Arabic Islam in its successful expansion into the entire Middle East. If, instead of Christianity, Islam was the power in Rome, or if Catholic Christendom expanded its religion and politics through the power of the sword, we would have had a different world. One cannot but speculate: Had there been no Christianity, what kind of fate would Rome have and what would it have resulted in? More interestingly, what if Mehmed II had heeded the calls by the Pope to become a sworded Christian? I know history is not an area of speculation, but it is no secret that historical developments carry with them several alternatives.

What the Italian cities did not achieve, Amsterdam and London achieved towards the end of the sixteenth century. Considerable research has been done to establish the reasons why capitalism had its final victory specifically in these areas and I will not dwell on it. I briefly list the reasons here:

1. These cities are located at the far North-Western end of Europe; because of this location, the ancient civilizations arrived at the Atlantic Ocean at a late and weakened stage.
2. The three major powers of Europe; France, Austria, and the Spanish Kingdoms, were fighting one another for control over Europe.
3. The big powers did not perceive them to be as dangerous as the Italian cities, hence they were not attacked with concentrated, sufficient force.
4. Their countries lead the expansion of the Reformation in Northern Europe.
5. Their location on the shores of the Atlantic Ocean gave them an advantage in the short and long-haul trade.
6. They had transferred all the material and immaterial culture of the Italian cities.
7. Feudalism was weak in these areas, both materially and immaterially.
8. A strong feudalism that could prevent the capitalistic development of transport, agriculture, and industry never existed in these regions. On the other hand, civilization probably developed here for the first time with capitalistic characteristics.

We could expand the list, but the reasons are all closely related to the geographic location of these cities. The geostrategic and geopolitical conditions of these cities presented the most favorable situation; this, in combination with the social conditions in these locations, made victory possible.

One of the important findings of anthropology is that, before the last glacial period, Africa played the leading role in humanity's development. However, because of climatic and geomorphological changes, this role shifted to the beautiful skirts of the Zagros-Taurus region where the Neolithic Revolution, arguably the biggest revolution in history, took place. These mountain skirts produced everything that was needed in terms of material and immaterial culture for the development of civilization. Not only was rich, fertile soil brought down from the mountain skirts to the Gulf Delta by the waters of the Tigris and Euphrates, the people from the mountain regions used their budding shipbuilding and navigational skills to transport themselves and all their cultural values on long, hazardous journeys down these rivers; with the onset of their first civilizational adventure, the cities of Eridu and Uruk had already synthesized these values. There, along the banks of the sacred rivers down to the Gulf where they poured into the sea, the culture expanded and flourished.

Uruk was not just another human culture—it was the start of a new miracle. The voice of Uruk's goddess, Inanna, is the main source of all legends, poems, and songs. Hers is the voice of a magnificent culture; the beautiful, clear voice of the woman not yet besmirched by the ugly voice of the scheming male. The flowering culture of Uruk scattered its seeds throughout its own geography: cities sprouted one after another. An urban zone had been formed. The strong and crafty man immediately noticed the source of real accumulation in the increasing trade possibilities of the cities. A cultural flow, directly opposite to that which came before, thus began. So started a period in which the Neolithic landscape became engulfed by urbanization. The drowning out of Inanna's voice by the ever-louder voice of the strong and crafty man reflected the fact that the woman was being rendered ineffective.[26]

I will not delve into the geographical adventures of the civilization that rests on power. Let me just say that it left behind thousands of kilometers of shoreline and rugged terrain all the way to the Atlantic Ocean, leaving behind a new culture on the shores of Amsterdam and London.

Thus, the material and immaterial culture obtained throughout time and all geographical locations has shaped the modern capitalist economy and nation under leadership of the two cities. But keep in mind that the Neolithic culture reached this region at a very late stage.[27] This corresponds with a commonly observed relationship between geography and culture: molding a new culture in an area where the old culture is deeply rooted is very difficult. The old culture will not easily accept the new one—it is only natural that it will defend itself. But when the seeds of a new culture are sown in a region where the old one has not established itself deeply yet, the region will turn green with the shoots of the new cultural seeds: it is highly probable that the new culture will become deep-rooted and permanent.[28]

That is why when the seeds of capitalist economy were sown in Northern Europe, a region relatively untouched by the ancient civilization, they took root so well in the two far-off nascently forming countries of England and the Netherlands. It was the last inheritance of the Uruk culture that was carried from one shore to another. The carriers of cultural inheritance have always been the merchants: as is often said, the merchants sense the most profitable places.

So, their remote locations in a marginal region never targeted by the power centers was in fact an advantage that brought good opportunities to these countries. They reinforced their leading positions by appropriating all findings by the Italian cities about capitalism and the routes discovered by the Spanish-Portuguese Armada. It was an act of assimilation: they made these gains their own. The wars between the big powers of Europe prevented possible external dangers. Internally, the productivity of the new economy (due to cheap labor and raw materials) was sufficient to render its birth, towards the end of the sixteenth century, in this geographical location successful and permanent.

The two powers, which only had some differences of form, seized the chance to represent the new economy around the world with this new alliance of theirs. The novelty of the economy led to the renewal of the state and to its evolving into a productive, successful type of statehood. Economic superiority contributed to their military and political superiority. Now, for the first time, merchant monopolies attained semi-official power by establishing partnerships (the West and East Indian Companies) with state monopolies. Now, for the first time, the disgraceful civilizational extortionists who hid themselves on the far edges and dark corners of society became masters whose legitimacy was no longer questioned. The ancient attributes of the aristocracy were bestowed on them by kings and queens. As the lion of Uruk no longer had the strength to stop Gilgamesh, there was no strength to stop his last heirs—the predators of London and Amsterdam. If they had any strength left, just as Gilgamesh had choked the lion, it would not have been so difficult for them to do the same.

The first and most powerful legend is that of the goddess Inanna's struggle against Enki, the guardian of Eridu (the first despotic and crafty male god or deified dominant man), in order to retrieve the 99 Mes created by the woman. Indeed, the queens of England and the Netherlands, who may be considered to be her heirs, have become symbolic figures reflecting all the vileness of the crafty and despotic male. This, indeed, sums up the whole adventure of the civilization.

Historical societal civilizations and capitalism

I am pursuing the answer to this question: Is the capitalist economy and its social formats a social and historical necessity? This part of my defense will be a reply to this question, which, in short, is: No, it is *not* a social or a historical necessity.[29]

The most serious mistake of Marxian interpretation (vulgar materialism) of historical materialism is its claim that capitalist economy is indeed a necessity. Even worse is the fact that these Marxists also adopted the linear development model of society—indeed, a presentation of Hegelian idealism under the disguise of materialism. This is thus nothing but a secondary derivative of Hegelian idealism. In reaction, Immanuel Kant (1724–1804) attempted, albeit rather hesitantly, to countermine this object-centered development by asserting the power of the subject, thereby emphasizing the role of morals as an option of freedom. Concerning freedom morals, Marxism lags even behind Kant. There is not much use in mentioning the right-wing liberal schools of thought since they see capitalism as not only a necessity, but as the final word of history.

Let me reiterate that positivism is more dangerous than religious obscurantism; it is also more conservative. If the truth behind capitalism, which rests on positivism, is not exposed and rendered ineffective, the option of freedom will have no chance. In fact, the two-hundred-year-old history of socialism and real socialism indicates that it has not surpassed the left-wing efforts to sustain capitalism. It is not a question of just finding where the mistake has been made—the paradigm itself is wrong. Hence, indicating any right or wrong elements within the paradigm will be of no consequence. Society *cannot* be approached in a linear manner, and all the social formats *cannot* be realized one after the other as if by divine order. Even the debate on partial (human) and total (God's) will of the

Middle Ages was superior to this positivist and materialistic approach. The factor responsible for the failure of the struggles that are waged in the name of socialism is this paradigm in approaching the society.

Clearly, my definitions in previous sections don't follow this approach. Viewing capitalism as a necessary social phase is to be under the influence of and to be an instrument of this system, whether intentionally or not. Let me say right now what I should say at the end of this analysis: *Capitalism cannot be a social format.* It may want to be one and it can influence society, but it cannot be a format of society. Some might argue that capitalism has been the sole format ruling the world for the past four hundred years, but to that I would say that it is one thing to rule and another to be a format. History has witnessed three social formats or modes: primitive clan society, classed state or civilizational society, and democratic, pluralistic society. The linear development approach that sets the societal formats as primitive, slave-owning, feudal, capitalist, and socialist, is far too dogmatic—or, indeed, idealistic and fatalistic. More importantly, the three social forms that I postulate do not linearly succeed each other. It is closer to a cyclic system that deepens and expands. I do embrace the notion of dialectical operation but I must clearly state that I do not agree with the interpretation that progress is achieved through extremes that eliminate one another. In my opinion the model of thesis, antithesis, and synthesis is a logical tool to explain the operational principles of the universe. A model of dialectic that is rich, that enables the existence of diversity and recognizes the need for symbiotic relationships, is much closer to nature's dialectical operation and will have more explanatory power.

We should not forget and be constantly aware that, from the smallest being to the entirety of the cosmos, all entities consist of contradictions that lead to creation as well as to their reciprocal relationships and mutual influences. A creation formed thus is both a sum of the separate elements and totally different from and more than its constituent parts. This is the kind of creation that can be observed in all change and development.

Society is not an entity outside of this creation. It has the same characteristics. In short, it too continuously generates antagonistic dilemmas. Hence, it allows for new and diverse formations that encompass both constituents but that surpass their total. This concept of dialectical change and the development of societies will yield more knowledge about concrete entities. Adopting this dialectical approach may lead to insight that will empower us to activate the potential of the free human. It will enable the development of free and responsible individuals by embodying society in the individual; as a result, the society, which has been influenced by free individuals, will become even freer. The opportunity to become free offers the best potential and chance to equality and democratization.

I must reiterate that when I talk about the triad dynamic of the social reality I am not making a new discovery. All that I am trying to do is to tailor the dynamism of universal genesis to that of society. If I am asked for the reason behind triad dynamism, I would have to say that it is due to *existence*. If existence too would require an answer as to *why*, then the question as to why we exist comes in. However, the fact of existence is incontrovertible. In the absence of *being* there would be no need for such problems and questions.

If we accept *being* and *existence*, then it is meaningful to talk about the manner of genesis. Those who focus on all the meanings of life and development of thought would have sensed that change and development arise from formation. Therefore, an extraordinary corpus has been created in the categories of mythology, religion, philosophy, and scientific thought. We obviously cannot deny such a corpus. They all are attempts to respond to the question of genesis. To this end some have employed the mythological, others the religious method; where these were insufficient, philosophy and science have come to rescue. Their functions have been similar but their responses have not. The reason, manner, and aim of genesis have continuously been questioned and each category has tried to come up with its own answer in accordance to its discipline. Science—the most ambitious discipline of all—has considerably elucidated the triad dynamic of genesis. When matter-energy and particle-wave mechanics are evaluated at the quantum level, both theoretically and experimentally, it can be proven that the new formation, which is the result of these formations, bears traces of its originating dichotomy (matter-energy and particle-wave currents have universality). Thesis and antithesis continue to exist within the synthesis, while at the same time becoming different. Change maybe in the form of progress or regress. Thus, it has been shown that this is the fundamental characteristic of *existence* dynamics. There is no need to re-prove it.

Let us look into ourselves. The child of a given father and mother looks much like the parents, where the child carries the genes, but is also becoming different (a very slow process), and becomes a different entity that represents them. We may look at this as a grain of eternal creation. Creation is able to win the existential war in this manner. What is the existential war? How does one remain *to be*? To continue to exist is to maintain itself through change. Why? Maybe to prove its existence, and to be able to gaze at the divinity and magnificence of existence through change!

Here is the absurdity: Whilst we could have attained a sound logic through observing the beings that are nearest to us, why did we—or why were we made to—become distanced to this essential truth? If we are to unravel this absurdity, then we will arrive at the fundamental issue.

I am talking about the web of narratives, disguises, and masks that have wrapped themselves around the operational characteristic of the social phenomenon since its birth. Why did communality need such masks and disguises? Why did intelligence split into emotional and analytic aspects due to this development? What were their functions? If we find the correct answers, we may be able to either interpret our communality as it is or change it the way we would like it to be. Human beings have the characteristics to interpret any given thing and change it in any way. The more interpretation and desire (or thinking and perception, and demand) correspond to creation dynamics, the better the new form's chance to develop. However, the more they drift apart, the bigger the danger of dogmatism or of deterioration of the communality. The development of emotional and analytical intelligence is due to such problems.

I must end this section of mostly philosophical interpretation. I will focus on it in the third volume, *The Sociology of Freedom*. I will explain in more concrete terms:

The communality called "clan" is not a static entity. Clan society developed as our species began to differ from all the other primates. Its fundamental problem is to stay alive. In general, the primary problem of a society is to continue and defend its existence in the face of forces that wish to end it. Such a problem has existed for societies at different times and locations. Defense may at times take the form of self-defense against the various dangers and risks and thus targets defending its own existence. When at other times if there is a positive environment and there are entities that allow for symbiotic development, then positive development accelerates. Here the species, clan, or society is enriched by the material and immaterial culture. If we try to explain it through the contradiction of "*I* and *the other*" of the contemporary sociological concepts, then the *I*'s adopt self-defense against *the other*'s that constitute a danger or a risk. In the case that they defeat *the other*, the *I*'s continue to develop, or if the *I*'s and *the other* are at equilibrium, the *I*'s preserve their existence but their development may slow down, whereas if they are defeated then—depending on the level of their defeat—the *I*'s lose their existence partially or totally. In the latter case, the *I*'s no longer exist as itself but become the object of another entity. Or the *I*'s will be assimilated to continue its existence as another entity. In such a case, distorted or degenerated categories are formed.

More concretely, the society, at more simple levels of formation, has constantly struggled against environmental conditions to not fall prey to predacious animals and to protect itself against illnesses and malnourishment. Whilst dangers threaten its existence, favorable conditions lead to progress. This adventure, which has taken place mostly in Africa and the last one million years in Asia and Europe, has been elucidated, to a degree, at fundamental points. Such early communality formed or aggregated around the mother-woman mostly due to her communal practices and to a lesser degree to the influence of her biological characteristics. The feminine suffixed structure of early languages confirms this. One should not overlook the mother-based characteristics of society. It is important to see the mother-woman as an "administrative," natural center of power due to her life experience and the raising of children. In early settlements, her appeal and pivotal position continually increases.

Fatherhood is a social relation that appeared much later, the society not knowing such a concept for most part. The concept of fatherhood has developed with patriarchy after the emergence of inheritance and the system of ownership.[30] The concepts of the child's place of attachment or belonging, and unclehood—that is being the brother of the mother—

emerged much earlier. Material needs were fulfilled through gathering and, to a lesser degree, hunting. Being a clan member was the most important assurance of life because being excluded from a clan, or to become isolated, would most likely result in death. It is thus realistic to view the clan as a sound social nucleus. It is the original form of society.

I have continuously emphasized that after long stages of development, and due to the favorable geographical conditions (the Taurus-Zagros mountain system), the transition to the Neolithic society was made. This stage can be viewed as the zenith of mother-based society and the emergence of surplus-product potential. Social sciences mostly call this order the primitive communal system or the Old and New Stone Age. However, I believe it is more meaningful to call it a mother-based society, as there were a series of stages involved. This stage comprises almost ninety-nine percent of the total duration of human society. It should not be belittled. It is not difficult to deduce that the strong and crafty man who was always at bay—mostly idle but slowly gaining strength due to some successful hunting heads—began to strive for domination in the face of the accumulation of the surplus-product and other cultural values at the heart of the communal mother-based society.

I have repeatedly pointed out that the patriarchal society mostly consisted of the shaman, the elderly experienced sheikh, and the military commander. It may be wise to look for the prototype of a new society within such a development. With "a new society" we mean a situation where hierarchy emerges inside the clan. The immanent division is finalized when hierarchy gives rise to permanent class-formations and a state-like organization. A society acquainted with class and the state has clearly changed its qualities. The fundamental dynamic of such change is to stop considering surplus-product as gift and to turn it into a commodity that can be exchanged, bought, or sold at the market. As the triad of market, city, and trade become a permanent component within the society, the movement towards becoming a state and class formation gains momentum. I will not elaborate on how such a development has occurred at different times and locations. This new society has been referred to as classed society, urban society, and state society, slave-owned, feudal, and capitalist society in various sociological studies.

Class, urbanization, and statehood are its obvious and permanent traits, and since *civilization* is the epithet accorded to these eras, it may be appropriate to call it "civilized society" or in short "civilization."

It probably has not escaped your attention that we don't use *civilization* to depict elevation or progress, but rather decline and suppression of social ethics. Civilized society, when compared to the old communal mother-based values, that is, moral perception, means a huge decline. This relationship is strikingly expressed in one of the earliest languages we know of, Sumerian. The word *amargi* means "freedom" and, at the same time, "return to the mother and nature." Such an identicalness established between mother, freedom, and nature is a striking and correct perception. Through the use of the word *amargi*, the Sumerian society, that had only just become acquainted with civilized society, wished to express the longing it felt for the old communal mother-based society from which it had not yet drifted too far away. It is quite instructive to learn what happened to the civilized society from the very first experience, the Sumerian original.

The equilibrium in the relationship between woman and man deteriorated against woman. This can best be seen in the very first attempt at writing an epic, consisting of dialogues between Inanna (the patron goddess of Uruk) and Enki (god of Eridu). This epic, written before the *Epic of Gilgamesh*, depicts the struggle between the communal mother-based order or society, and the hierarchic patriarchal society (the transitional society to civilization). It is clear that the process was extremely unfair and full of struggle. There are some arguments and historical data indicating that there may have been a primitive democracy at the early stages of Sumerian society. The elders' assembly had not yet turned into a patriarchal order and the very vibrant discussions there point to a democracy of sorts. Concepts such as *God's command* (in fact a principle of the one-sided military-despotic order originating from a masked person, such as the strong and crafty man) had not yet been formed. Indeed, the conversation style in the epic of Inanna is very vivid and depicts all that has happened within the society—the injustices and all the disasters that struck the women, their accumulation, and children. If there were more data available, it is highly probable that we would have been able to notice that there was also a transitional period of democracy—one that surpasses the democracy (slave-owned, classed democracy) of ancient Athens.

We can theoretically assume that the transition to both the civilized society and the democratic society formed within one another. The harsh arguments in the early elders' assemblies are the initial reflections thereof, the footsteps of democratic society. During this stage in all societies we witness a similar contradiction: the democratic society and civilized society contradiction; or, in more understandable and concrete terms, the contradiction of state and democracy. The problem of democracy exists in all places where the state exists. And, vice versa, in all places where there is democracy, there is the risk of becoming a state. Democracy is not a type of state nor is it correct to say that a state is a form of democracy. It is important to be extremely careful about the characteristics of the relationship between the two.

This contradiction is yet another point that has been much doctored throughout time. What has developed from the heart of the old society: democracy or state? This question has lead to extensive discussions and contortion. The fact that democracy and state developed within one another denotes the struggle, contention, and wars that occurred during the process. The best-known example is the discussion and struggle for a republican democracy versus a sultanate within Islam. *The Charter of Medina,* drafted by the prophet Muhammad, is quite similar to *The Social Contract* drafted by Jean-Jacques Rousseau. This can be seen clearly in the Koran and *hadiths.*[31] However, the tribal aristocracy—and in particular the hierarchic order of the Quraysh tribe—wanted a sultanate similar to that of the Byzantines and Sassanids. The dispute already existed when the prophet Muhammad was alive. Indeed, another way to interpret the dispute between Medina and Mecca is whether the new order would be a republic (the Arabic *jumhūriyya* means "people's democracy") or a sultanate (a monarchic order where power is handed over from father to son). The quarrel began as the prophet Muhammad fled Mecca in 610 BCE. The quarrel led to the killing of the prophet Ali in Kufa (a similar conflict, of a similar intensity, had raged in this city, 170 km south of Baghdad), and in 661 BCE it concluded with the pro-sultanate Muawiyah faction emerging victoriously from the fifty-year-old dispute. At the time, the very strong tribal hierarchic order did not allow an opportunity for the republic or even a primitive democracy to flourish. I believe a sociological study of Islam from this perspective will result in quite striking and interesting results.

Another striking example from history is the case of the Persian Empire. After long discussions and disputes, the legacy of the Median Confederation was turned into an empire. The decisive role in this was played by the Achaemenid lineage. There are many indicators that point to an intense era and resistance led by the Median priests (560-520 BCE). The story of Cambyses is a striking example in this regard.[32] The establishment of the Median Confederation is an example of a typical primitive democracy at the time. The *Histories* of Herodotus has interesting narratives in this regard.

Another well-known example is that of the Athenian democracy. The wars waged against the Spartans, Persians, and Macedonians are a reflection of the struggle of whether to establish a democracy or an empire-kingdom. Albeit primitive and class-based, there has always been a dispute and struggle over whether the society should be a democratic or a civilized society. The quarrel in Rome over being a republic or an empire shows that even famous personalities like Caesar can be killed in such quarrels, thus signifying a severe contradiction. Examples can be multiplied and the Great French Revolution, as well as the Russian Revolution, can be expanded upon in order to further develop our understanding of, and interest in, the topic.

The French Revolution began against absolute monarchy in 1789 and resulted in a republic (radical societal democracy). It went through an extremely violent period, the so-called Terror.[33] The period of the Triumvirate was followed by the era of the Napoleonic Empire.[34] To date, five republics have been declared, and the sixth is still being discussed.

The Great Russian Revolution began with a more radical democracy, the Soviet era.[35] However, it became acquainted with revolutionary dictatorship, and during the Stalin era the dictatorship became permanent. In 1989, the 200th anniversary of French Revolution, it returned to democracy. It still wishes to develop its democracy. Hundreds of such examples have been experienced during the era of capitalistic modernism.

I presented these brief examples in order to illustrate the web of relations between civilization and democracy, and the tense, conflicting and stormy ambiance resulting from this web.

Another important point to consider is that both new societies wish to build their existence atop the communal society. The communal society is still ongoing, continuing its existence, albeit as remnants amidst the fabric of societies. As described earlier, communal society is an irrevocable "mother cell" society, and one should not doubt its permanency that will last as longs as the human species exist. As a mother cell plays the role of nurturing and repairing the body structure, rebuilding it when necessary, the communal mother-based society continues its existence in all societies with such a duality. In democratic and civilized societies born from the communal mother-based society's structures, and despite the conflicting, intense and at times reconciling ambiance, the communal society has not and will not disappear. I am aware that I often emphasize this, but I do so for important reasons, and it has important results which I shall continue to expose.

I continuously refer to conflict between democratic society and civilized society. However, the possibility of compromise cannot be excluded. On the contrary, compromise is essential—or rather, should have been essential. The main reason for their continuous existence, in terms of the dialectical understanding that opposites do not destroy one another, is that the one cannot exist without the other. The existence of one is possible only through the existence of the other. As I pointed out before, both democratic and civilizational breakthroughs have come from within the communal mother society. Democracy is based mostly upon the substratum majority and multitudes that have been betrayed, oppressed, and exploited mostly by the hierarchic upper-strata, whereas civilization is based mostly on the section of the upper strata that pursue the oppression, exploitation, and ideological hegemony. No doubt neither are completely isolated from one another and from the communal mother society—although intertwined, they have distinct differences.

At this point, there is a need to review our understanding of the concept of society as a whole and we should continuously remind ourselves of it. Societies should be understood to be the integral sum of classes (including hundreds of sub-groups and millions of families within each class), all communities who have not yet been subject to class division or who resist class division, global as well as local units (religions or languages, economies, tribes, nations and transnationals, chaos and order) that have tense, calm, conflicting, solidarizing, and various multiple intertwined relationships and contradictions. Societies should not be understood as being unique but as the integral of sum of thousands and thousands of instances of uniqueness. Amidst this huge complexity a societal order that is closest to peace can only be created if democracy and state strike a balance. Absolute peace requires the state of having no state. While theoretically this can be envisaged, practically we are far from it.

Only a long-term democratic life that includes the entire society, even the society of the state, can lead to absolute peace. At this moment in history we can only talk about peace in terms of no-clash periods based on the equilibrium of the forces in question, that is of the state and democracy. If democracy attempts to absorb the state completely, then at this historical moment chaotic features will outweigh—as demonstrated by experiences in many countries. If the state continuously imposes the absence of democracy, then despotic dictatorship systems form and in the present historical moment this again results in chaos. Becoming civilized, also called the historical process, has continued for the past five thousand years. Democracy has had a more restricted opportunity. But society, the overwhelming majority and multitudes, has always awaited, and struggled for, democracy. Maybe thousands of years from now, although it may have a different form, state and democracy will continue to exist intertwiningly as a category.

The challenge is, just as much as dissociating state and democracy, to determine systematic rules under which they will live in coexistence without denying each other. It may be necessary to draw new types of constitutions. The present claim that the state and democracy are interwoven is totally deceptive. It cannot be more than efforts to hide one another's defects. In the absence of overcoming this position there can be no coherent discussion on state and democracy. The two most modern revolutions, the French and the Russian Revolutions, instead of clarifying and improving the debate regarding this topic, have made it more complicated. There is an urgent need for political theory to at least determine and define a state that is open to democracy, that is, a state that does not ban real democracy or consider itself to be the epitome of democracy. Similarly, it must define a democracy that does not deny the state, that is, a democracy that will not rapidly turn into state itself and that does not continuously see the state as an obstacle to be destroyed. There is a true need for theoretical work that responds to the complexities of the practical aspects experienced. I believe that there is a need, and indeed that it is possible, to have modes of state and democracy that will be in less conflict and will improve each other's productivity. It is in this way that we can develop the much needed and strongest political possibility. Present states essentially do not acknowledge democracy. States are extremely hulky and bulky, and democracies are like caricatures of states, extremely distorted and dysfunctional. No doubt, this is the fundamental problem of political philosophy and praxis. I will delve into these topics more extensively in the next volume, *Sociology of Freedom*.

I am aware that I am presenting a paradigm, a theoretical framework, far different from the traditional liberal and socialist paradigms. I will attempt to elaborate on the short framework outlined above, which is a response to the question of where to situate capitalism "as a form of society." Clearly, not only do I not consider capitalism to be a form of economy, I also do not consider it to be a form of society.

So, if it is not a form of economy and not a form of society, where does capitalism then fit in? To form a clear picture, we must, above all, attempt to see the web of relations called capitalist economy within the integrity of civilized society. It is of the utmost importance to understand that the capitalist economy is nothing but an exchange economy (or commodification) that descends on market relations and competition. It then establishes itself through monopolist acquisition by exploiting fluctuation in price and the difference in price formed in different regions. From this definition, it should be clear that it is not a sector that generates exchange value. It relates to just a trivial part of the general economic life. However, due to its strategic position, this triviality is a determinant of economic life. It is a huge amount of accumulated exchange value in the hands of a few, which puts it in a position of superior power where it can manipulate both supply and demand. In the past even the state did not possess such authority.

We understand very little about the way in which this superiority came about, but because the way it functions depends on the perpetual growth of capital, the impact its functioning has on society is bigger and more subversive than its birth. To call this revolutionary is a betrayal of society, especially of the historical, democratic society!

When will the science of political economy admit that the growth of capital (the infamous law of profit that the politicians varnish and shine by invoking the sacredness of the term *law*) is nothing but disguised plunder? Why am I not calling the strong and crafty man a capitalist? Only because his appropriation is based overtly on power and war. War means ambushing: it does not see the need to camouflage itself in law, religion, or any other cover. But there is a need to remunerate capitalist economy. The previous state-economy relationship depended on seizure by force; the tacit law and tradition of the hierarchy allowed looting as an inherent right—the strong crafty man was on the way to statehood. This is where the capitalist economy differs from the classical state. It is not that the state and the economy are in conflict—it is just that civilized society's development level does not allow plunder in the form of overt looting because such plunder is no longer productive. Indeed, it stepped in the moment the slave-owning and feudal states started to become ineffective, thus grasping the opportunity to label itself "the new economic order."

The slave-owning state monopoly of antiquity was very productive, as can still be seen from the Pharaohs' tombs and the remnants of the Greco-Roman cities. The capitalist sector did exist at the time, but was quite restricted—the productivity of the state monopoly did not allow the sector much scope. When the slave-owning system's labor order became unproductive, the feudal labor order became widespread. Why the slave-owning society became unproductive is not under discussion here, but let me just say that it was due to its view of life and labor, its spread over extensive areas, its enormously costly structure—including the enormous cost and exhaustion of occupying distant geographical areas and of enslaving humans—and the thousands of democratic and freedom struggles and rebellions, both internally and externally.

The system of legitimization and exploitation upon which the constructed civilized society (mostly the Islamic Middle East and Christian

Europe) rested, differed from the one inherited from Sumer through the Greco-Roman and Egyptian civilizations. The two religions presented very strong legitimization armor and, since serfs and peasants had more say over themselves than slaves, civilized society indeed managed to renew itself. The first three centuries of Christianity (when it represented the conscience of the poor), the struggle for equality and freedom by Islam (disguised as interdenominational struggle), thus the general efforts and quests of the democratic society, played a dominant role in the renewal of civilization and its becoming more tolerable. However, that this phase was reached at all was due to the remnants of the old communal societies, the tribes and slaves that have run off, and the resistance and rebellion of the poor and not, as claimed by the ideologues of civilization, due to the sublimeness of the civilization or its honorable development.

The new legitimization tools renewed coercion and exploitation, which in turn led to the renewal of its fundamental tools: class, city, and state. In the new environment of serf-seigneur, city-market, and subject-state, the advancement of the capitalistic elements became much easier. From China to the Atlantic Ocean, towns flourished around markets allowing acceleration of commodity production as well as expansion and depth of exchange. Because of the difference in price between the markets, the monopolist merchant's profits reached unprecedented levels. For the first time, there was a balance between the influence of town and rural area. In a way, the Islamic Civilization was a trade civilization, functioning as trading agent between the Far East and Europe. It presented Europe with all that it required for trade, both in terms of material and of immaterial culture. Other fundamental tools of civilization had been provided since antiquity. With Islam, the transporting of city, class, and state from the Middle East to Europe ends. Arabs and Jews played leading roles in this transfer—changes started by the Greco-Romans were completed by Arab and Jewish scholars, craftsmen, and merchants.

The Middle East civilization's most important deficiency was the capitalist sector's inability to reach beyond the city and to play a leading role in an entire country: this is why it could not achieve what Amsterdam and London did. This was mainly because of the despotic central authority, which was far more repressive than the autocratic regimes of Europe. The political structures in China and India were even more centralized and had an even more asymmetric and crushing superiority than that of the Middle East. This rule was only prolonged and strengthened by the migration and invasion of Turkish tribes and the conquests of Genghis Khan and Emir Timur. Japan remained a semi-feudal political structure, similar to that of Europe. Thus, as the sixteenth century approached, the ancient Asian civilizations did not have the strength to take a new direction. Hence, if anything were to happen, it had to be in Europe. So Europe, almost a peninsula at the western edge of Asia, was the new civilizational laboratory.

When the old civilization was brought to Western Europe, this area with its freshly established cities and inexperienced, adolescent feudalism, lay fallow before the trade and capitalist sector that came with the civilization. The Europe of the time could hardly be called a civilization—Christianity succeeded in being a moral vaccine by the end of the tenth century. Had an ancient civilization such as that of the Middle East developed in Europe, the development of the capitalist civilization there would not have been certain, as new civilizations can only develop in virgin soil. The difficulties in maintaining the old and the inexperience of the new (feudalism) created a vacuum that allowed a third force to rise above the rest. Had, for example, the Arabs in Spain, the Ottomans in the Balkans, or the various tribes attacking from the south of Siberia (the last of which the Mongolian tribes) been able to establish an old-fashioned empire in Europe how would history have proceeded? So, chance also was an important factor for Europe.

These speculations are important if we want to clarify the factors that led to the birth of the capitalist sector and its hegemonic character. It should now be clear that capitalism is not an inevitable developmental stage of civilization—it is the result of the combined effects of coincidences. Sheltering in the cracks and margins of ancient civilizations, it established itself above and against the market. Through the money games it devised, by exploiting the long-haul trade and by colonial looting, it has taken more than its share. When it arose, this group of big merchant-speculators grasped the opportunity to establish its hegemony, initially over Europe through the two unassertive cities, and then over the world. It has used the opportunity well.

These speculators were a conservative group, without truly creative or inventive ideas—its only talent that of making money with money. The only social area it was resourceful in was profiting from famine and war and utilizing price disparities in different regions of the world to make more money. This was not civilization's first introduction to money, market, city, trade, or even to banks and deposit slips—these tools were invented thousands of years earlier. Civilizational renewal did not occur out of the blue—the weight of the money factor in the civilizational history of the world (not the world's history, that is to say, the history of the societies struggling against the civilization!) prepared the way for this. But it did not cause a fundamental change of its essence.

A striking characteristic of Europe at the beginning of the sixteenth century was that money attained the power to command everything. Indeed, money became the real master and commander: whoever had the money wielded the power. The main reason behind this was the frightening growth of commodification, urbanization, and marketing. No other empire or ruler, not even the ancient Asian powers or the Roman emperors, exercised its reign by basing itself entirely on money. If they did have any wealth anywhere around the world, these emperors would have them moved to the palace instantly. But, in sixteenth century Europe, when the capitalist sector gained one success after another, the kings begged for loans. The might of money and power had entered a new phase. For the first time, political power knelt down before money. Money had gained so much power that it could take over the political power. Napoleon's remark about money was actually an attempt to comment on this state of affairs.

Initially, the capitalist sector took no part in production or even in small scale trading. It had nothing new to contribute to the fundamental relationships of the economy; neither did it bring anything creative to commodification or exchange, which had been in existence for millennia. Thus, its only skills lay in discovering how to use the power of money, turning money into capital, and the art of making money with money. And let us not forget that these merchants masterfully sniffed out the routes, towns, countries, and markets where the most money was to be made and that they were *the* experts on the networks through which money and goods were circulated.

We would be mistaken if we thought that Europe came under the command of money due to the mastery of this group of merchants. The facts that we have reviewed show that its role in this civilizational development is but marginal. For money and market to give rise to the capitalist economic sector is *not* inevitable. In fact, Asian civilizations had money and market power long before Europe; had there been a direct causal relationship between these factors and the capitalist economy, capitalism would have been generated there. The victory of capitalism cannot be attributed to science, arts, religion, and philosophy either; on the contrary, these disciplines have always been suspicious of and opposed to it.

Something that I have always tried to remind: How was it possible that the power held by the woman fell into the hands of the male, who was not very productive or creative? Why did the woman become so miserable and fell captive in his hands? The answer, of course, lies in the use of force. When, besides the leading position in the family-clan, the economy was taken from her too, atrocious captivity was inevitable. She has been convinced to cease to be herself. In fact, it is more horrific to be the *housewife* of the *strong* man. A comparison of this instance of usurpation to that of the power that money as capital has gained over the entire society is quite instructive.

Admitting its attainment of the commanding power is also an admission that money is no longer an economic phenomenon. The brilliant historian Fernand Braudel makes a most significant statement when declaring that capitalism is anti-market and hence anti-economy, even non-economy—an opinion that I share. Capitalism, which suffocates everything in the economy, is the sworn enemy of economy. Let me repeat: *Capitalism is not economy, but the sworn enemy of economy.* I shall later discuss this in more depth. Is finance economy? What about global finance? Environmental disasters? Is unemployment an economic problem? Are banks, deposit slips, exchange and interest rates economy? Is production for the sole purpose of profit, growing like cancer, economy? We can increase the list of questions, but there is only one answer to them all: *No.* Money-capital is no more than a pretext for attaining power. No new economic forms, capitalist community formats, or even a capitalist civilization has been generated through the fraudulent games of money-capital. Instead, the society was seized; an unprecedented act in history. A seizure not only of the economic power, but of all cultural power, including political, military, religious, moral, scientific, philosophical, artistic, historically accumulated material, and immaterial power. *Capitalism is the most advanced hegemony and power in history.* If you examine the last four hundred years, the Age of Capitalism, can you find a single cell or tissue related to society that capital has not taken under its hegemony, not established its power over?

The crafty English sociologist Anthony Giddens talks about the three discontinuities of modernity, namely the capitalist mode of production, nation-state, and industry.[36] His definition of modernity, based on these three discontinuities, seems realistic. But he surely must realize that what he is really doing is theorizing a new stage of the salvation of capitalism in its homeland: another attempt at theorizing capitalism as eternal. So, where right-wing liberalism proclaims it to be the end of time, left-wing liberalism eternalizes it. Thus, once again, with its last global assault, capitalism attempts to imprint upon us that it will exist forever.

In the next section, as I evaluate modernity, I will continue my analysis of capitalism—especially in terms of the nation-state and industrialism. I will try to track it down to the bases of its power. I will show how capitalism, whose aim from the very start was to become a global power, used the nation-state and industrialism, supported by a synthesis of various modes of explanation, to succeed in this. This new Leviathan's first task was to break down the existing modes of explanation in order to render it difficult to understand—a fragmented explanation is an incomplete explanation. My method may be seen as unusual, but I believe that it will render a competent analysis, and thus knowledge, of social relations. The subtitle of this section, "The Thief in the House," is inspired by Braudel's description of capitalism's "real home" as the zone of the anti-market, where the great predators roam and the law of the jungle operates.[37] This description evokes in me images of the underground palaces where the Sumerian god Enki and the Greek god Hades played their power games, shrouded in invisibility. As the kings and gods of capitalism do not feel the need to mask the power games that *they* play, "At the palace of the naked king, the unmasked god and the Commander Money" is a fitting subtitle.

The Mortal Enemy of Economy

The saying goes, "children speak the truth." When someone wants to know the truth, they ask the children. Once again, both due to my respect for all the children, and in order to be able to get to the source of the truth, I need to reinterpret my childhood imagery.

When I heard that Emin, the son of our neighbor, had begun to read the book called *Ilmihal*, my interest in Islam and the mosque increased.[1] In return for memorizing a few prayers, I succeeded in slipping into the ranks right behind imam Müslim. I later heard and never forgot what Müslim said about me: "If Abdullah is this quick, he will fly off." So I had started off well. I still remember my queries and discussions with my primary school friend Aziz about what kind of place a school is, and what teachers are like while embracing the trunk of the olive tree. When they talked about the school, I would have a monster like image in my head (the modern Leviathan). I was not mistaken, because the school was the location where we were made to memorize all aspects of the nation-state (the new god). Much later, I read Hegelian philosophy and saw how the new god came down to earth as the nation-state and began its walk in the shape of Napoleon. When I began to interpret what it meant for the teachers (the new priests) to have the children memorize all this I realized that as a child I recognized the truth. As I began primary school, Müslim's "god of the mosque" became insignificant, while the primary school theism of Mehmet—the teacher from Çorum—was on the rise. Another image I recall is how the headlights of the truck driver Haydar would blind me at dawn as I was half asleep on the pergola. The fascination I felt for the truck has permeated into my memories like a semi-god. The new god had a car. Much later, when I began to understand industrialism as the strongest pillar or attribute of the new Leviathan, I once again was sure that my childhood imagery provided me with another truth.

I must say, though, that no theism has become as monstrous as industrialism. Our village was around fifty kilometers from the Syrian border. The projectors at the border would hit my eyes like the lightning from a thunderbolt, creating the third state-god mixed image of my childhood.

The Republic of Turkey is one of the early examples of a semi-colonial country turned into a nation-state by capitalist modernity. When first established, such a state bears the stamp of the Republic of France. At the beginning, democracy and state are intertwined, just as in France, the Islamic Republic of Iran, the very first Islamic Republic in Medina, and even in the early USSR. As the democratic elements are pruned in time, these republics are transformed into unitary nation-states—a capitalist power format. (I will delve into these topics more comprehensively in the relevant sections.) The early examples always need to be interpreted with great care. I would like to describe my imagery of the republic in a novel, but for now let me say this in short: As I entered the final year of Faculty of Political Sciences at Ankara University—one of the most distinguished schools of republicanism—my emotional and analytical intelligence had become paralyzed. I could no longer sense or understand anything and had been turned by the Leviathan into an utterly ignorant person, totally hollow. I was to notice this about myself only later in life.

I was able to break free from the effects of the old religion of my village many years later through what I had memorized particularly from the real-socialist school—a denomination of capitalism. I must say that I had turned into a terrible skeptic. It was as if I was suffocating as I contemplated things. Much later, when I realized that what imposed itself upon me (whether in the guise of the Republic of Turkey or that of Soviet Real Socialism) was the modern Leviathan, I slowly began to come to my senses. I was up against the god of the modern religion (besieged by the numerous images and idols) which was more horrific than the gods of all the other religions.

After I had become aware of how it emerged and gained control, I understood that this religion and its god were not for me. From then on, I understood and felt that the more I was successful in not being immersed in this religion and in not deviating from my course, the more the option of free life would develop for me. For the first time my emotional and analytical intelligence cooperated in making me come to my senses. Indeed, I am still trying to interpret what happened back then by writing these lines. For now, let's get back to what capitalism is and is not.

Marx and Engels described their sociology, their "scientific socialism," as a synthesis of English political economy, German philosophy, and French socialism. These three schools of thought all attempted to develop a theoretical analysis of modernity—of the controlling forces reshaping life in Europe. While the English school of political economy set out to prove that the new economy was the victorious power (sounding more like the proselytes of a new religion), German philosophy saw the nation-state (the new form of the god-king) as the main force, and French socialism (as the alliance of civilization and democracy) theorized on behalf of the entire society that the strongest force was the society of secular-positivism (the new religion of the system).

The revolution of thought that started in sixteenth century Europe was induced by the capitalist monopoly's tremendous, subversive influence. In our attempt to depict this revolution of thought there are some historical examples we must recall.

Our first example is the birth of the Sumerian priest-state at the fertile cradle of the temple—the Ziggurat. The conditions under which the state-like organization organized itself around the surplus product should be evaluated together with the revolution of thought that took place. The central questions would have been: How can the surplus product be tucked away? How can the fundamental legitimization tools (so that the society would believe in the new order) be developed and rearranged? The remedy that was found was the state organization and the construction of new gods—the initial example of all civilizational religions. A very radical response was generated. The state—for the very first time—was organized as the priest-king. Economy—for the first time—was organizationally intertwined with the state and brought under control as state socialism. Traditional hierarchical forces were being constructed and masked as the new gods of air, water, sky, earth, and the city. The initial enslavement of humans is symbolized in the creation epic as "the creation of humans from the excrement of gods." The location of all these inventions is the ziggurats. The highest level of the ziggurat is the pantheon (the unity of gods, the authority of the hierarchical upper layers); the floor below this is the floor of the priest-king (the creator of the system, the first hegemon and administrator). The lowest floor is left to the slaves and artisans that produce the surplus product and value. Indeed, we ascertained the formula underlying the entire civilization system when we established that the temple was the prototype of the city, state, and class system. All instances of the system, including the European one, have carried traces of this first example, the prototype. I thus see the Sumerian example as the superb, original source of civilization—none of its descendant versions or adaptations as splendid and impressive as the original.

The second version of the Sumerian system was that of the Hurrians from Upper Mesopotamia, intermingled with the Hittite civilization. The Ionian-Greek version was the third—with the only difference that the Greeks surpassed the mythological discourse and constructed the philosophical style. The main reason behind constructing the philosophy of nature and society was the increasing difficulty in explaining the city-states through mythology. Although the legitimizing power of the mythological narrative continued its effect on the lower classes, those who had to battle with concrete administrative problems needed a more convincing narrative. City life resulted in problems which required a philosophical explanation to the kind of social life experienced there. But the Olympian pantheon that began with Zeus was still quite effective. Socrates paid for his early skepticism with his life, but his students managed to make his teachings, albeit in draft form, the main source of Greek philosophy. It would not be wrong to call Plato and Aristotle especially the fathers of philosophy. The Hebrews can be described as the tribe who made the transition from the Sumerian and Egyptian mythologies to the first monotheistic religious expression. This was the construction of a different version from a separate branch that later gave rise to Judaic, Christian, and Muslim derivatives by merging with various other side branches, especially Zoroastrianism and Greek philosophy.

The new material and immaterial cultural accumulations which generated the enormous power that enabled sixteenth century Europe to surge forward rested upon the original source and historical versions of the civilization system. To deny their role and to posit Europe as the start of history is tantamount to creating a new mythology or religion, one doomed to fail from the outset. Ideological constructions such as positivism, secularism, liberalism, and even socialism, all had their own novelties but were all formed under the profound influence of the historically original source. Essentially, their concepts and contents had been developed within the preceding versions. These rest not only on the Greco-Roman philosophy, science, arts, and law, but in the absence of the Egyptian and Sumerian heritage, the European Renaissance, the Reformation, and the Enlightenment cannot be explained.

There is no doubt that Europe made its own contributions towards the new version of the system. Especially the expositions of Francis Bacon, Montaigne, Machiavelli, and Copernicus, blending science, philosophy, and religion determined the nature of the new version. However, civilization did not only introduce city, state, social class, merchant, money, and market—it also introduced philosophy, religion, science, and the arts. Europe proved able to examine and take the most from the ancient history's material and immaterial culture, constructing a synthesis. The Indian and Chinese civilizations did not succeed in this; the Middle Eastern civilization could not gather the strength required for the final step forward. It is important to keep these historical facts in mind when pointing out that the European civilization is the third biggest version within civilizational history.

Anthony Giddens uses the concept of *discontinuities* when attempting to determine Europe's contributions; thus, he tries to illustrate the originality of the European system. Undoubtedly, the European civilization did bring its own innovations, but Giddens' discontinuities (capitalism, nation-state, and industrialism) are only partial proof of its originality. I will attempt to evaluate the sociology of Giddens to show that he too tries to salvage capitalism. But in order to do this, we first need to do an in-depth evaluation of the three fundamental topics he analyzes.

Here I will briefly return to the three main sources of Marxism. Distinguishing between the three is important for understanding the sources of European thought. However, Giddens failed to establish the similarities between them. (Could it have been to avoid exposing himself?) The common ground between English political economy, German philosophy, and French socialism (and thus also Marxism) is the ideology of the Enlightenment. What really should be analyzed is this ideology, because it is still *the* influential and dominant ideology in the world. Although sociology is presented as science, it does not bring any innovations because it falls within the framework of the same ideology. If I am not mistaken, the famous sociologist Immanuel Wallerstein admits this when interpreting European thought (which includes Marxism): "It is simply not true that capitalism as an historical system has represented progress over the various previous historical systems that it destroyed or transformed. Even as I write this, I feel the tremor that accompanies the sense of blasphemy. I fear the wrath of the gods, for I have been molded in the same ideological forge as all my compeers and worshiped at the same shrines."[2] He is referring to the ideology of the Enlightenment. The famous admission by Theodor Adorno (1903–1969), one of the strongest representatives of the Frankfurt School of critical theory, that "There is no right life in the wrong one."[3] Nietzsche and his successors criticized the Enlightenment ideology much more openly. Nietzsche argued that all the concepts of the Enlightenment were obtained from religion; on the other hand, Carl Schmitt disclosed the religious roots of all the concepts and hypotheses of political philosophy. The long list of rich literature and exemplary individuals shows that skepticism about the European way of thinking is deepening.

The complex and dreaded character of the civilization in Europe cannot be blamed solely on the terrible colonial and imperialist or religious and nationalist wars. The European civilization has brought economy under its control and has manipulated it. It has also brought on the reign of economy, and of economy becoming the state. These are all equally to be blamed and have reached levels incomparable to any other time in history. At this point, no one can deny many of its "discontinuities"; indeed, from certain perspectives, capitalism, industrialism, and nation-state do constitute important "discontinuities."

However, none of these descriptions, including those of the ideology of the Enlightenment, explains the "discontinuity" of European civilization. Whether intentionally or not, all devotees ultimately propagandize their own religion—the few exceptions do not negate but affirm the rule. We should not ignore the religious and metaphysical character of the European thought system which was shaped by a complex material civilization which had its own origins; its roots in the depths of history that passed through several versions. As with any religion, its devotees too are obliged to defend and eternalize the material culture their thought system represents. It is their strategic duty to spread it to the whole world. Thus, the European thought system has conquered the mind of the entire society on the local, national, and global levels: from the initial priests to its schools and academies; from official universities to military barracks; from the factories to the shopping malls, press, museums, and remnants of the old religions; from hospitals to prisons and graveyards the system has used its techniques of political power and military might to wrap itself around society like armor. The whole society has been sealed in an "iron cage."[4]

When religions or their associated thought systems are officialized, they turn into ideology. Ideologies, on the other hand, are the principles of a program for the defense of a group of people and their interests. The European thought system, or religion, that has become official around the world is now an ideology. As the civilization, it now has to use all its power to defend, perpetuate, and strive for the sovereignty of its upper classes.

Why has the ideology of the Enlightenment become so effective? Because it is the most advanced cosmopolitan religion which appeals to the members of all the religions that preceded it. It is national. A sociality and nationality that does not worship the nation-state is unthinkable: someone without a nation-state is deemed faithless. Nation-statist ideology is the weakest religion of all and therefore not *that* difficult to accept when compared to the religions of the past. It is continuously nourished with scientism. Its material life style has been turned into its religious ritual. Its immaterial cultural tools, and above all its media organs, ceaselessly propagandize it. It fully controls political and economic life. It has now become global.

I know that these generalizations are painting an image of a world inextricably ensnared. But a civilization presenting itself in this way must, like the Roman Empire, be living through its final stages with absolutely no self-confidence. No matter how magnificent and strong it seems because of all that it has destroyed, the activated ecological defense of the environment and the plurality within society have long ago begun their struggle against it. Just as the turning of civilization into an empire continues, so does the turning of democracy into a confederation. And remember, as I am part of this world, my criticism is not addressed solely to the European; it is addressed to myself, to my region, to my world—to the entire conquered humanity.

Capitalism is not economy but power

The insight that capitalism is not economy should lead to a work at least the magnitude of *Das Kapital*. Let me say outright that the ideas I will express here have nothing to do with power reductionism. Neither will I accept any criticism that I am linking capitalism (in terms of it being an economy) with the state. What I am talking about here is the formation of a *political* power that controls the economy but is conceptualized as "capitalism," "capitalist," and "capitalist economy." This power became influential for the first time in sixteenth century Europe and later became the true dominant political power in the Netherlands and England under the aforementioned labels. That it makes use of economy does not affirm that it is economical in character. Fernand Braudel openly states that capitalism is anti-market, a monopolist plunder externally imposed on the economy, and he is the first sociologist and historian to have realized it. Although he is aware of having ruined one of the creeds of European thought, he is unable to put it into words. The question then arises: What is this thing that externally imposes itself, that is anti-market and not economy? The answer to the question is yet insufficient. Is it a political power, religion, or a school of thought?

When a theoretical concept becomes too complicated it may be instructive to examine the practical developments. Let us examine the example of Venice. In thirteenth century Venice, there was a group of big merchants that, at the same time, were in control of the town's administration. Because they fought with their rivals they acquired armadas; hence, there was military power in Venice, too. They were patrons of the arts and influenced the Renaissance. They strictly controlled the economy and society—an integrally intertwined network of such relations in which money was the adhesive. What term, then, can be coined to denote this integral network of relations? Venice was able to control the economy through the group called the big merchants and hence was able to siphon off an important portion of the surplus value. In order to achieve this, it had to either *be* the political power or control the political power. When force was needed, it was able to use the military power.

This group, controlling everything in Venice, was the merchant monopoly. They were the ones controlling the state, the army, and the bureaucracy. They were the patrons of the church and art community. This group transcended the state. It externally imposed itself upon the economy but was not economy. It imposed hegemony over society that transcended the hegemony imposed by that of the state. What should we call this group then but the concentration of power itself? If this group had succeeded in being an influential power over all of Italy, we would have called it a national power; a nation-state had it taken over control of the entire society; an economic power had it taken control of the entire Italian economy. If, on the other hand, it had expanded to all of Europe and then to the world at large, it would have been called the European and World Empire.

Let us now examine the situation in sixteenth century Netherlands and England on the basis of the above hypothesis. The continuous pressure applied by the French and Spanish Kingdoms was decisive. These kingdoms aspired to become empires and wanted to turn England and the Netherlands into their provinces. Yet the king of England and the Prince of Orange wished to preserve and expand their political independence. To achieve this, and to prevent becoming absorbed, they desperately needed power— political, military, monetary, and intellectual power. They welcomed thinkers and artists to their countries—Descartes, Spinoza, and Erasmus. Jewish moneylenders streamed in. The foundation for a new kind of army was laid, a professional army with professional training, discipline, and techniques. In order to foster the development of social support and solidarity, they placed an emphasis on freedom. They overcame the internal political quarrels. But, more importantly, they showed an economic skill that proved effective across Europe. Thus were the Netherlands and England able to successfully defend themselves. More than that, they were able to utilize the situation and establish their hegemony towards the end of the century.

Let us now re-ask our questions: What should we call this intertwined and interconnected web of relations? How should we define its system? Were all these developments achieved by a new, creative economic class? An economy was rendered productive—who brought this about? Thousands of craftspeople, farmers, workers, small-scale merchants, shopkeepers, market—and money and deposit slips that increased circulation. Most importantly, such an economic productivity increased the surplus value. But who received the lion's share of the increased value? It must have been those who regulated the economy through monetary, political, and military power. If there was no money, there would be no retail and productivity decline. If there was no army and no political power there would be an invasion, which would also reduce productivity. So money and its derivatives have an influence, but such supervision is maintained so that economy is brought under a certain level of control and, in return, the growing surplus-value can be usurped.

We can assume that, as in the thirteenth century Venice, the group controlling the economy in the sixteenth century England and the Netherlands had a good relationship with the political and military powers. The enormous need for money that the prince and king would have had as head of their armies implies that they would either have belonged to this group or had strong ties to it. While they sought recognition as champions of individual freedom through their support of artistic and ideological movements, they did not refrain from supporting movements opposing their rivals.

Let me ask once again: How do we conceptualize this movement as a whole? Could we call it "economical" while not a single member is involved with real economic practice except to seize the surplus value?

Who are they then, the members of this group? They are the ones who, from outside the economy, impose themselves on the economy and multiply money by increasing value and money in circulation; who then pass the money on to the state in the form of debt; who then, perhaps in return, become partners of the state.

It is clear that those who indirectly control the economy are capitalism, the capitalists, and the capitalist economy, although, for the most part, they are not intrinsically involved in the economy. What then is their real endeavor? Their interest is power monopoly—combining their economic monopoly with the power monopoly. They wage war. When they win an internal war their power within that country increases. This means more surplus value. Victory in external wars means colonial gain and hegemony, which in turn means the plunder of monopoly.

Let us look at the English and Dutch examples to get a more concrete picture of how such a situation developed. The English and Dutch first used their alliance to achieve hegemony across Europe. By the end of the sixteenth century the oppression of the Spanish Empire had been shattered and its ambition to build a Europe-wide empire had been dealt a fatal blow. The end of the seventeenth century witnessed the defeat of the French monarchy's hegemonic desire of Europe. They struck a fatal blow to the Hapsburg dynasty's dreams of a European empire by supporting Prussia against Austria. They brought an end to the era of religious wars with the closure of Thirty Years' War, and with the 1648 Treaty of Westphalia they laid the foundation of a system based on the equilibrium of national states. The response of France, in terms of the 1789 revolution, ended in a strategic hegemonic loss for France during the Napoleon era. By this time, most of Europe's colonial wars had been won. The Industrial Revolution that took off in Britain at the start of the nineteenth century opened the door for British world dominion. After Prussia's victory over France in 1870, the German giant slowly awoke, but its attempts to become the European and world hegemonic power were defeated during the two World Wars. The USA, essentially the second England, profited from both World Wars, and after World War II became the new hegemonic power of the world. The Russian Soviet Empire—repeating what Germany had done—came out of this hegemonic war defeated. The USA is now striving to become a world empire, and in order to prevent its collapse it is, at the same time, seeking to extend its life through defensive wars.

The stream of political power that started at the city of Uruk converged with many tributaries to form the course that reached the Atlantic coast of Northern Europe. After a deep swirl during its stopover in England and the Netherlands the main stream of civilization continued its flow to the coastal waters of New York City, having gained speed and a new color when the discontinuities converged with the main stream during this swirl. Nation-state, the new version of the traditional state, and its industry, the biggest economic revolution second to the Neolithic Revolution, are two very strong tributaries. More than anything else, these were the two factors that accelerated and defined traditional civilization to give it the form that we know today. The main stream of civilization is now disappearing in the ocean near New York City. Currently, there are speculations that the shores of China will be its next stop. I believe that the chances of its arriving there are less than its chances of not arriving. The chances are higher that civilizational society will dissolve. Because of the monstrous levels of social and environmental problems worldwide, the chances of democratic societies stepping in and constructing their own civilization have become a real possibility. A confederative union of democracies has a better chance to deal with global problems than the empire cult left over from the old state systems.

Once again the question arises: Where is capitalism? Where is it—in terms of economic contribution—in relation to the nation-state and industry? I cannot find an answer within economy despite my sustained effort.

It may be viewed as strange, but I believe the true owner of the economy, despite all the attempts to invade and colonize, is still the woman. If we wish to meaningfully evaluate economy from a sociological perspective, we must see the woman (bearing, carrying, raising and nurturing children until they can be independent, as well as being the artisan of the house) as the fundamental power. This sociologically based answer is far more respectful to the truth. It does not ignore the relationship between economy and biology. As the gatherer of plants for millions of years, as the main actor in the agricultural revolution to date, not only inside the house but in many areas of economic life, it is the woman who has always spun the wheel. The ancient Greeks determined this truth thousands of years ago and acknowledged it by naming woman's household management *economy*. Second in line after the woman are of course those who fall into the category of slave, serf, and worker. Endless, merciless methods ensure their labor and keep them under the strictest leash in order that the civilizational powers can seize the surplus product and value. Those third in line are somewhat freer: the various craftspeople, small merchants and small farmers, artists, architects, engineers, doctors, and those who are self-employed.

These are the social groups—or classes—that have spun the economic wheel throughout history. No capitalist, seignior, agha, or landlord can be found amongst them. It is clear that they are *not* economic powers but occupying, exploiting, colonial, and assimilationist powers who externally and monopolistically impose this on the people and their labor. It is not only capitalists such as the large-scale merchant, industrialist, and banker that is externally imposing and anti-economic; the seignior, big landowner, politician, high-ranking military members, and the civilizationalist intellectual can be included in the list of powers that are not economic but who externally impose themselves on the economy.

Evidence that capitalism is anti-economy

The evidence that capitalism is not only *not* an economy, but that it is *anti*-economy is striking.

1. Economic crises

The "priest class" of positivist-scientists intent on proving that capitalism is an economic system have the wrong perception of the capitalist problem, a perception which they transmit to others. There is only one explanation for economic crises, namely that capitalism is the sworn enemy and opponent of the economy. Some crises are said to be caused by overproduction. While the majority of the world is starving, the minority produces in excess! These deliberate depressions are the best proof of capitalism's anti-economy position. The reason for causing these depressions is very clear: the profit of the monopolies. When the allowance left for the workers is no longer a sufficient purchasing power, the so-called depressions are generated. Who comes to the help in such a situation, which fake priest or so-called economist? Keynes! What is his solution? The state should increase expenditure. How? By increasing the purchasing power of the worker! How is this dirty game exposed? With one hand, you empty the worker's pocket while with the other you fill it up! This certainly is a policy aiming at persuading all the workers and the societies excluded from the main civilization by saying, "This is not the worst yet." It is clear that we face a political relationship. When there is a desire to suppress any act of democratic force against the civilization the dissidents are starved, then they are made to beg and only then are they fed. This is one of the oldest tactics of war: If you want to seize control of a people or a city, you first put them under siege and then you starve them. They shall be fed only if they surrender.

There are many examples which we can use to prove that the essence of the fake depression theories of capitalism is nothing but this starvation technique. An analysis of the infamous depression of the 1930s will help us understand the logic. What happened there? The Soviet Union, who did not accept the hegemony of England, was becoming a permanent and successful regime, at the same time threatening the capitalist world. The Germans and their allies were in resistance against the treaty of surrender that was imposed on them. China, under the leadership of Mao Zedong, was conducting a massive peasant rebellion. Around the world, including in Anatolia, colonized and semi-colonized countries rebelled through growing national resurrection movements against the English hegemony. The response of the English world hegemony was the deliberate depression that started in 1929. On the one hand, there were piles of goods; on the other, starved peoples and workers. The redress proposed by John Maynard Keynes of England reveals it all—a chance of survival for the world's workers and peoples that resembled breadcrumbs, the so-called social state policies. What was the end result of these capitalist social state policies? Gradually, the world democratic society that began with the September Soviet Revolution was assimilated, distorted, and its development impeded until, in the 1990s, the Soviet system was eventually subverted from within. These policies were initiated in the 1930s at the time of Stalin's anti-democratic policies—indeed, his dictatorship. Why? Ostensibly to eliminate the 1930 depression. What was eventually eliminated? Stalin, his successors, and the Soviet economy. What was the result? States that had succeeded in their national liberation struggles were drained of their social contents (that is, from the democratic revolution and democratic society) and integrated within the hegemonic capitalist system. Clearly, elimination of resistance against the hegemonic system is the main objective of these depressions and, through deliberate state policies, such an objective was met with the Great Depression: the hegemonic system was maintained—at least, a critical phase was overcome.

2. *Crises of famine and disaster*

The production of goods can be stopped deliberately, or humanity's despair in the face of illnesses and disasters can be exploited. Given our modern technical tools and equipment, a serious famine or epidemic is unthinkable. But when there is an existential crisis for the hegemonic system, such artificial depressions are generated and illnesses and disasters are used against dissidents. Once again, we see the link between the device called "capitalist economy and society" and the power of the official hegemonic civilization. Once again, the siege method is used: Starve them, exploit any epidemic or disaster situation, and then step in as the liberating angel (or god!). Your servants shall praise you abundantly, Sir!

3. *Engineering of war and peace:*

Capitalism is not just anti-economy but also anti-society. Theoretically, it is not possible for the entire society to become capitalist, as Rosa Luxemburg proved decades ago. If every society is divided into two, workers and capitalists, you cannot produce goods for the sole purpose of making profits! A very rough example of this is a factory with 100 workers manufacturing 100 cars. The society consists of the 100 workers plus the one capitalist (because the society consists only of workers and capitalists—what we call "pure capitalist society"; this is of course the mistake made by at least some Marxists). To realize a profit 100 cars must be sold. Let's say the 100 workers buy the cars from their salaries. What is the owner left with? Nothing. So, for civilizational society to sustain itself, there is a need for the continuous existence of, as I call it, the anti-civilizational democratic society that does not become capitalist. Capitalist civilization, as the new hegemonic power, can only continue its existence by being anti-democratic-society. In times of action against it, this need intensifies and civilizational society can only exist by being an enemy to democratic society—either through waging war or through making peace. There are innumerable events and wars throughout civilizational history, including capitalist history, that confirm this.

4. The unemployment crisis

Capitalism as a system must keep an army of unemployed in order to keep the profit margin (obtained from the surplus-value) high. If there is no unemployment, it must be created: *unemployment is an intentionally created process*. The most ordinary animal and plant have their uses; how then can a human be left unemployed and rendered useless? Indeed, there is no room for the concept of unemployment in the universe. However, unemployment *is* artificially created as a distorted product of analytical intelligence—the most savage act of social life. Unemployment is continuously fed. No event exposes the capitalist system's animosity to the economic life better than *unemployment*. There has never been a concept such as the unemployed slave, even during the pharaohs' regime that we criticize so harshly. Only in capitalism does one have unemployment, that is, an implacable animosity against economy.

5. Refusal to resolve the economic crisis

Capitalism is also the enemy of economic technique. The present level of science and technology is so highly developed that it has the ability to sustain any society, both in terms of its political system in the form of democratic society, and to resolve all its economic problems. The capitalist system's law of profit prevents the optimal application of science and technology from meeting the need of the people. The current level of science and technology have the capacity required to find various solutions for an economy that is based on the needs of human nutrition. But the law of profit does not allow this capacity to be used. On the contrary, capitalist civilization sustains itself by generating continuous crises, unemployment, and overpopulation. Hence, capitalism is not only the enemy of the economy but also of the science and technical development that can bring about an economy that functions at the optimal level.

6. *Exchanging morality for capitalist principles*

Capitalism is also the enemy of morals and moral values, which are the fundamental principles of economy. Humanity can only see to its own economic needs if guided by the principles of morals. In the absence of morals the entire society will be lionized, leaving no cattle-like people. But this will mean the end of time. That is, if capitalism cannot be restricted and eventually stopped, it will turn the society either into a society of ants (like in China and Japan), thus bringing the society to the brink of collapse, or into a society of lions (like the society in the US). Clearly, if all societies are to become like those of the US, or China and Japan, the continuation of human societies is less likely. Capitalism has indeed sacrificed the moral principle for the principle of the capitalist "economy." In the past, some societies sacrificed female children because they were "redundant"; if such morals exist, the society may be sustained through the sacrifice of human beings. If we only realized that war waged for the sake of capitalism is but the *ritual of human sacrifice*, we would understand what immorality we face in the guise of the principle of the capitalist "economy." This immorality destroys not only the inner social fabric of society, but it subjugates the environment and nature to the extent that not only human life but all animate life is under threat. What could be more immoral and hostile towards living beings than this?

7. *Suppression of women*

Capitalism is also the enemy of the woman—the creator of economy and, as our analysis shows, the fundamental force in the economy. However, throughout civilizational history, she has been pushed out of life. The most brutal period began when, with the start of the capitalist civilization phase, she was ousted from the economy. Thus, until the Neolithic Period woman was the one who "manages the household, the economy," woman's reality now is that of "one destitute of economy." This is the most striking and profound social paradox. The female population of the world has been left overwhelmingly unemployed. Although housework is the most difficult of work, it is seen as valueless. Although childbirth and child rearing are the most exacting of tasks, they are not always regarded as valuable but often as mere trouble. On top of being an unemployed childbearing and child raising machine that is inexpensive to obtain and can be run cost free, the woman can be used as scapegoat, carrying the guilt for all that is wrong. Throughout the history of civilization, she has been placed on the ground floor of society. During the capitalist period, she is the object of inequality, freedomless-ness, and democracyless-ness, not only at the ground level but at all levels. Moreover, the capitalist system has developed the rule of sexist society—its intensity and focus unmatched at any other time in history. This ruling has become so widespread and multiplied that the woman has been turned into the object *and* subject of the sex industry. This torturous approach has been spread across all social strata. In turn, the male dominated society has been allowed to reach its peak during the capitalist civilization, taking its revenge on the one who "manages the household, the economy" and proving its hostility to women and the economy. Indeed, no other society has had the power to develop and systemize the exploitation of the woman and the economy to the degree that capitalism has.

8. *Economy turned into a paper game*

Capitalism exceedingly proves that it has nothing to do with real economy. In its current phase, the global phase, its hostility towards the economy has reached its peak when it turned economy into the money and paper game of stock, exchange, and interest rates. Never before in the long history of civilization could the economy have been turned into such paper games, to the extent that it has been transformed into a virtual system. In the past, it was seen as the most sensitive element of society, and sacredness (its roots go back as far as the Sumerian society) was always attributed to it. Nourishment was seen as the primary problem that needed to be resolved. Every religion has an economic pledge as an aspect of its elucidation, the festivals are celebrated in commemoration of economic abundance, or at least of overcoming crisis. Economy, which is so important that it can be viewed as the sum of the factors that can influence all areas of society, has lost its position as the focus area of the emotional and analytical intelligence. The result is that the economy has become dependent on the money and paper games, that it has been transformed into the most irresponsible area of analytic-speculative intelligence. As Marx rightly pointed out, economy has become detached from real life and has been turned into speculative gambling. Without any need for labor, just by fluctuating the exchange and interest rates and stock prices, billions of dollars exchange hands globally. While half of the human population is bordering on the poverty and starvation line, it is hard to imagine any other system so in opposition to the real economy. Capitalism, in its present so-called "age of finance," has once again proven what an irrelevant, anti-economy, and hostile system it is.

9. Crises of production and consumption

By taking direct control of them, capitalism radically breaks away from the essential structures of the two main areas of economy: production and consumption. This is done through the policy of maximizing profits by generating production and consumption crises. This includes a devastatingly high level of armament manufacture (especially of nuclear armaments), continued investment in high profit yielding carbon-based energy supplies (despite its destruction of the environment), genetically modified agricultural products, space technology, big investments in ground, marine, and air travel (despite it being very expensive and the massive pollution it causes), and an unwarranted investment in various trendy goods. Thus, on the one hand there are heaps of goods that became redundant because the consumer no longer finds them attractive; on the other hand, there is the death of millions through starvation and illness, because they, the armies of unemployed, have no consumer power!

The hostility and harm done by capitalism is unequaled by any war or natural disaster in history. This "economic" form called capitalism realizes itself by suppressing and exploiting economy and by changing its chemistry.

Undoubtedly, much substantiating analysis is needed in respect to the points raised above. However, as this is my defenses before the court, I will have to leave it at this. I will, however, continue to expose other aspects of capitalism as a civilizational phase in the following sections.

Capitalism in Relation to Society, Civilization, and History

How can we come to an adequate understanding and interpretation of the capitalist system (which is clearly not economy, but is indeed anti-economy)? Where exactly should we situate it in terms of location and time within the social and civilizational reality? We can only reach a meaningful conclusion with regard to capitalism by probing into the actions and conflicts between and amongst the civilizational forces and systems, and the actions and wars led by the anti-civilizational forces against these.

If I am repetitive, I apologize; however, I believe a summary is needed here so that I can present a complete picture.

The Primitive Communal Era
Until about 20,000 years ago

The foundations of the economic culture were laid during the matriarchal Primitive Communal Order.[5] Food attained from gathering and hunting was consumed immediately and by-products such as fur and fiber were used extensively. The regulatory authority of the clan was predominantly the woman-mother—the initial, but motherly, hegemon. Conflicts and relationships forming inside the clan society occurred mainly to protect the clan from the dangerous environmental conditions, and to benefit from those environmental conditions that offer nutrition. Under such conditions the clan identity was vital and indispensable. As yet, the concept of *husband and wife* did not exist. The mother that bore the child was recognized, but who the father was, was of so little importance that it was usually not known. The clan took shelter on riverbanks, in caves, and sometimes sheds. As yet, concepts such as *homeland, borders*, and *property* did not exist. *Belonging* was identified only with the clan. Clanship was symbolized by some object or totem.

This appears to have been the life-style for at least two million years in Africa and about one million in Asia and Europe. This life-style was the basis of human society for 98.5% of its existence; thus, out of all the social orders, this lasted the longest by far. The entire human race lived under this social order, and at the end of the last glacial period made the transition to the Neolithic era—although the level of development differed from region to region.

The Neolithic Era
Ca. 15,000 to ca. 4,000 BCE

As the last glacial period ended, approximately 17,000 years ago, the Mesolithic (or the Middle Stone Age) Period began. It was of short duration, and after this period the transition to a historically important stage, the Neolithic (or New Stone Age) Period was made. Although termed "Neolithic" (because of the "new" tools made from polished stone and obsidian) the essence of this era is the agricultural and village revolution that developed on the slopes of the Taurus-Zagros Mountains. Archaeological evidence indicates that this society developed ca. 10,000 years ago, probably due to the favorable weather conditions in these parts. The beneficial weather induced an abundance of flora and fauna that were then domesticated, forming the heart of the new culture of agriculture. This led to improved nutrition as well as the development of weaving and, ca. 6,000 BCE, pottery. The transition from cave life to village life was made and, especially in the crescent formed by the mountains that stretched from the eastern Mediterranean to Zagros, the transition to the cultural period of Tell Halaf began.[6]

The main locus of this development was Upper Mesopotamia, where society entered a period during which new inventions of production tools and methods flourished—the "industrial period" of the Neolithic. The mother-woman rose to the level of mother-goddess in this culture—most likely she played the decisive role in the construction of the new society—and the matriarchal order left its mark on clan society. Conflict with the male slowly began to develop.

Due to geological and climatic changes the groups now referred to as Semites could no longer easily make the crossing from the south into Asia and Europe over this main region (a factor that must have played an important role in the shaping of the Semitic culture). Neither could any groups from the north enter this region with ease any longer. While one of their branches made it to the American continent (presumably over the Bering Strait around 12,000-7,000 BCE), the rest spread over

China, Central Asia, and Eastern Europe. The Indo-European group in the middle came to play a leading role due to favorable weather and nutritional conditions, while the group in the Fertile Crescent became the dominant group; this was a position that they maintained for a very long time—indeed, until the onset of the civilizational phase.

The Fertile Crescent culture was here to stay—and to spread. It expanded to Lower Mesopotamia ca. 6,000 BCE, to the Egyptian Nile valley ca. 5,000 BCE, and to the Balkans, Iran, and northern Black Sea, as well as to Europe and China ca. 4,000 BCE. Although much commentary is made about the Chinese Neolithic that developed by their own dynamics, my personal belief is that they rested predominantly on the transmitted culture of Upper Mesopotamia. This belief is reinforced by archaeological evidence regarding the spread of cattle husbandry and the use of obsidians. Of course, since we are talking about very long periods of time, each main region also had the opportunity to develop its own Neolithic Period, but all the prominent signs point to the Fertile Crescent as the focus of the initial cultural spark. The expansion was not based on colonialism or occupation—the vast, free fields did not allow for such relations.

This initial global movement has left its permanent mark on the world and continues to influence it.

The Sumerian Civilizational Era
Ca. 4,000-2,000 BCE

A new phase, the Ubaid cultural period, prevailed in Lower Mesopotamia from ca. 5,500 to 3,800 BCE.[7] Although it rested upon the Fertile Crescent culture (mainly that of Tell Halaf), this period is of historical importance in its own right because it started the transition toward patriarchal society, development in pottery, the growing importance of trade, and the onset of the era of invasion and colonization. It can be called the Proto-Uruk culture. Of special importance are the emergence of the patriarchal society in this era (as it is pre-civilization) and the concomitant loss of the preeminence of the goddess culture and women being coerced into recognizing men's superiority. A major development in hierarchical rule occurred when, in this culture, the tripartite structure of traditional civilization's rule declared itself for the first time in rudimentary form. It was namely in the Ubaid cultural period that the combination rule of the shaman (a type of priest), the sheikh (experienced ruler of the society), and military chief (who has the physical power) first took root. (The religious, political, and military culture of the Middle East carries deep traces of this period!)

This was a prolific culture and by 4,500 BCE its effects were felt in Upper Mesopotamia. It subdued the Tell Halaf culture; it "colonized" it, as it were. Archaeological data indicates that by 4,000 BCE Ubaid trade "colonies" existed as far as Arslantepe, Malatya, and Elazığ in eastern Anatolia. With dynasties, the culture of extended families also spread. These elements did not exist in the previous culture. The trade culture was here to stay. There are also traces of destructive activities. Archaeological remnants of some destroyed villages denote occurrences of deliberate destruction and invasion. With this culture came the first serious assertion of hegemony.

The period between 4,000 and 3,000 BCE is now widely referred to as the Uruk cultural period. The Uruk culture based itself on the Ubaid culture—the major difference being the emergence of the first city-class-state society, hence the onset of civilization and written history. And, of course, the transition from the patriarchal to the civilizational culture *was* a major historical event. The fundamental agent of change was the artificial-irrigation necessitated by the Lower Mesopotamian climate. This method of irrigation required a big population and irrigation tools—two important prerequisites for urbanization. Such a large population of workers brought the question of sustenance and the craftsmanship required to produce the irrigation tools. Settlements thus had to be city-sized but this, in turn, necessitated solutions to the questions of city administration and the legitimization of the administration itself. Moreover, there was a need for protection from ongoing predatory tribal attacks. When those conditions occurred together the tripartite consisting of the priest, the ruler-king, and the military commander was born. The Epic of Gilgamesh, dedicated to the first Uruk king, reflects this historical development in a most striking and effective way.

We can consider class division as predominantly the product of urbanization. The urban society surpasses the tribal and dynastic units. Moreover, because of the inherent conflicting nature of the hierarchical and patriarchal administrations, a huge part of the population more than likely would have been excluded from these tribal and dynastic structures. Even if it was only to have access to food, the city became the center of attraction for the population detached from these structures. Inevitably, those who for various reasons were excluded from their tribes and dynasties would have constituted the section that became the workers, the ruled. At this point, the birth of class division became inevitable. The social relationship of class division was an important element of the Uruk culture. The state would emerge as the natural extension of this web of city relations.

The city administration did not accommodate tribal or dynastic rule. It required a professional administration exceeding blood ties. Moreover, in order to legitimize itself, the need for a system of persuasion too imposes itself. The priest (who was most probably the constructor of the initial "draft" state) and the temple (the initial model of the city) came to the rescue. The ideological and mental construction of city, state, and class division as institutions was the job of mythology and religion. The Uruk culture is a striking example of material culture's influence on the immaterial culture. The opposite is also true. Under the heavy impact of the constructed immaterial culture it was nearly impossible to ascertain the exact nature of the material culture. It was rendered invisible by a vast ideological construct. The main duty of the new state ideology was to make the material conditions indiscernible by manipulating the people to internalize its language and content over thousands of years. This function could clearly be seen in the Sumerian society. While the state was portrayed as a divine establishment, the working class was projected as the subjects created by god. The intermediaries between the state and the ruled were reflected through the concept of angels. The highest authority in the administration was elevated to main god, whereas his deputies, as secondary gods, formed the pantheon, that is to say, representing the upper-level state management and its meeting arrangements. The presence of the ancient generation of goddesses still evoked the memories of women's influence prior to urbanization. All social relations, expressed partly mythologically and partly religiously, attained their own legitimization in a totally different metaphysical world. City, state, and class division were ideologically recreated.

Being ideologically recreated (an immaterial culture of immense function) is indeed an interpretation of material development including even that of nature. Based on this, and in particular on the reflective language used, new meanings were derived and people were persuaded and life was blessedly lived in this new legitimized world. In the face of this ideological rebirth, the question, "Is there a real, material (physical) birth?" has almost lost its meaning, or, even if it is seen to be meaningful, it shall be portrayed differently.

The Uruk revolution, as the initial urban revolution, is as important as the agricultural revolution. There were many later derivatives. It is true that there were also urban revolutions in China and in Central America. But they were localized cultures that were either unable to form a main civilizational river or dried up in their own place of birth. The main condition for being a civilization is to either be the main stream or to be able to join the main stream. There are no pure civilizations. Besides, behind the Uruk culture was the ten-thousand-year-old Neolithic heritage.

This new culture is called the "civilization." This can be interpreted to mean urban. We have thus defined the whole civilization by defining its material and immaterial structures and the manner in which these were reflected. Structurally, the Uruk culture was expansionist. The cities grew in many ways due to increased productivity. In turn, the increase in population led to the emergence of many neighboring cities. Formerly, the Fertile Crescent's village culture had led to villages becoming widely established. The early villages spread out from Nevala Çorî (Urfa, Siverek at the banks of Euphrates) to Çayönü (Diyarbakir, Ergani at the banks of a branch of the Tigris). From there it spread to Çemê Hallan (near Batman Creek) and all the way to Kirkuk (since 10,000 BCE). This is exactly what is meant with the blooming of cultures. The Uruk acculturation followed the same path.

The growing number of cities meant increased competition. City, at the same time, meant market, and so the new culture carried competition along with itself. Trade had already become a favorite occupation, and an agriculture and transportation industry had emerged under the leadership of craftsmen. Now the rivalry between cities would naturally put the question of hegemony on the agenda. Hence, the transition from city-state to primitive empire (the rule of all the cities by the same person or dynasty) would soon impose itself.

The trade needs of Uruk brought the Neolithic region into the civilizational and colonization phase early on. My understanding of the available data is that, following the colonies of Ubaid culture, Uruk's expansion area and colonizing activities were more developed. Especially advanced were the Uruk colonies that were found on the banks of the Euphrates River. Archaeological findings also prove the existence of the Upper Mesopotamian culture, which had not stopped developing since the Tell Halaf culture. This culture rebelled against the Uruk colonization movement (3,500 BCE) but at the same time, there were mutual dealings between the two cultures. Numerous mound excavations prove the urbanization of this region around 3,000 BCE, a development that resulted from its strong internal dynamics.

The increasing number of findings suggest that the urban culture was transmitted to Lower Mesopotamia—as it was to Egypt, Elam, and Harappa—from the main regional source. In particular, the recent excavation of Göbeklitepe near Urfa (Klaus Schmidt and his team established its time of origin to be ca. 10,000 BCE) led to findings that may change present-day convictions. The remnants of a structure (most probably a temple) of vast dimensions were found. Although the significance of the erected stones is not clear, what *is* clear is that the structure reflects an advanced culture. New studies may well reveal some other settlement as the cultural center.

Only a very strong culture would have been able to respond successfully to this Uruk expansion. Previously, the culture of this region had resisted another cultural expansion (the Ubaid culture, which most likely started ca. 5,500 BCE) and maintained its own culture. The permanence of the cultural structure in the region can be explained by the continued resistance to the migration from the south and north throughout the Mesolithic and Neolithic Periods. This reality (that is, the dissolution of Uruk culture within the local culture) is indicative of the strength of the opposing culture—a situation that has continued to date. Uruk's superiority lay in its production and its state-power, derived from its huge population. In fact, here we almost have the original model for the Netherlands and England.

My personal interpretation is that the cultures of Egypt, Elam (present day southwest Iran), and Upper Mesopotamia successfully responded to the Ubaid and Uruk expansions by creating their own urban culture. As a matter of fact, more and more archaeological findings indicate that urbanization in these three historical centers accelerated from ca. 3,000 BCE, enriching the development of the civilization.

What happened in the urban and rural regions around Uruk is more important. We know from history that the Uruk Cultural Era ended ca. 3,000 BCE and that a new period began with the First Dynasty of Ur, a development probably resulting from intense urban conflict. Indeed, this is what the tablets tell us: hymns like "The Nippur Lament" and "The Curse of Akkad" are all elegies focusing on the fate of these devastated cities. (How this resembles the events in Baghdad and the surrounding areas!) The period of the First and Second Dynasty of Ur continued till 2,350 BCE. Around 2,350–2,150 the Dynasty of Akkad was founded by the infamous Sargon. Sargon, who can be described as the very first emperor, proudly boasted about how he was able to construct his hegemony, indeed empire, all over the Fertile Crescent by waging his bloody wars—terrible atrocities told as if they were tales of honorable deeds. He is said to be of Amorite origin and according to the Sumerian list of kings he himself was the builder of his capital, Agade (Akkad). But ca. 2,150 BCE others with Zagros origins destroyed Akkad under the leadership of Gudea, who then founded his own dynasty, the Second Dynasty of Lagash. At about 2,050 BCE, this dynasty also fell apart. It was replaced by the Third Dynasty of Ur, which existed for only a hundred years. When the clock of history pointed at 1,950 BCE, it was the beginning of the magnificent Babylonian Era.

In the battle between the cities an interesting contradiction occurred. The society mainly responsible for the creation of civilization, its main source, was the Sumerian civilization. Its point of origin probably was the Fertile Crescent, but it seemed to have become a people, a society, firmly settled in its new location. Their language differed from that of their two neighbors, the Amorites and Gutians. Although there were many words they shared, Sumerian was closer to the Aryan language group and differed distinctly from these languages with their Semitic roots. The attacks of the Semitic Amorite tribes were frequent. In fact, the city of Akkad, the Dynasty of Akkad, and Sargon were all of Semitic Amorite origin. (According to the Sargon legend, Sargon grew up in the Sumerian city castles and took part in their administration before making himself king of the Sumerian city-state of Kish and subsequently set out to conquer the other Sumerian city-states.) The Gutians saw the Sumerians mainly as allies even though they were Aryans who initially came from Zagros. What is really interesting is that there is an extremely similar situation in today's Iraq.

As a result, the emergence and development of civilization as a system, up until the beginning of the second millennium BCE, was characterized by bloodshed, ubiquitous exploitation, the construction and destruction of cities, the formation of alliances, colonization, and the establishment of hegemony. The slaves worked the moist, fertile land solely for their daily feed. But with the development of agriculture, trade, and craftsmanship in the neighboring cities and the Neolithic regions, they produced a huge surplus product. With such production at its disposal, the civilizational system, based on this material culture, constructed a magnificent immaterial culture in which its own clique of rulers was elevated to gods. The slaves who worked the land, the producers of the surplus, were belittled; they were reduced to the excrement of the gods. It must be well understood that *this* was how the creation legends depicted material life. The real creator, the woman-goddess, was reduced to a being created from the right rib of the male—the legends' clear and striking reflection of mother-woman's dependency. Thenceforth, life would be analyzed and understood according to the language of these legends.

The true material life has not been able to create its own language and interpretation. At times it might attempt, vaguely, to mention the truth of former times. But because no one will understand, the true material life will thus continuously experience an absence of meaning and muteness. Let us not forget: the language of truth and its ability to express itself has not yet been created!

The Babylonian and Assyrian Civilizational Era
Ca. 2,000 BCE to ca. 300 BCE

These two civilizations, which brought about very specific changes, appeared in different times and at different locations.[8] However, their appearance in history and their complete cessation from the rule of the Sumerian dynasties make them more significant in terms of culture and contemporaneousness. On the strength of the similarities between the two languages and cultures and from indications in surviving texts, we can assume that they were of Semitic (specifically Amorite) origin and shared a common civilizational heritage with the Akkadian Dynasty.[9] The last moments of the glorious Sumerian era were lived in the ancient city of Nippur, the most important spiritual and cultural center of Sumer (and probably the first city to provide an academic education).[10] Nippur went through periods of decline in importance. The new city that emerged nearby, under Akkadian cultural and linguistic influence, was Babylon (1,790–1,750 BCE).

The emergence of this city can be seen as the beginning of the new civilizational era.[11] In fact, with the fall of Sumer's last and Third Dynasty of Ur at the dawn of the second millennium, the new status quo became clearer as the hegemony of the Mesopotamian cities passed to Babylonian rule. The Akkadian language attained importance as the new civilizational language, making its presence felt throughout the civilizational region as the language of hegemony and trade. In time, it became the Aramaic language, the *lingua franca* with which all civilized people communicated with one another, playing much the same role as English today.

The Akkadian culture, in civilizational terms, inherited the contents of the Sumerian culture. The transformation in mythology can best be seen in the elevation of the god Marduk. In the most important myth from the period, the creation myth *Enûma Eliš*, Marduk is elevated to main god and the woman-goddess is vilified completely. Thus, the new religion symbolized and deified the male-dominated culture.

The Greek equivalent of Marduk is Zeus and his Roman counterpart is Jupiter; his equivalent in the Indo-European culture is Gudea (*Gott* or *God* of the Germanic peoples and *Xwedê* of the Kurds both have the same Aryan root); and, in the Arabic culture it is Allah, Brahman in the Indian, and Tao in the Chinese culture. These male gods all represent the same divine generation. The commonality of civilizational phases and the cultural similarities are displayed most dramatically in the names given to the gods representing the various societies. It is no coincidence that these gods—and even their names—all made their first appearance around 2,000 BCE. This is due to the deeply rooted and common culture that lies at their foundation. Thus, the male dominated culture in symbolized form (the seizure of the mother-woman and her house economy by the tyrannous, cunning male) is deified. The mother-goddess—called Star by the Aryans, Inanna by the Sumerians, Kibele by the Hittites, Ishtar by the Semites, and Kali by the Indian cultures—gradually fades away while the male-gods are exalted. The years around 2,000 BCE also signify a defeat and belittling, reflected in culture and language, as the woman is pulled down to society's basement. Her enslavement occurs even before man and tribe are enslaved within the material and immaterial culture of the civilization. The cursed slavery to which she has been subjected ever since is the most profound— the deadliest, most humiliating—enslavement of all enslavements. Indeed, the institution of housewifization and patriarch (giving the man-husband unlimited power over the woman) emerged from this cultural foundation. The continuation of this status of women in the Arabic and other Middle Eastern societies that share this cultural foundation attests to this. Honor crimes are only a small element of this culture.

The Babylonian city stands out in history because of some of its characteristics. In the first place, it absorbed the entire culture of Nippur, the last of the Sumerian cities. Thus, it can be deduced that it channeled the cultural accumulation and prominent people of all the contemporary societies to Babylonia at its empire-forming stage. Indeed, the famous tower of Babel and the "seventy-two languages" present there cannot be anything but truth turned into legend. Hammurabi was the most famous emperor of Babylon and, after Sargon, the second known emperor in history. Although the Code of Hammurabi might have been a continuation of a previous tradition of codes, its influence and the mark it has left on history is of primary importance. The "Law of God" and "code of law" of the civilizational culture most certainly carries traces of the Hammurabian period. After Hammurabi waged a series of bloody wars the Babylonian Empire came to dominate all the surrounding cities and imposed its hegemony on the neighboring tribal cultures, as well as those within its own borders.

The Old Testament tells the story of the Prophet Abraham's escape, or exodus, from Ur (today's Urfa). This escape seems to be closely related to the tyranny of the Babylonian Nimrod. Indications are that Hammurabi's reign was from about 1,700 to 1,650 BCE. Since the Prophet Abraham's exodus probably occurred in about the same period, we can well understand the contention between Abraham and Nimrod. The tribe led by Abraham was one of the many in the region subjugated by Hammurabi that subsisted on agriculture, animal husbandry, and trade. Just as today, there were numerous transitional societies in this region that were influenced by cultures of both Aryan and Semitic origin.

The symbolic value of the partly-religious, partly-mythological story of Abraham and his tribe is widely acknowledged. The fact that the Prophet Abraham is considered to be the founding father of the three monotheistic religions and that he has not left a single religion unaffected attests to its importance. One might expect that many tribes and cities, along with Hammurabi, resisted the Babylonian Nimrods, who at the time reached a period of their utmost authoritarianism. Tribes and even villages and cities still under strong influence of the communal life will resist and rebel against the imposition of empires in the name of whatever god. Societies that have not yet known any form of slavery are enslaved only with great difficulty. They may even prefer total annihilation to enslavement. There are many such examples in history.

The Abrahamic religion and narratives represent this anti-Nimrod resistance culture. This resistance culture can initially be discerned against the background of the Babylonian Empire at around 1,700 BCE. The second source—and branch—is the narratives around the Prophet Moses and his opposition to the Egyptian Pharaohs at the end of the thirteenth century BCE. They tell the resistance story of communities that were partly enslaved but, in the tradition of the Prophet Abraham, rejected the culture represented by the Egyptian Pharaoh. The sum of these narratives constitutes the Biblical tradition. In the long run, and increasingly, it constituted itself as a new culture against the Nimrods and Pharaohs, the strong rulers of the time who represented themselves as the god-kings. After the Prophet Moses, this tradition was represented by even more powerful priests (including those in the tradition of the High Priest which began with Aaron the brother of Moses, followed by Samuel, Isaiah and others). Later, roughly during the years 1,020 to 900 BCE, the Hebrew tribes built a strong kingdom in what is today's Israel and Palestinian territories under the leadership of the Prophets David and Solomon. In the absence of a careful interpretation of the movement and influence of the Hebrew tribe throughout history we shall not be able to understand and analyze civilizational history and the various forms of resistance and rebellion—the ideological, mythological, philosophic, religious, political, physical, economic, tribal, and national movements—against it.

In 1,596 BCE, the first Babylonian period was ended by the Kassites, a people of Hittite and Hurrian origin. The interesting and important thing here is the alliance formed between the Kassites and the Hittites. This is seldom studied by historians. However, it is important to do so if we want to understand the history of the peoples of the region. Not only could it not have been that easy to defeat such a strong cultural, political, and military tradition as that of the Babylonians; it would also have required a very strong counter-culture. Resistance in the Abrahamic tradition entailed *hijra*— that is, they escaped; it only turned into political power where there was a power-vacuum. The tradition formed in the Taurus-Zagros region, around about the time of Uruk and Ur, is of vital importance. The last example of these, the Zagros tribal federations, was represented by Gudea who brought down the Akkadian Empire at around 2,150 BCE. (Interestingly, the name Gudea, a priest-king of the independent state Lagash during the Guti reign, is the same as that of the word for the main god of the Aryans; it seems that he entered a kind of counter-civilizational process.)

Although historiography never mentions such a tradition, a thorough analysis of the tradition (that is, of the tribal federation) formed at the Zagros-Taurus area is crucial. It was the people from this area who were the creators of a more settled agricultural culture and the construction of a tight village network. They were on the brink of urbanization, could even have achieved it (the huge temple hills of Göbeklitepe near Urfa certainly suggest this). Those that created a culture such as this about 10,000 BCE could surely have created an urban culture more advanced than that of Uruk and Ur. A society with such a sophisticated architecture and mythology could have created a society surpassing that of Ubaid's cultural colonies and the political and trade colonies of Uruk and Ur.

It is also highly probable that a wide variety of tribal communities resisted colonization and constructed a federation against the common danger, after which they formed a more permanent political unity. These communities (whom the Sumerians in 3,000 BCE called Hurrians) constructed two strong political unities at about 1,650 BCE. One, the Hittites, had two centers, namely Kanish and Hatushas. The second unity, the Mitanni, was centered at Washukkani (or Xweshkani: "good and pretty fountains") located at modern Ceylanpinar and Serekani that fall within the borders of Turkey and Syria respectively. As indicated by many ancient documents, the Mitanni had expanded from Kirkuk (in the Zagros) to the Nur Mountains. After those of Egypt and the Hittites, theirs was the third biggest political and cultural power of the time. They shared a common culture and language with the Hittites. The two communities had strong blood ties and political marriages were common. The Hittite emperor Suppululiuma, who ruled from 1,344 to 1,322 BCE, is rumored to have told a Mitanni prince "I gave you the hand of my daughter; come now so that we can rule the region together." Many Egyptian hieroglyphs attest to Mitanni power, as do the many Mitanni brides in the palaces of Egypt (amongst them the famous Nefertiti).

Puduhepa, the famous Hittite queen with Hurrian roots, was the last representative of the woman's trail on the culture of the region. The Gutis and Kassites, as well as the Mittani as the new political formation, reflected the subdivisions of the Hurrians.[12] The word *Hurrian* is derived from the Sumerian word for "highlanders." The kings and princes of the Hittite state apparently all had Hurrian names and married Hurrian princesses. Personally, I think that while the Mitanni were a political unity or a confederation-like formation formed at the southern skirts of Fertile Crescent, another branch of the Hurrian community organized themselves as the Hittites in the north all the way to the Black Sea mountains and the northern Taurus region, representing themselves as a strong state or even a primitive empire. The cultural background, their kinship, diplomatic relations, and more importantly the Hittite-Kassite alliance may be seen as the affirming elements. It could be said that this cultural resistance in the north and the political unity it has thus developed heralded the end of the first Babylonian period. Babylonia in its second period (1,600-1,300 BCE) continued to exist either under the hegemony of this political unity or under some settlement where they ruled together. It was the most magnificent cultural and trade center of its time, much like today's Paris.

The Babylonian culture has profoundly influenced the three Sacred Books. It has left its mark in many areas. It can also be defined as a trade depot, regional market, and university city. One can easily describe it as the international (or rather, the inter-peoples and inter-denominations) center of the then civilization. All of the political, commercial, and intelligence games developed in Babylonia. One should not neglect its role as the center of conspiracies. Its depiction in the Sacred Book is striking. In short, it duly played its role as a civilizational center. From this perspective, it is much like today's London.

The third Babylonian period (610-330 BCE) began as an alliance established with the Medes when Nineveh was wiped off the map around 612 BCE and ended with the invasion of the region by Alexander around 330 BCE. It was the last big empire of Mesopotamia and it gradually lost its role as the civilizational center. It is as though it suffered from fatigue after 15,000 years of being the leading power in the development of the culture of humanity in the valleys of the Tigris and Euphrates Rivers and spreading this culture to all continents. And as if, with much hope, it is preparing for a new period today.

The Assyrian era can also be divided into three periods. This was the strongest political, military, and trade power in ancient history. It was the main link between the Sumerian and the Greco-Roman civilization. It is remembered for tyranny, bloodshed, and creative trading and its destruction was celebrated as a holiday by all the peoples of the Middle East (including its own people) because it marked the end of Nimrod- and Pharaoh-like despotism.

Its first period (2,000-1,600 BCE) embodied the emergence of the trade aristocracy and, strikingly, the merchant and the political power were frequently represented by the monopoly of same person. It could be said that the political and trade power monopolies were first constructed by the Assyrian communities. They rested on the trade accumulation of Ubaid, Uruk, Ur, and Babylonia and developed trade in all civilizational areas and with neighboring Neolithic villages and nomadic communities. Establishing trade colonies in important centers, they were the first ones to work as independent capitulationists and had widespread networks of trade routes. It can easily be surmised that they used violence ruthlessly in order to secure all these strategic relations. Nineveh, much like Amsterdam, was smothered with riches, silver and gold. Just as Amsterdam was rivaled with Paris, Nineveh was rivaled only with Babylonia. Both had expended much effort to influence and dominate the other. Hence the economic, commercial, political, and military clashes were plentiful, yet neither ruled the other.

The second period was during the rule of the Mitanni-Babylonian alliance (1,600-1,300 BCE) when the role of trade remained preeminent. It was during the third period (1,300-600 BCE) that their military and political power was really built up and they became the most terrifying power of the time. They invaded everywhere, including Egypt, with the notable exception of Urartu. This was possibly the bloodiest manifestation of civilization as can be seen, for example, in the devastation of the Kingdom of Jerusalem. It was a global power similar to that of today's USA. The egoism inherent in all empires was most developed in the Assyrian Empire. They repudiated the culture of living together, compromise, and peace. Their role in the creation of the tradition of empire cannot be underestimated.

The decisive role in their destruction lies with the people of Hurrian origin. It is known that for a long time the Mitanni cracked down on the Assyrians (1,600-1,300 BCE). Although they brought down the Mitanni, they could not end the resistance of the people of Hurrian origin. The tribal communities known as the Nairi (Assyrian for "people of the water") resisted Assyrian rule for a long time (1,200-900 BCE), much like the present day tribal confederacies in the Kurdish area previously known as Botan. Later, the political union Urartu came to the fore and they resisted Asur from 870 BCE until this union was destroyed in 610 BCE. This 300-year-old resistance became a very strong political formation with the present-day city of Van as its center, and left its mark on history. It is highly probable that there was a mixed political superstructure and that initially the Assyrian language would have been dominant. It is thought that a language with elements of Hurrian, Armenian, and Caucasian languages might have been used, a language structure which would have reflected the mosaic of the resistance. Most probably through a strong political formation and by acting in unison against the common danger they preserved their existence. The Scythians of Caucasian roots are also quite active at the time. The Urartu were the masters of iron and bronze, developing both weaponry and cooking utensils. Their superiority in castle construction and architecture signifies their importance even better. The Urartu state, although not the one that finally defeated the Assyrians, certainly had done most of the damage. It left a mark that cannot be easily erased from civilizational history. The alliance between the Median Confederation and the Babylonian city-state (a result of a long-term diplomacy by Babylonia and efforts of the Median Magi priests) in 612 BCE finally defeated the Assyrians. This heralded the start of the Median Period and the third Babylonian Period.

The most important observation to be made from the Assyrian civilization is the strong interdependence of trade monopoly and political monopoly, and the reliance of these monopolies on war. It is one of the most important stages of political and trade monopoly in civilizational history. We can conclude that the initial central link between the Egyptian, Chinese, and Indian civilizations was established by the Assyrian trade monopolies well before the Persian Empire had established any such link. They had created a commercial world, a sort of globalization in its own time.

Once again it becomes clear that commercial monopoly is not economy. There is rather an external imposition of a regime of terror on the economy in order to seize what has been created and accumulated by the peoples and tribes. It is also clear that without a state there can be no commercial monopoly. The previous political monopolies were all a type of slavery-based agriculture but now, for the first time, trade had reached the level of agriculture. If we equate commercial monopoly with capitalism, then it will follow that commercial monopoly is a more effective exploitative power than the political monopoly that seizes the surplus product of agriculture. Trade, rather than agriculture, leads to and stimulates empire as a form of administration or government. A simple example is that of road safety; this is a requirement for long-haul trade and it can only be secured by an empire. There can be no doubt that its focus on violence led to the development of, and became inextricably linked to, the resistance of society to the new economic impositions.

Agriculture, the market, small-trade, craftsmanship and numerous independent private sectors are clearly contributing to economy. In all of these areas human labor has proven its value in advancing productivity. It is therefore not so difficult to see that there is absolutely no need for political, military, or commercial economic monopoly. If the Assyrians had not existed would economy have come to a complete halt? On the contrary, it is most probable that a peaceful environment would have led to a different and positive economic life. The state, as an anti-democracy administration, is not only *not* necessary, it is also a power that destroys society and economy through its bureaucracy, its wars, and its plunder. I am not talking about the importance of the city and of stratification or, for that matter, their necessity. However, I question the relationship between the despotic power (which has disguised itself under divine and ideological covers and has built a firm military and political wall around itself) and civilization. Even if there were some positive aspects to urbanization, I would like to repeat myself by showing how civilization has become so negative through the most backward and conservative barriers. Administrative coordination and usurpation by monopolists are not the same.

I want to emphasize that the interdependency of political, commercial, and economical monopolies is not unique to capitalism, but that it has existed since the beginning of civilization and the onset of urbanization and dynasties. These three monopolies, like a tenacious chain, together with the positive aspects of the civilization, have crushed and encapsulated democratic efficacy and are continuing to do so into the present day.

Let us now continue to examine the links in this chain.

The Egyptian, Indian, Chinese, and Phoenician Civilizations

Discussing the contributions made by the Egyptian, Indian, and Chinese civilizations to the main stream of civilization will require a vast amount of study which is not possible under present circumstances. But for the moment it may be sufficient to question why they concentrated predominantly on agriculture and apparently did not show the will or strength to go beyond their own regions despite the advances made in these civilizations. I believe the reason they survived for such a long time is that they did not establish a long-haul trade monopoly. There does not seem to be much evidence of these three civilizations engaging in external trade on any significant scale. Domestically, too, the internal structure of agriculture and trade did not allow much opportunity for monopolies. Political monopoly can only last if it is far removed from economic monopoly, and there are fewer objections to political and military power when it prevents external dangers and internal chaos. Hence, its life is prolonged. In the final analysis, though, they too are economic monopoly rentiers although they are not totally submersed in the economic monopolies.

Egypt contributed to European culture and civilization to the extent that it could influence the Greco-Roman culture. As far as its influence on the rest of Africa is concerned, it is as if its culture never existed. Egypt did not make any attempt at trade and isolated itself from the Middle East as well. It may be the early example of state socialism. None of the similar examples are as impressive as that of Egypt. Egypt totally, and India and China partially, joined the medieval civilization via the Middle East. Islam, on the other hand, played a major role in funneling all these elements into its own reservoir and presenting them to Europe.

There is no need to discuss the Hittites separately, as they spread the civilization to Anatolia as an ally of the Hurrians and Mitanni. Their influence on the Aegean shores meant that their contribution to the new civilizational development in the Greek Peninsula was as significant as that of the Egyptians and Phoenicians. They stopped the expansion of the Egyptians in Syria and they had a hand in stopping the Assyrian and the preceding Babylonian expansion.

The Phoenicians of the Eastern Mediterranean established the long-haul trade that the Egyptians could not; the success of establishing the first trade colonies all over the Mediterranean belong to them. They were also the first to bring the Egyptian and Middle Eastern cultures to Europe. An alphabet and the art of shipbuilding are important to civilization—the Phoenicians taught the Greeks the alphabet. They were the ones that constructed the first ports. Moreover, their role in transferring the immaterial culture is of great importance. Their contribution to the history of civilization is as influential as that of Urartu.

The influence of the Kingdom of Israel was more of an immaterial character. More importantly, the Abrahamic tradition generated the monotheistic religions. It is as though they had a historical reason to bring about an immaterial state, as opposed to the material states of Sumer and Egypt. But one should not evaluate the Hebrew tradition from a narrow

Judaic perspective. Whereas the prophets, writers, and intellectuals emerged on the immaterial branch of this tradition, the merchants rather emerged on the material branch. Their influence on both branches has profoundly affected world civilizational history. In order to understand civilization as a whole we need to thoroughly analyze all aspects of the Sumerian, Egyptian, and Hebrew traditions. Thus, to describe Europe only in terms of the medieval period and, partially, the ancient Greco-Roman culture is not satisfactory; moreover, it is insufficient and incorrect. Later, I shall describe the terrible results of such insufficient study.

The Median-Persian Era
700-330 BCE

The influence of the Medes on civilization has not yet been explored. Some of the best known facts about them are that they had Hurrian roots and lived in Zagros, that they were related to the Persians, and constituted a branch of the Aryan tribes. The intense suppression that they endured at the hands of the Assyrians caused them to be known for their resistance. Their priests, called the Magi, educated and organized the people and are believed to have played an important role in management. We know that the Medes formed a confederative union around 700 BCE and lived in the region called Media where today's Iran, Iraq, and Turkey border each other. At times, they were friendly and at other times in conflict with the Scythians who came down from the Caucasus. When they defeated the Assyrians around 612 BCE they not only became famous but more opportunities opened up for them. It is also known that they defeated the Phrygians at the banks of the Kizilirmak (Halys) River. In the meantime, a competent sage called Zoroaster (Zarathustra) emerged from amongst the Magi priests and a spirituality with high moral content developed around him. Zoroastrianism is neither purely a religion nor purely a philosophy. Although this spirituality is different from the Hebrew tradition, they mutually influenced each other to a great extent. The influence of Zoroastrianism was especially felt during the time when the Babylonian Emperor Nebuchadnezzar captured the Israelites around 595 BCE. In Greek civilization, the Medes were viewed as more important than and superior to the Persians, and they are the most mentioned people in *The*

Histories by Herodotus. The Persian Achaemenids were able to take over the Median political formation due to a betrayal from within. Cyrus, the founder of the Achaemenid Empire, was raised in the Median palaces. The Persians and Medians jointly founded this empire; thus, calling it just "the First Persian Empire" is not accurate.

For about 300 years the Persian-Median Empire (extending from Egypt to the inner parts of India, from the Chinese borders to the Greek Peninsula) achieved the broadest political unity of its time. It was divided into twenty-two provinces, forming a sort of semi-state. The Persian-Median Empire contributed to the civilization in the areas of bureaucracy, the creation of good roads, the postal system, and the biggest and most magnificent armies of that time. They also attached importance to the moral tradition.

Although Greek civilization derived many of its cultural elements from the Medians and Persians, it was in this era that the separation between East and West became more evident. Still, there was an extensive interaction between them with many Greeks working at Persian palaces, and thousands more becoming soldiers of fortune in the Persian armies. The Persians accumulated vast wealth and kept the Aegean region under their domination for two hundred years. This later led to an almost passionate opposition against the Persians. To break free from Persian suppression and to obtain the wealth they possessed became almost a national objective. It is not coincidental that Alexander could emerge as the new Hercules. He had been influenced by the *zeitgeist*. It is instructive to remember that he was a student of Aristotle, and Greek philosophy itself was influenced by problems associated with opposing such suppression. Still, the influence mythology had on him was far greater. It served to form a sort of resistance culture. The Greek's resistance against the Persians are similar to that of Medes against the Assyrians. Although Alexander was Macedonian he was a child of Greek culture. Indeed, it was the synthesis between hundreds of years of resistance culture—especially philosophical enlightenment—and a free Macedonian tribal spirit that led Alexander to shatter the Persian Empire.

The Greco-Roman Culture and Civilization

The Greco-Roman culture and civilization is wrongly interpreted as the start of Western culture. This culture and civilization did not emerge in the West, or Europe, for it to be called "Western" culture or civilization. All the major cultural milestones, including the Christian medieval period, have their origin in the Middle Eastern cultures and civilizations, that is, in Mesopotamia and Egypt. These had been transferred to Europe by the fifteenth century, albeit with some delay. We are trying to establish how a daisy-chain of a culture originating from a *specific location* and formed within the scope of Braudel's *longue durée* of fifteen thousand years has been funneled into Europe. Although the Greco-Roman civilizational link was formed within the European geography, it has taken everything from this Middle Eastern inheritance.

In terms of material and immaterial culture, no important originality or "discontinuity" emerged after the sixteenth century. Even the philosophical leap forward, which can be seen as a novelty, is unthinkable without the culture taken over from the Babylonians, Egyptians, Hittites, Urartus, Medes, and Persians. Even Plato himself admitted that the Greek sages, like Solon, Pythagoras, and Thales, have for many years traveled around Babylonia and the other Eastern centers of wisdom to find their own philosophical views. The Greek and Roman mythologies are, in essence, the fourth or the fifth version of the Sumerian (and partially that of the Egyptian) mythologies with new names. We can thus say that the Greek and Roman mythologies are the result of the sum of the Sumerian, Babylonian, Hurrian, Hittite, and Mitanni mythologies. In fact, the material culture of the Neolithic had reached Europe's most important centers of settlement by 4,000 BCE. Sumerian and Egyptian culture reached it around 2,000 to 1,000 BCE. The synthesis that had begun around the end of 2,000 BCE in the Greek Peninsula only came to fruition around antiquity (ca. 1,000 BCE) after it had a first trial between 1,600 and 1,200 BCE. Homer and Hesiod were early products of this period. The fermentation that began in the Italian Peninsula with the Etruscans at about 1,000 BCE resulted in a kingdom around 700 BCE and in a republic at about 500 BCE.

The Greco-Roman period (500 BCE to 500 AD) contributed important authentic aspects. It established a chain of cities second only to Uruk. Greco-Roman urbanization was undoubtedly characterized by sophisticated aesthetic appreciation. Features of Greco-Roman civilization, such as class division and elements of governmental administration, existed thousands of years prior. They had not, however, developed nearly to the extent they eventually did in Greco-Roman civilization. Similarly, although material and immaterial cultural elements like trade, market, money, alphabet, science, philosophy, morals, and mythology had existed for thousands of years before, they were all exceptionally refined during the Greco-Roman civilization and constituted a very important second version. So, to say that Europe's material and immaterial culture could have emerged from these two Peninsulas in the absence of the mentioned inheritance is not really meaningful. For a very long time Western history's understanding of the issue of its roots had been inadequate and incorrect. More correct interpretations have developed in post-modern times.

What is unique to Greco-Roman culture is that the state regimes of kingdom, republic, democracy, and empire developed in sequence and within each other. Initially, democracy and kingdom were intertwined: in the later Greco-Roman period republic and empire were intertwined. But finally, just before the collapse of the Roman Empire, empire as a form of regime became very important. In a way, it represented the last and most comprehensive culture and civilizational system of the slave-owning society. This is a crucial characteristic and as a result it will either collapse or transform. As it turned out, the Roman Empire could only transform after its collapse. The Greco-Roman civilization, after experiencing one of the long-term phases of history, went through its most mature period and then plunged into a deep crisis.

To understand this, we need to understand that agriculture in rural regions and craftsmanship in the urban centers both result in an important amount of surplus product. This abundance of surplus product lays the foundation for state-like organizations. Surplus product is essentially related to laborers that will work for sufficient food and will attain skills. The primary form of labor used is slave-like labor. This type of labor makes possible state monopoly: a monopoly consisting of the trilogy of ideology, politics, and the military. This system develops in tandem with urbanization and improves the division of labor in conjunction with craftsmanship; hence, securing the formation of commodification, market, and money chain. Trade monopoly comes into play and gains the opportunity to seize some surplus product. In essence, two monopolies come about within the state or between states: competing against one another, they gradually come into conflict with each other over the surplus product that has resulted from agriculture and craftsmanship. While there is no sharp division between them, the concepts of state monopoly and trade monopoly are critical for analyzing various political and military relations and conflicts.

We can define *civilization* as a social system that is made up of material and immaterial cultural wholes. The nucleus of these is in turn shaped by the ideological, political, and military apparatuses that position themselves around the city and the forces that can loosely be called the agricultural and commercial monopolist cliques. Because the dominant form of the exploited labor is controlled in a slave-like fashion, one could readily call such systems "slave-owning civilizations." We can distinguish between two different forms in the rivalry and conflict experienced throughout civilization: first, within civilization itself (and generally between monopolies, and especially amongst the agricultural and commercial monopolies), and second, all the social forces that are in conflict with the civilizational forces (the oppressed class, tribe, people and artisan). The nature of war is nourished by these two forms. The reason why material culture and immaterial culture have to be continuously developed under circumstances of intense rivalry and conflict is in order to win. Thus, formations (which we can call "chain reaction") in the history of civilization will commence.

We can view the era up to the Greco-Roman period as a period of crisis, the result of the chain reaction which we have summarized. The crisis was always sustained due to the collapse or weakening of agriculture and trade in some areas, for various reasons. The main reasons for such crises could be climate, excessive production, internal and external conflict, internal and external migration, efficient production methods, more advanced systems (philosophies), and organizations in the ideological, political, and military areas. Members of monopolist cliques that do not wish to go under, but desire to increase their share, use conflict and war as if these were tools of production. This is because they are monopolies that have established themselves over the economy. In particular, states and civilizations that are primarily commerce based will evoke war more often due to the frequent crises in trade. In contrast, states and civilizations that are dominated by agricultural monopolies with a suitable climate and regular irrigation are more stable and more likely to be peaceful. Thus, such conditions prevent frequent occurrences of crises. In general, civilizations with Mesopotamian roots are more expansionist and are constantly fighting. At the heart of this lies the extreme dependency on trade. Ubaid, Uruk, Ur, Babylonian, Assyrian, and Persian civilizations continuously lived in an atmosphere of colonization, expansion, and war. This is closely related to the indispensable role of trade in the production processes.

The Greco-Roman civilization continuously embarked on expeditions and waged war, both at sea and on land, during the Athenian and Roman period. This must be seen in relation to trade being the *sine qua non* of the Mediterranean world. Mesopotamia had been the cradle of agriculture and trade since the formation of civilization. For similar reasons, since 600 BCE, the Persians from the East and the Greek and Romans from the West started "thousand years' wars," both against their own main regions of production and trade, as well as against Mesopotamia, due to their dependency on Mesopotamian trade and agriculture.

Without trade, but in particular without Mesopotamian trade, there would be no civilization. Either one or both would fall, or they would find an equilibrium. The winners have indeed been losers. Periods in which an equilibrium was reached while there were no winners have occurred for long periods of time. For example, Ubaid and Uruk were both in conflict and in equilibrium with one another. And both of them were previously in conflict and in equilibrium with the society in Upper Mesopotamia. There was terrible conflict between the Ur and the Akkad dynasties, yet they also achieved an equilibrium between them. They were both later obliterated from history. Akkadians and Guteans went through periods where they fought, eliminated, and balanced each other. The Babylonians and Assyrians also balanced and fought with one another. Over all, there frequently were terrible wars and periods of equilibrium amongst the Hurrians (including the Hittites, Mitanni, Kassites, Medes, and Urartuans), Babylonians, and Assyrians. Amongst the Egyptians and Hittites, too, war and equilibrium was attained. Finally, though, the "thousand year" Greco-Roman and Persian-Sassanid wars (550 BCE — 650 CE) occurred. This is the way civilizations make war and peace within themselves (involving internal cliques) and against one another.

On the other hand, the resistance and rebellions of peoples, tribes, slaves, and cities, including craftsmen—who forcefully wished to be bound to the civilization or, indeed, to be subjected to slavery and trade extortion—constituted the other main category. Civilization is a bloody, torturous, exploitative, and enslaving system based not only on the surplus-value of capitalism but also on the five or six thousand year old surplus product.

Islam and Christianity

Islam and Christianity are no doubt both civilizations. The differences and similarities between them are both interesting and important. Although much has been said about their position and influence within civilizational history, interpretations with a scientific base are rare. This is mainly due to the nature of the human character that was formed under their influence. Thus, to step outside of Islam and Christianity in order to develop a different paradigm may be a task successfully completed in the future. Secular and positivist interpretations are themselves religions, similar to that of the coarsest idolatry, and are devoid of any content that could be helpful in the analysis and overcoming of religion in general, and Judaism, Christianity, and Islam in particular.

The Reformation and Enlightenment represent the modification of Christianity to suit the requirements of capitalism. Thus, it can be said that the Renaissance did not enter into a conflict with Christianity. The anti-religious and anti-Christian character of the Enlightenment did not only deprive it from the quality necessary to surpass religion and Christianity, but also was far removed from offering a consistent critique and interpretation.

Islam, on the other hand, was never criticized by its followers. Instead, from early on it entered denominational conflicts as a result of which it became rigid. It has not been subjected to philosophical interpretation like Christianity. It has not gone through its own Renaissance, Reformation, or Enlightenment at all. The "neo-Islam" currents, which are merely reactionary and provocative movements, mean nothing other than nationalist and fascist rule under capitalist conditions.

Islam and Christianity may be interpreted as the second phase of civilizational history. The crisis that the Roman Empire entered into in the fourth and fifth century CE was in general a civilizational crisis. During these centuries, the general dissolution of the nearly 4,000 year old slave-owning civilization accelerated. Historians describe these two centuries as "dark." Humanity, living under the yoke of civilized society, was in need of a profound liberation and the concomitant intellectual and material (structural) tools. There was a quest for purpose and the tools to realize this purpose all around. The existing mood was as if everyone and everything was about to awaken from a nightmare. There *would* be a dawn, but that dawning day would be uncertain. The old beliefs and their icons were no longer worthy of anything; even the Roman emperors no longer visited the shrine of Jupiter. The emergence of Christianity, Manichaeism, and Islam were in accordance with the spirit of the time—a time during which the intensity of thought and the search for faith was profoundly felt.

A more important question is this: Although both Christianity and Islam were certainly political movements, why did they insist on presenting themselves as "divine" and "theological" movements or, in short, as religions? The answer to this important question is to be sought in the liberationist, intellectual pursuits, as well as the atmosphere of the time. Thought, discussion, understanding of program, and organization must follow the previously shaped examples.

The tradition that played the most important role in this was the Abrahamic tradition of prophets. The prophets were the first to bring news of liberation; only a prophet would be followed, no one else—even if they laid claim to being "liberators." Since this tradition was very deep-rooted, no other option would have had much of a chance. Indeed, Manichaeism attempted to proffer a different tradition, but although its contents were more enlightening, it did not really succeed because of this old tradition. Even to date, the Middle Eastern movements presenting themselves under the garb of religion are linked to this historical tradition.

Therefore, when one attempts to interpret Islam and Christianity, one should understand that they are outright political movements clothed in religion. As I briefly mentioned before, there certainly is an ideological part to these traditions as well. The Abrahamic religious tradition, with roots that can be traced back to the mythological-religious icons of the Sumerian and Egyptian priests' temples, is mainly theological. It is concerned with the concept of god and its rituals. They made a big effort to develop a different interpretation to that of the Egyptian and Sumerian gods and rituals. There have always been contributions of interpretation attributed to very famous prophets. Moses, Samuel, David, Solomon, Hezekiah, Isaiah, and many others can be considered prophets that made such contributions, and that had the grand liberationist mission to dispose of the contemporary despotic regimes.

The reason why all traces of Manichaeism have been lost must be due to the lack of any strong tradition preceding or succeeding it. And even though the Abrahamic tradition had been around for 1,500 years, it only had a partial success, that is, until the period of Jesus Christ. It could not defeat any of the civilizations that had Egyptian and Mesopotamian roots. The tiny Kingdom of Jerusalem it established was not very influential or long-lived. Its most important success was to continuously be the hope of the oppressed and those seeking liberation. It had thus become the conscience and center of attraction for all those who had suffered at the hands of the Nimrods and Pharaohs—of all despotic rulers—for the poor and for those with ideals.

If the phenomenon of Jesus Christ were seen in this light it would be better understood. When, following the Roman conquest of Judea, the collaborationist priests sided with the Roman rulers, the atmosphere was once again conducive to new prophets. Moreover, the Roman slave-owning system dissolved the Middle Eastern community structures, and many "unemployed slaves," proletarians, were generated as a result. Many cults and prophets came to the fore, and Jesus Christ was probably only one of a number that were crucified or condemned to similar deaths. Christ (as liberationist) became the symbolic name for the general movement of the poor. One may see this as a primitive socialist movement. Initially, it was definitely the movement of the poor and the escaped slaves. Jesus' last action was his march to conquer Jerusalem: he was after a new kingdom—a kingdom of the poor—a Spartacus that did not wage war. But the movement changed after the time of the twelve apostles and, especially, immediately after the initial outlines of the Bible (which one can call the ideological material) were compiled and separate groups were formed. Then it became the movement of the masses.

Saint Paul and some other apostles were very active and they monitored the Roman and Sassanid Empires. Three important groups joined the movement en masse: Greeks from central and western Anatolia, Assyrians from the East and the regions of the Sassanid Empire, and Armenians from northeastern Anatolia. Many Jewish intellectuals, and in particular Saint Paul, were quite active at the time. They rocked the social foundations of the Roman and Sassanid Empires, generating quite a strong political movement. The acceptance of Christianity as an official religion was followed by Byzantium's (Constantinople's) separation from Rome and the formation of the Eastern Roman Empire. This is where the contradiction lies: the doctrine that had emerged in opposition to Rome became the official religion and ideology of the larger part of the Empire. While it sped up the split in the Empire, this transformation also prolonged its life-span.

The history of Eastern and Western Roman Empire is well-known. It seems obvious that at the time there would have been much discussion and divergence between leading Christian rulers. As a result, many denominations emerged. Although the argumentation appeared to have been theological (Monophysites vs. Dyophysites), in reality its essence was purely political. While some denominations went underground again, the majority became the most powerful political and economic partners of the two Romes; politics and economy pouring out from under their ideological masks. Christianity ceased to be a religion and was transformed into a civilization. It was this theological and political act, as summarized above, that allowed Europe for the first time in its history to make the complete transition to civilization under the guise of religion.

Christianity successfully completed its first historical mission by moving to northern and northwestern Europe in the tenth century. Later, especially during the spread of capitalism, its expansion became global. The Christians of Anatolia and Mesopotamia (the Greeks, Armenians, and Assyrians) also embarked upon the transition to civilization, initially with the Byzantine Civilization and later around independent churches. This transition to civilization, however, retained a stronger moral aspect. Being "Christian peoples" strategically influenced the destiny of these people; in particular, being targeted by Islam would lead to tragic results.

The emergence of the Islamic civilization stems from a similar tradition. Mecca was essentially the intersection of the main trade routes between the Red Sea and the Golden Horn, Yemen, Ethiopia, and Damascus. The Arabic Quraysh tribe's hierarchical and aristocratic rule had been established early on. They were a tribe of merchants with a certain amount of commercial capital. At the time, along with Judaism, Zoroastrianism, and Christianity, there were many other belief systems around; for example, the Quraysh were pagan.

The Zamzam well, the initial place of worship in Mecca, is said to have been miraculously created when Ishmael, the son of the Prophet Abraham and Hagar (two breakaways from the main Hebrew tribe), migrated there. A hut, in which later some idols were placed, was constructed around the well. There were three important idols at the time of the Prophet Muhammad: Allāt, Manāt, and al-'Uzzá.

The Prophet Muhammad was born into the Banu Hashim clan, part of the Quraysh tribe. The countries claiming to be Islamic steer clear from sociologically studying Islam in general but they especially avoid studying the life of the Prophet Muhammad. It is as if they are scared of something. A true enlightenment cannot be developed if religion, as a social lifestyle and system of thought, cannot also be studied sociologically. If the Middle East cannot achieve such enlightenment, then it cannot but be the guinea pig of the US and its allies. Indeed, in order to better understand the Prophet Muhammad, we need to do sociological research. Society will not lose as a result of it. Europe had the Age of Enlightenment exactly because of such research into Christianity. If the Middle East is not able to realize its own enlightenment, then it cannot develop its own thought revolution. An analysis of the Prophet Muhammad could be the first step in this thought revolution. The period he lived in, his personality, and his actions are all subjects for such an analysis.

In return for a share, he organized expeditions to Damascus for the female merchant Khadijah's trade caravans. He had been influenced by Syriac priests, and no doubt his contact with the Jews and the importance of their trade would have been an additional influence; however, from the start he had many conflicts with them.

Muhammad's marriage to Khadijah brought about a new situation. Once again there were rumors about the "Final Prophet," with many—including women—laying claim to this title. I believe that the young Muhammad learned much from Khadijah. She clearly would have been a very competent individual, as it could not have been easy to be both wealthy and a female merchant at this time. I think it highly probable that she would have been the one who whispered to him that he was the prophet. What united the two of them was most definitely the quest for power in embryonic form. The Quraysh aristocracy was in no position to form a state because of its backward traditions (such as their use of idols). The Jews and Christians were ineffective and not approved of. Besides, there were also material conflicts between them.

The story of Hagar and Ishmael is an Arabic folktale and it gave Muhammad inspiration. He began to get to know and analyze the beliefs and cults of the time, and he came to understand that none of these beliefs and cults would succeed in establishing a political union amongst the Arabs. He set out to achieve this union with Khadijah's encouragement. He had all he needed in terms of ideological tradition, as the Arabic branch of Abrahamic tradition was available to him, and it was not difficult to learn whatever else was needed from the talented Syriac priests.

Muhammad's first revelation as a prophet came at around the year 610 CE, a period of the fiercest conflict between the Byzantine and Sassanid Empires. This conflict could be considered a great fortune to the Arabian Peninsula, but there were two obstacles in the way: the Quraysh and the Jewish colonies. From the very beginning, prophethood entailed political leadership—otherwise it would not have been successful. And, indeed, every message delivered by the Prophet Muhammad resembled those typical of statesmen. And so, it was a move forward for the new rising empire of the Middle East. Under the leadership of the Arabs, the Jewish ideology was renewed and modernized—transcending its narrowness and opening it to all peoples. The new way of worship symbolized a new lifestyle and, due to good strategy and tactics, it spread to all four corners of the world. One could call Islam the first comprehensive internationalist movement. In short, an exemplary civilizational political movement, together with its ideology, political program, leader, strategies, and tactics, would leave its mark and advance in history.

It is interesting that the word *islam* also means "peace."[13] The Prophet Muhammad most probably foresaw a period rather riddled with conflict, and in this way wished to show that he gave priority to peace. But to realize his goals he had to overcome a number of obstacles. The three main targets he had to tackle were the Byzantine, the Sassanid, and the Quraysh aristocracies. Confrontation with the latter in Mecca ended in the *Hijra* (the migration to Medina) at about 622 CE. It was during this time in Medina that he prepared the first social contract. This new contract was approved by the majority of the tribes, but not by the tribal and clan aristocracy. Indeed, the heaven he promised his followers was laying their hands on the possessions of the Byzantines and Sassanids, while the hell he warned of was the old way of life. When he drove back the first attacks of the Qurayshans (amongst others, during the Battle of Badr, Uhud, and Hendek) the outcome seemed more or less clear: it would be only a matter of time before the first Arabic republic (or democracy) was born. Discussions and meetings were plentiful—the mosques evoked assemblies. In fact, contrary to common belief, the first mosques were not places of worship but of meetings and discussion.[14]

The aristocracy and its leader Muawiyah, who briefly lost his throne, began to regain power through new maneuvers after the death of the Prophet Muhammad in about the year 632 CE. The murder of Prophet's son-in-law, Ali, a staunch believer and a person of principle, paved the way for Muawiyah and his family to regain their sultanate. The house of the Prophet lost all its political power when Husayn ibn Ali was tragically killed at Karbala and a new clique of Arab merchants laid claim not only to the peninsula but also to the looted Byzantine and Sassanid possessions. They initiated a large conquest movement which won many successive victories. The first to lose to them were the Jews and Christians of the Arabian Peninsula, but at around 650 CE all Sassanid territories and most of Byzantium and North Africa had been conquered. The new conquerors were knocking on the gates of Constantinople.

We may compare this rapid expansion to Alexander's swift conquests, achieved by combining the Macedonian tribal spirit with that of Greek philosophy, and the resulting material and immaterial culture. Similarly, the synthesis of the Arabian tribes' courage and the spirit of the new religion, that rested on a deep-rooted heritage, made possible these Alexander-like wars of conquest. This formed the second stage of the civilization, its most important branch. It achieved the last major cultural-civilizational advance of the East.

The most interesting point in the story of Islam is that the declaration thereof and its expansion occurred simultaneously: it was *born* as a power. In contrast, Christianity only came to power three hundred years after its advent. The oppressed, the poor, and those who really contributed to it, were rapidly excluded from power and instead the rebellious, fresh, and hungry spirit of the tribes started constructing the civilization through a mighty state, organized around the heavenly palaces and mosques. And thus, although it started as a small city merchant clan, an empire was constructed in no time (between the years 640 and 650 CE). A sociological analysis looking at its religious perspective together with its political significance and implications would be most instructive.

I personally think that this rapid establishment of political power can be explained by the long-term power vacuum in the Arabian hinterland, the social chaos created by tribal conflict, Prophet Muhammad's personality, and the fact that the character of the Byzantine and Sassanid Empires was that of the first stage of the civilization. Islam had not only conquered all the traditional civilizational areas of the Middle East but went all the way to parts of India, Central Asia, the heartland of Caucasus, the farthest regions of Southeast Asia (that is, Indonesia and Malaysia), and way beyond the two most important peninsulas of southwestern and southeastern Europe, the Balkans and Iberia.

A religious word like *Islam* cannot really explain such a large military and political movement. It only serves to disguise the reality. *Islam* is a symbolic name. The concepts *Allah* and *prophet* were developed by the Hebrews much earlier. The Medina Jews' criticism that "you are stealing our religion from us, and using it against us" must have angered Muhammad very much.

Sociologically, one can trace the roots for the glorification of the king and his deputies back all the way to the Sumerian and Egyptian mythology. However, Muhammad brought a different context to the concept of *Allah*.

It is like the energy of the universe, a more advanced concept. But Islamic scholars have not yet developed a sociological interpretation of this issue. The dictates of faith in Islam are more like theoretical principles, and different forms of worshiping exist to keep the connection with practice alive. Most of the directives were needed to meet the moral and legal requirements of the time. They stipulate productivity in trade and agriculture, and thus the canonical jurisprudence (*fiqh*) developed. Islam made a harsh intervention against the ideological lifestyle of the initial phase of the slave-owning civilization. An infidel was "the other" that had to be annihilated. Ideological pluralism as a right was only granted to those who adhered to the Abrahamic tradition.

Objectively, Islam is far more open to secularism than Christianity. But the radical struggle against the old lifestyle had many adverse outcomes as well. The historical cultures of peoples had either been annihilated or assimilated on the ground of their beliefs: Zoroastrianism, Manichaeism, and Christianity are examples of this. Clearly, the new life-style it brought resulted in feudal aristocracy: instead of a god-king there would now be the duality of God and his shadow, the Sultan. Eventually, despotic sultanates were inevitable. Islam as a religion did not have, and still does not have, the ability to prevent despotism. Christianity was even worse because of its susceptibility to monarchy, with priests becoming more advanced partners in power. Still, these two religions, as far as they constituted the state, in some ways kept the sections of society excluded from the civilization under better conditions than that of classical slavery. However, they took care to keep them at a level of servitude that was even worse than the slavery imposed on them before. Neither religion was totally opposed to slavery. Both had the characteristics to strongly protect the hierarchical and state power. Both also encouraged the development of nations.

In terms of time and location, these two religions (and we can include Judaism here) joined the main stream of civilization to constitute its second phase. They, however, could neither redress the problems experienced amongst the ruling monopolist cliques, nor the demands for freedom and justice of the democratic social forces that had been excluded by the civilization. On the contrary, this second phase has aggravated the problems of warfare, freedom, and justice, as I will outline below.

First: New monopolist powers were added to the already existing structures of monopolist power. Yet there had been no qualitative improvement in efficiency and yield of craftsmanship and agriculture. More parties were now fighting over the surplus-product. Emirs (princes) became as monopolist as the sultans (monarchs) and dynasties multiplied. Those who claimed a share increased. Just like the middle class, when they could not get as much as they wanted, they continuously started wars—and the wars waged by feudal lords in Europe and Russia were severe. The monarchs on the other hand increased the problems associated with income by enlarging the bureaucracy.

Second: There were also those who accepted these two new religions with liberation, freedom, and justice in mind. However, when their expectations were not met, they continuously resisted in various denominations.

Third: There was no development in terms of immaterial culture. While the old culture, which was described as "dark," was destroyed, no new culture was developed. Instead, there were endless discussions on theology and on different denominations. As a result, mankind no longer had a hold on the real world and its history. History had been reduced to religious stories. The will power of human beings was ignored and people were turned into shadows. Humans were captivated by the imagery of heaven and hell, and they began to not care about the world and living while the monopolist cliques built heavenly castles and palaces for themselves. Urban culture and philosophy fell behind the old ones.

Fourth: Even worse was the slogan "a single god in heaven and a single sultanate on earth." Their war to expand their rule around the world had made antiquity look innocent. The war in the name of god was more destructive than the war of the gods of the first phase; the expansion and colonization were much worse during this second phase. The wars of *ummah* became more systematic and persistent than ones in antiquity. Sectarian conflicts became really difficult to settle.

The situation in Europe at the onset of Capitalism

Neither Christianity nor Islam has found a solution to the final crisis that deepened with the fall of the Roman Empire at its slave-owning stage.

The system that they developed, the so-called "feudal order" or "Medieval Civilization," is no different to the solutions preached by the Sumerian and Egyptian priests. Thus, all that these ambiguous metaphysical recipes managed to achieve—both in terms of political program and in terms of praxis—was to plunge society into a "dark ages." Many of the cultural values that had still existed during antiquity vanished during this time. Rome's crisis only deepened under its heirs. The societies, on the other hand, were lined up as groups awaiting their turn for heaven and hell, figurines in rank that would march off to war in order for this end to be achieved. The living had almost been excluded from life itself. But what was the concrete situation?

The Greeks, Armenians, and Assyrians, the initial people to embrace Christianity, lost the majority of their historical and cultural domains of influence due to the Islamic conquests. Greece was bent on strengthening its own identity against Rome; the Syriac Armenians and Assyrians wished to do the same against both the Byzantines and the Sassanids. Instead, as a result of the Islamic conquests, they lost most of what they had and experienced the most tragic of situations. The Kurds and Persians were able only to ensure their own survival. The Turks and Arabs were greatly advantaged by these conflicts, which enabled them to expand their dominions. Russia, however, was one nation that benefited from these conflicts because of Christianity. The Turks, Tatars, Mongolians, and even the Chinese, suffered big losses in their conflicts with the Russians.

Christianity enabled the European tribes to consolidate their gains and stabilize their losses. National identities at first started to develop because of the shared belief but the ecclesiastical aristocracy, and later the feudal lords, caused the loss of a significant portion of the old cultural elements. The superior aspects of the Neolithic culture were overpowered and assimilation was imposed. Nonetheless, the historical reality is that the first aspects of nation and nationality had appeared and these would prove to be permanent.

The natives of Africa, America, and Australia could not preserve their main cultures when confronted by Christianity and partially by Islam: they have lost their identities. Indian cultures, too, have been on the losing side, and thus far China has not dared to expand in the face of these religions.

The medieval civilization—I call it the second phase of civilization—not only failed to solve the cultural crisis but exacerbated it. Consequently, the situation in Europe became strategically important: should Europe lose the battle for civilization, Europe would lose its cultural identity like other parts of the world; should Europe win, its strategic superiority would be certain. The "civilizational battle," of course, was the battle between the two strategic powers of the Middle Ages. It was the battle between Christianity and Islam *in* Europe and *over* Europe. The situation was far more complex than what is commonly thought.

At the onset of the fifteenth century, Christianity had completed its expansion into Europe and the period of sacred kingdoms and feudal lords began. The Holy Roman Empire of the Germans claimed that they were the ones to continue the legacy of Rome, but there were rivals who disagreed. The French Kingdom was one, so was the newly emerging power of the Austrian Habsburgs. The Russian Czardom, after the fall of Constantinople, had long since declared itself the true representative of Christianity and the "Third Rome." The Polish Kingdom, the latest culture to become Christianized, did not wish anyone to snatch the badge of sacredness from it and thus was at the forefront of the claimants. England and France were caught up in their Hundred Years' War and thus kept out of the struggle. The Iberian and Balkan Christians were waging their own defensive struggle against their Muslim conquerors. The Italian cities were not only leading the Renaissance; they were moving towards capitalism as well. Rome was deeply involved in the intense commercial rivalry amongst the Italian city-states, and so no one expected it to be able to come to the fore and secure unity amongst the cities, and thus becoming a role model for Europe. The Italian cities' only contribution was to prepare a strategic opportunity by leading Europe into urbanization and by spreading merchant capitalism throughout Europe. But, as we learned from the events of the sixteenth century, this opportunity turned out to be Europe's best chance to win the battle for the civilization. The Crusader wars did not deliver the expected outcomes and, as the fifteenth century started, the future of Europe was uncertain.

In the meantime, Muslim Arabs continued to pose a strategic threat to the Iberian Peninsula. (They had invaded France but were ousted.) The loss of Iberia could have meant that Christian Europe would be colonized and lost forever. After all, the Ottomans had advanced swiftly into Austria and Hungary by invading parts of the Balkans and had even reached Poland. Had they not been stopped, the political and cultural existence of Europe might have ended just like that of Rome. The Ottoman Turks and the Andalusian Arabs knew very well that if they did not win a conclusive war against Europe, they would be the ones suffering consecutive losses. On the other hand, the Golden Horde states (as the western part of the Mongol Empire) could attack Western Europe via the northern Black Sea at any time.

But some elements of a deeply rooted, pre-civilization culture did survive in Europe. The tradition of tribal democracy was still fresh in the cultural memory and people had not profoundly experienced the civilized slave-owning system. Their understanding of Christianity was quite superficial—their minds had not been totally conquered yet. This was especially true for Northern Europe where the bond with natural life was still very strong. Despite going through the fastest period of urbanization yet, democratic characteristics predominated because their cities did not really experience kingdoms and empires. They all had semi-democratic rule, and confederations were being established among them and they did not easily recognize other, unelected hegemonies. The kingdoms and fiefdoms were all newly established and did not possess the necessary skills or experience to represent Europe. (Such experience and skill that had existed was greatly depleted during the Crusades.)

On the other hand, with the oldest civilizational world behind it, Islamic civilization *was* experienced and well versed in issues relating to power. Not only were they not defeated during the initial Crusades, they still controlled the trade routes and they were still superior in trade. Thus, they were completely self-confident. Furthermore, because they represented the "final" religion and prophet, they were more dogmatic than the Europeans.

An analysis of all these facts will make it clear that the civilizational crisis in Europe was profound. The threat of Islam, and hence the Turkish and Arabic threats, grew by the day. Christianity's foothold in Eastern Europe was lost with the fall of Constantinople in 1453. In 1480 Mehmed II sent 20,000 troops to the southern Italian city of Otranto, from where he hoped to conquer Italy.[15] Islam posed a total nightmare to Europe—

not only because of the religious threat, but also because of the belligerent tribes it dragged along. Christianity was not a form of civilization capable of dealing with such a nightmare. It incurred a continuous string of losses. The only battle left was in Vienna; if Vienna fell, stopping Islam and the Turks would have been extremely difficult.

Hence, it is understandable that the Italian cities embraced merchant capitalism and delivered the Renaissance. Besides the commercial and cultural-intellectual innovations these movements engendered, it was a matter of survival. This is why the developments in the Italian Peninsula would determine Europe's fate.

The two powers promising to resolve the problems created by the darkness of a collapsing Rome and to bring liberation and enlightenment, in fact deepened the crisis because of internal problems and by seeking each other's destruction. Indeed, these powers led to renewed problems of liberation and enlightenment. Europe could either resolve the crisis—developed by these two powers and left in her arms—or, just like Rome, drown in it.

At this point, the predominant question is whether capitalism can become the solution to the problem at hand. Circumstances at the time of its birth may provide a chance for it to resolve the problems stemming from Islam and Christianity of the late Middle Ages (that is, the fourteenth and fifteenth centuries). The experiences of the Netherlands and England during the sixteenth century shed light on these chances for a solution. However, a closer look at these aspects will show that there also exists the danger of spreading the crisis worldwide—with the crisis of the third phase becoming more profound than the first two phases. The fact that capitalism itself can only exist as a military, political, and economic monopoly makes it the fundamental element of crisis in the history of civilization. It is both the result and producer of crisis. It can spread crisis over time and location but this cannot be a solution. The events that have taken place between the sixteenth and twenty-first centuries are enough proof of this.

The subjects of the next two main sections are the nation-state and industrialism. I will question these fundamental tools used, for the first time in history, by capitalism to resolve social questions before concluding with an assessment of capitalism as a regime and a civilization of crisis.

The Modern Leviathan

The Descent of God on Earth

Conceptualization of *capitalist modernity* cannot be done by economic consideration alone. Not only is it insufficient, but it is also a methodological diversion preventing us from comprehending its relationships and its essence. Therefore, it leads to fuzzy judgments and conclusions. As shown by my definition and analysis of capitalism in Sections 1 and 2, it can operate in the economic area only as an external imposer and a monopolist power. Therefore, it may be better to search for its essence elsewhere. This may also lead to far more accurate findings due to better method. We will continue searching for it there where it most often tries to hide and disguise itself: in the area of state.

Karl Marx searched for capitalism in the economic arena by using methodological, philosophical, historical, and sociological analyses. He concluded that capitalism, characterized by a system of intense crises with a favorable outcome, has a monopolist structure. It does not follow from capitalism's domination of economy, nor from it imposing a structure on economy, that capitalism is economic in nature. The diversification of money as a tool for accumulation of profits and capital by fluctuating market prices is not possible unless accompanied by political power. There is a need to analyze this political power and its characteristic of coercion together with the consequences thereof. Conceptualization of *capital* through abstract analysis of political economy will, whether knowingly or with good intentions, lead to methodological errors and fall victim to capitalist paradigms. I am aware of the dangers of proposing an easy and superficial thesis in the absence of a comprehensive analysis, and in criticizing Marx (and the dogmatic and positive approach of those calling themselves Marxists, who, unable to progress beyond being disciples, became tedious and repetitive and unable to further the discussion). However, a hundred and fifty years of theoretical and practical experience has affirmed many times over that *Das Kapital* serves as the new totem and that it has not really served the workers. This failure, I believe, is mainly due to its erroneous consideration of capitalism as economy and, hence, the futile search for its meaning in economic terms. I believe that making monopolist state policies the cornerstone of economy (despite all its non-economic features) blurs the mind and covers up the problems of capitalism. At the same time, this is an "enlightened" aberration with tragic consequences both politically and ideologically.

Although I am no expert on Hegel or Marx, I consider them to be important; hence, I must comment. Their influence on modern capitalist society was vast and therefore I associate the right to comment with notions of freedom and equality. When Marx and Engels named German philosophy as one of the sources of scientific socialism they must have referred to Hegel, whom they were immensely influenced by, as can be seen from their critique.

Ideologically, Hegel was the peak of metaphysics and the biggest contemporary representative of dialectics. He was a true German philosopher; by this I mean he was the prime mover of German nationalism. Marx and Engels were moving in the right direction as they studied the backwardness of German capitalism, the German bourgeoisie, and the status of the bourgeoisie within German philosophy. Initially, this attitude of theirs was reflected in their critique of Hegel's *Philosophy of Law*. Subsequently, the formation of the League of Communists and the work done on the *Communist Manifesto* consolidated their position in practical terms as well. I believe that because the 1848 Revolutions fell short of expectations they constituted a profound breaking point. The early indications of deviance into economism started here. I am not arguing that they should not have given such a big role to economy or that it is not necessary to study economy. Moreover, I am not criticizing *Das Kapital* for being wrong. My main point of criticism is exactly the point on which Marx and Engels criticized Hegel, and that is the priority given to the state and law by Hegel. In my opinion, Hegel started his analysis at the crucial point, where one should start. I believe it was Marx and Engels who made a historical mistake, namely falling into economic reductionism. This misconception is the fundamental reason why the one hundred and fifty years of socialist struggle for freedom and equality—that is, for a democratic society—did not fulfill the expectations. By saying that Hegel was right, I do not say that I embrace his theoretical and practical policies. I only say that he determined the correct point of departure. I emphasize this in order to remove any misunderstanding.

The problem is a general problem in Europe and relates to the problems associated with the assumption of power by a statist Europe. How would the modern Leviathan be formed? The solution, according to Hobbes and Grotius, lay in the absolute necessity of the state and its centralization. With this they created the doctrine of absolutism. They saw modern absolutism, as a state model, as the solution—the tool that would make possible the transition from the feudal to the capitalist era. However, such a tool could not really resolve the crisis. The state problem continued as strongly as before. The fact that capitalism was dominant in the Netherlands and England and that these countries developed hegemony over Europe, severely affected—devastated—France and Germany. France lost repeatedly in its struggle for hegemony. Germany, on the other hand, had not yet secured its "national unity." All other candidates in the European power struggle, still waiting for prosperity, were deeply troubled by problems of statism. Monarchism and absolutism could not fully overcome these problems. A well-known example illustrating this is France's Sun King: the absolutism of the magnificent Louis XIV was neither successful against the alliance of the Netherlands and England, nor could it resolve the growing internal problems of the state. What could the other European states have done? Their material and immaterial cultures, as well as their conflicting interests, did not allow them to adopt the state model of the Netherlands and England.

The French Revolution erupted as a result of these conditions and problems. Hence, now there was not only the state question but also the questions associated with the revolution. Lenin discussed these together in his 1917 book, *The State and Revolution*. The problems associated with power developed into a total crisis. The capitalistic hegemony which had developed in order to resolve the feudal crisis, far from resolving the crisis, made it more profound and universal. Absolutism collapsed, a republic was declared, and a terrible period of terror began. What followed was a mad emperor whose empire, like an ordeal descending from heaven, devastated the whole of Europe. The French overwhelmed Europe with much theory and many wars. What was the guillotine compared to this? (I am thankful for Hegel's insightful description of the state as *God descending to earth* and Napoleon as *God's march on earth*. This is an explanation that I benefited from and was most charmed with. Finding another statement which so perfectly explains both the new and the old state won't be easy. In one sentence, he manages to explain what all holy and many secular books attempt to explain. This is true philosophy. It is possible to say that the English practice economy well, the French sociology, and the German philosophy. But I have to emphasize that synthesizing them all may have disadvantages!)

In order to deal with the European absolutism that surrounded him, Napoleon (as far as I know the first to do so) drafted the state model that can be called the "nation-state" model.[1] He was urging France to become statist in its entirety and to bring Europe to its knees—a plea that succeeded. Napoleon was not in favor of a feudal civilization; indeed, he wished to eliminate it with a revolution. What he wanted was to emulate Alexander or the Roman Principate and Caesar. But the circumstances of this era, the material and immaterial culture in Europe, did not allow for the existence of such an emperor. England, on the other hand, with its more insidious and refined methods, carried out a masterful act of imposing its hegemony in line with its political economy, thus playing the central role in Napoleon's downfall. Napoleon was about to go mad.

Apparently, Napoleon did not learn his lesson from his exile on the island of Elba. After his escape, he vigorously continued his attempts to master Europe. Despite his brilliant war tactics he was defeated at Waterloo and had no hope of making a comeback. With his death on Saint Helena, the small island in the middle of Atlantic Ocean, his last words were about France, armies, and Josephine—words that perfectly characterized a nation-state activist. While the French and the British waged war in order to establish their hegemony, the Germans—specifically Hegel—created an appropriate doctrine. Magnificent ideological work was done—it was not called German ideology for nothing. In practice, the North German Confederation under leadership of the Kingdom of Prussia was gradually composed and on the rise. England supported Prussia (formally between 1756-1762) in order to halt the progress of the French and Austrian states (empires at the beginning stage). With the 1870 victory at Sedan over France and the establishment of German unification, Germany confronted England as the second hegemonic power. Germany was dissatisfied with the way the world was shared out amongst the colonial powers and demanded its own share. But with the conclusion of the First and Second World Wars it lost all of its hegemonic claims, having been defeated just like France.

It has been shown that from the French Revolution until 1945 capitalism continuously (not cyclically) experienced a profound crisis. The German Führer Adolf Hitler started the Second World War. There have been many analyses of fascism, but all the definitions—whether made by the Marxists, liberals, conservatives, or anarchists—have been misleading. None of them had the intention or the power to explain what really happened. The magnificent intellectuals of the Jews, the victims of the Holocaust, also contributed to this misunderstanding. This is because Hitler was the result of everyone's collective *intellectual dirt* and political praxis. But, of course, who is to acknowledge this?

I find two assessments by Adorno, the German philosopher with Jewish roots, very meaningful. The essence of the first one, his analysis of capitalist modernity, is: "Wrong life cannot be lived rightly." Secondly, in relation to the Holocaust camps, he says: "In the name of all that is divine and all that is holy, humanity's right to speech is over."[2] I may be wrong, but as I interpret these words to mean that there could be no explanation for genocide. The mask of our civilization has fallen off. It has no right to speak. The Frankfurt School of philosophy is on the trail of truth. But the realization of being involved in this crime and its psychological drawbacks affected and disillusioned these intellectuals deeply. It is important that Walter Benjamin and Theodor Adorno grasped and admitted the part played in this by Jewish ideology. The European Union, in its present form, is an attempt to cover up this *intellectual dirt*—I don't believe they have cleaned what is beneath. The depth of the crisis continues.

The third biggest globalization move (in the age of finance) is the practice of controlling the crisis by spreading it in depth over time and location. The official dissolution of the Soviet system in 1989 is also a proof of the nation-state character of the USSR and its role in the permanent crisis. The USA, the new hegemonic power after 1945, is the victorious power of the Cold War. It has declared the Middle East, the major long-term crisis region of the system, a strategic war zone. What is the symbolic meaning of the execution of Saddam Hussein, the former Iraqi Head of State (the "Sun King" of the nation-state in the Middle East)? There is a need for a comprehensive discussion of this issue.

The phenomenon of nation and its development

The division of society into primitive-communal society, state society, and democratic society is related to the formation of classes and problems associated with administration. The division in terms of nationalities is determined by developments in language, culture, law, and politics. It is more meaningful to talk about different types of nations instead of a single type of nation. This will make it possible to talk about nations that have been constructed on different bases.

It is instructive to consider a general social phenomenon when trying to render meaning to the category of nations. The paramount question for all clans and communities is one of entity: What kind of society or community am I? It is an inquiry into its own identity. Just as every person has a name and identity, it is possible—and necessary—to talk about a name and identity for all communities. If there are social phenomena based on differing natures, then it is only natural that they will have an expression of their identity. Name and identity are important for different clan societies to have interaction. Besides, it is absurd to think that all the developments in science and society that have advanced human life and established communication could have happened without naming one's unique features and not have an epithet. It is of course possible to be multilingual, multicultural, and to have a plurality of political and legal systems. In this huge network of relations, yet again, a name and an identity are a must. There can be a bilingual and bi-cultural nation, but this does not remove the need for designation and an identity. Multiple identities and diversities require the correct choice of methods of coexistence. Indeed, societies can neither emerge nor be governed in any other way.

The fact that each clan always had a unique totem is an indication of the ancientness of this reality. The totem, in short, is the identity of the clan. It is still possible to observe this relationship in some clans and tribes existing today.

The Sumerian society reflected the connection between designation and belief by expressing itself in its own temple identity. The temple is a fictive network of relations. With the temple, society's ability to render meaning to itself attains an analytic level. Evaluating the relationships as a whole at the temple—that is, its identity—enables the understanding of that society to a large extent. The city temple, city god. and city goddess are indications of the kind of power and conceptions the society has. The value ascribed to the sacred places results from the value of the identity still embedded in these places. This is because it is also how the community identifies itself. This is what we call "self-consciousness." Having an identity is to have consciousness of the self; indeed, it is the most effective consciousness of one's self.

In monotheistic religions, the identity of society is the religion and God itself. A society without a religion and a religion without a society cannot be envisaged. The resulting relationship is so strong that religion and God can be described as society's manifestation of the awareness of its own existence. For example, one can recognize Islamic societies primarily by the religious consciousness they have absorbed. They have other signifiers of belonging as well, such as sexual, political, tribal, class, and intellectual identities, but these all carry the stamp of the overarching religious identity.

In antiquity, the city rather than the nation was the bearer of identity. For instance, identity was attached to Athens and Rome. Citizenship of Athens or Rome was a most distinguished identity—one not easily attained. This shows the strength of the city's character and the honor in which it was held. Greek and Italian identities were not yet that significant. During the Middle Ages, the identity of being a people started to develop. The various religions played an important role in this development. For example, Islam brought awareness of being Arabic and of Arabic supremacy. Judaism was equated with Jewishness. Christianity was an extremely important identity of the Armenians, Assyrians, and Greeks as a people, who became Christians very early on. The religious and ethnic identities mutually fostered one another.

One of the most important functions of monotheistic religions is that of surpassing the tribal identity. Although it may not be as strong as a national identity or consciousness, the awareness of being a people has also played an important role in the Middle East and during the Middle Ages. The monotheistic religions were influential in the development of this sociological formation of being a people. When religion plays a part in a group identifying itself as being a people, we can talk about that religion being proto-nationalism. For the Turks, religion was a very important tool in forming an identity. If there were no Islam, the existence of Turks and Arabs as peoples would have had less significance in the Middle East; two counter-examples are that of the Jewish Khazar Turks and the Christian Arabs.

The spread of Christianity in the European Middle Ages was intertwined largely with the development of the awareness of being a people. In their previous tribal communities, just as with Arabic and Turkish tribes, the consciousness of being a people from a common background was very weak. Before modernity, Christianity was a factor that objectively raised this awareness. It did not designate these societies to be French or German, but a shared religious consciousness in all these tribes was a huge step towards the development of a people with a common identity. The second step was the political development of the formation of kingdoms. So, after development of a common religion, the formation of the tribes into a mutual kingdom is the final big step into becoming a nation. France is a typical example of this process.

The development of the market results in the increase of social relations; the birth of the nation is near. Nationhood is therefore the sum of social relations that develop around tribal consciousness, religious consciousness, common political authority, and the market. It may be more meaningful to talk about a nation-society. Becoming a nation is not the same as becoming a state. For example, even though the French kingdom was destroyed, the French nation continued to exist. It may be instructive to describe being a nation as a community that is unified by language and culture. But it is both a narrow and an inadequate definition to say that language and culture alone determine what a nation is. These of course are not the only bases for being a nation; politics, law, revolution, arts—especially literature and music—and market economy all play their role in becoming a nation. Nationhood has no direct relationship with economic and political systems, although they may be mutually influential. It is a very ambiguous matter, and thus any analysis in this regard should be done in a sensitive and balanced way.

The majority of today's communities have become nations. Although there are marginal groups that have not become nations, the majority now are nation societies. It is almost as if there is no individual without a nation—belonging to a nation may even be considered a natural social state. But in the long history of civilization being a nation has never, before the onset of the capitalist system, acquired such importance. Or, rather, what has been done in the name of nation has prepared the ground for terrible catastrophes.

An excessive emphasis on the elements that constitute a nation has created disaster. The most important factor in the formation of nationalist ideologies is the link between nation and politics. Nationalist politics will always end in fascist rule (as will nationalism fueled by economy, religion, and literature). The capitalist monopoly has "over-nationalized" the elements contributing to nation forming, such as politics, economy, religion, law, arts, sports, diplomacy, and patriotism in order to attain a systemic unity in the name of resolving the crises. Thus, every nation thinks that it will be the strongest of all by not leaving a single social entity out of the power relations. The results have been terrible with a bloodbath in Europe and eventually two world wars that had historically unprecedented consequences. This is not an act of becoming a nation but one of turning nation into a religion: the religion of nationalism. From a sociological perspective nationalism *is* a religion. I will elaborate on this in due course. Even religions have been aware of the potential dangers of an identity such as this, and in previous centuries opted for consistent and internationalist approaches (*Ummah* and Catholicism). The capitalist era has been the most sordid period in the history of civilization.

The most beneficial model for a nation is *democratic nation*. It is very important to understand this: In order to resolve the problems relating to nation, democratic society is the most constructive type of society. Nations can be formed and developed best within the system of democratic society. If they are to mutually support one another instead of using nationhood as a reason for warring and fighting, then the historical stage of the nation of nations, the über-nation, may be possible. Only within a democratic system will nationhood *not* give rise to fighting. Only then is it possible for nationhood to contribute to peace and fraternity in solidarity and cultural plurality. I will discuss this topic in detail throughout the book, as it is of the utmost importance.

To resolve and move beyond the problems related to the existence of multiple nations, the solution isn't to deny the various nations: it is not to "over-nationalize" the factors constituting a nation, to reduce a nation to its constituent factors, or to allow these factors to become the vehicle for ultra-nationalist formations of government by politicizing them. The solution lies in developing the awareness of democratic nationhood and in developing ways to realize democratic nationhood.

Defining the state

State is, and has been throughout history, one of the most frequently used terms. But, at the same time, it is one of the least understood and defined concepts. Despite the ignorance as to what it really entails, analyzing the concept *state* remains a fundamental issue in order to move beyond the social crisis. It is not only important to analyze the concept in historical context; the contemporary state must be analyzed as well. The worst aspect concerning the ignorance surrounding the concept is that even those who are running the state do not know what kind of vehicle it is they are driving. As for those who are excluded from the state (if there are any), they have misunderstood what the state is (the disaster of real-socialism is a good example of this). This lack of true understanding has led to a dead-end reminiscent of the state of confusion after the destruction of the Tower of Babel. More often than not, the state is seen as the area where problems are resolved. It is assumed that, if you have a state, you have rid yourself of all problems. But this type of reasoning is only one step away from envisaging the state as god-like.

A deep sociological insight will reveal that the historical development of divinity has been intertwined with becoming a state. The intertwined development of state and God resulted from the contribution the priest made to state formation. In the Sumerian temple, the pantheon of gods acquired an identity with an ideological component. In the construction of the state, the priests used this pantheon as the ideological mask of the political administrators. One step up from priest-king is the god-king. Originating in the Sumerian temple, this concept of the god-king or emperor was used until the time of the Roman Empire. The Abrahamic religions successfully turned this concept into that of the god-prophet or god-envoy, thereby incorporating a human figure.

The distinction made between divinity and humanity in Greek mythology (the third version of the Sumerian mythology) is also quite interesting. For example, Hesiod's *Theogony* is organized as a narrative telling how the gods came to exist; it is as if he prohibits any link to be made between the gods and humans, considering it to be shameful. He insists on keeping the relationship of gods and goddesses distinct and separate, placing it above humans—like a caste system. The Brahmin caste in the Hindu faith is a faint image of the god-king but the gods are stricter about this separation. They do not easily accept a god becoming human or having any relations with humans. Expressed scientifically: It is never admitted in ideologies that the state is a human construct. This is quite clear in mythology and religion, and partially in philosophy. The protagonists of these ideologies are trying to shield the state and maintain its divinity through a rigidity of belief. The conceptualizations, such as the state is sublime, sacred, and a fundamental vehicle of salvation, have their roots with the Sumerian priests, who were the initial builders of state. The state was constructed inside the temple's womb.

Hegel described the nation-state, which he believed Napoleon had set in motion, as *God descending on earth*. To him Napoleon symbolized the nation-state, calling him *God's march*. Hegel's observations are quite insightful and instructive in the light of our discussions above. Nation-state is not only the *final* form of god-state, it is also the most dangerous form of state. On the other hand, in the socio-scientific interpretation, defining *state* in terms of this web of relations is very new. Sharing my long held thoughts on this matter is a fundamental duty and I hope that it will open new horizons. It may be a good start to define *state* with reference to *power*. We can describe power that has been turned into various forms of legal order as a state. A concentrated power within the entirety of institutions, whose rules are determined and are set in a framework, define the state well, at least in terms of law. But such a definition is not sufficient. However, if we unite this approach with that of historical and social development, then we shall attain a definition that is broader and more meaningful. This will present a more complementary view of what the state is because it deals with scope and form at the same time.

I am aware of the various definitions of *state*. But it is not instructive to repeat the cliché definitions that have been memorized both in the liberal and socialist camps. Let me first of all point out what *state* is not:

— Its role is not to silence or stabilize the class conflict. The commonly repeated definition of it being mostly a tool for class coercion is also not enlightening.
— Its role is not to remove the state of chaos either. Its claim that it is there to ensure security and order is far from the truth.
— It is definitely not the area to resolve problems; on the contrary, it is a platform to turn problems into a crisis and to ensure their continuation.

— Its relationship with divinity and sacredness is nothing but ideological and mythological.
— It means nothing in terms of being the administrative and creative power of nation, religion, and culture.

The above statements can be multiplied, but it must be underlined that they are nothing but propaganda. The state does deal with the situations described; however, history shows us that the state has not really played any other role than that of turning the world into a slaughterhouse, assimilating and creating a lazy society, and turning the human into the fool of speculative intelligence. I do not deny the role the state plays in administrating society. I do not find the definition of *state* and the forms of being without a state as formulated by the anarchists very meaningful and implementable either. The reality of a hundred and fifty years of socialist practice showed that neither of them was successful. The fact that they made many correct statements regarding *state* does not eliminate their mistakes about fundamental issues. The liberal's proclamation of "reducing the state as much as possible" is in a way more meaningful. They have realized that the state is the imposition of economic monopolies. But the fact that they passionately defend capitalism as the most productive economic system shows their true face and reveals their dishonesty—even though they leave all those who incorrectly define *state* far behind.

It is more revealing to define *state*, in a narrow sense, as being the economic monopoly that is based on surplus product and value. The state organizes and monopolizes itself as a superstructure over society through the use of various ideological and coercive tools in order to squeeze the surplus product and value from society. If viewed from this narrow definition of *state*, politics is the art of administering the realization of surplus product and value. Then, roughly formulated, *state* is the sum of surplus product and value together with ideological tools, instruments of coercion, and the art of administration. If we are to evaluate the state throughout its historical development, then all these factors can be determined. If these factors are not considered as a whole, any attempt to define *state* as any one of these tools will not allow us to decipher this web of relations called the state.

— It is correct, but insufficient, to call the state the extortion of surplus-value.
— The state may be defined as an ideological divinity, sacred entity, or the descent of God's shadow on earth. But this only serves as an ideological cover for all its tyranny.
— The dictum "the state is tyrannical" is the weakest moral judgment of all and has the least scientific value since it excludes all the other factors.
— The definition of the state as an art of administration and management is as dangerous as moral interpretations because it ignores all the other factors and disguises the real essence of the state.

Undoubtedly, though each and every factor mentioned has an inevitable place in the existence of the state, it cannot be said to define the state alone. Most definitions of *state* highlight a specific factor and inevitably define it inadequately. It is possible to classify states throughout history in various ways:

Distinctions in terms of the social classes that derives the surplus product and value:
1. The slave-owning state
The form of state in which the human being belongs to the state and to the special masters of the state, not only with their labor but with their body and soul in return for food. It is the main mode of exploitation of the ancient civilization. The slaves are the fundamental tools of production.

2. The feudal state
It embodies a limited softening of enslavement. The difference between serf and the old slave is that the serf has now the right to establish a family. Because it gives way to more surplus product and value, it is the method employed during medieval civilization.

3. The capitalist state
It is the mode of state that bases itself upon the social class of the worker, who sells his labor in the labor market like a commodity. It may be more appropriate to call it a section or structure instead of a form. It is the state of the age of capitalist civilization.

Distinctions in relation to the ethnicity of the administrative elite:

1. The priest-state

This designation is used because it carries the stamp of the initial creators, the priests. Concepts such as *temple*, *sacred state*, and *god-state* all belong to this category.

2. The dynastic state

Here, *state* is defined according to the dynasty in power. We can call it a family state. It is a mode of state administration that has had widespread influence throughout the different eras of civilization and even in today's administration of states. It is a state where a family or dynasty constitutes the real administrative group.

3. The tribal or people's state

Such a state is more under the influence of a tribe or a people. Its existence is felt more during "medieval" times when consciousness of being a tribe or a people develops. The status of the state in religions such as Christianity, Islam, and Judaism, and in terms of peoples like those of India and China may allow for such a definition.

4. The national state

This is a state based on societies that have become nations. It is not just the state of the new era (the capitalist era in the strictest sense). The democratic era too bases itself on it, or rather, state and democracy each take on a role in the administration by way of reaching a compromise. When they govern together (that is when the regime of the state and democracy is effective), then one can call it a *national* state. It is quite different from the nation-state because there may be different nations in a national state.

5. The nation-state

This is a state consisting of a single nation, and all the members of the nation are integrated with the state on the basis of the religion of nationalism. The nation and the state have almost become one. It is capitalist civilization's main mode of state. The fascist state is the counter-revolutionary form, or a continuous regime of crisis, that the nation-state becomes in capitalism. Therefore, it is difficult to differentiate between the nation-state and the fascist state.

Categorized in terms of being elected or appointed to power,
or power being handed down from father to son, or seized by force:
1. The monarchical state

This is a state where a single person symbolizes the state. There is no distinction between the state and the ruler: they are one. This person may be a monarch, a king, or an emperor. One could become a monarch either as a result of the crown being passed from father to son or by obtaining it through force. This mode of state has existed in all ages of civilization and reflects the weakness in the institutionalization of the state.

2. The republic

This is where the main administrative group attains office through elections. It does not really matter whether it is one person or many people because its essence remains unchanged. At times *democracy* and *republic* are confused. It is a terrible mistake to make. Republic is a mode of state. The elections are done in order to choose the administration of the strongly constructed institutions of the state—not an election for democracy as the people's governance. Democracy is a totally different system, a mode of administration that is not state-like. Democracy, too, has institutions and requires elections to fill them. But democracy and state diverge from one another in terms of their essence. All the intellectuals of the Enlightenment, including the Marxists, confused these notions. This even pertains to Lenin. There is a qualitative difference between the official civilizations—with the state being their nucleus—and the condition of having democracy.

Therefore, it is quite important not to confuse democratic governance with that of state rule (whether there are elections or not). Moreover, the state is a method for ruling more than for anything else. It is the institutionalization of rule that rests on many thousands of years. The role of elections in this is quite limited. What is being achieved through elections is that *various monopolistic cliques (such as agrarian, commercial, industrial, or financial) within the state* will try to outmaneuver each other. The stronger one will be elected. Thus, there is no such situation where there is democracy or the victory of democracy.

There is also no such situation in any democracy where everyone shall be given assignments through elections. Those who have not been elected can also play a role in the administration of the democracies. But it is fundamental that the democratic society determines its own administration through elections in short intervals, so that there is a chance for various improvements and productivity, creativity, rights, as well as freedom and equalities.

Distinctions based on the groups that seize the surplus-value:
1. The agrarian state

It is quite revealing to call it as such. When it was first established it was organized as the administrative authority which would seize the surplus agricultural product. There were many such states or agrarian states where the power of agrarian cliques was present.

2. The mercantilist state

This is where the state bases its method of surplus value and product appropriation on commercial organization. Assyrian and Phoenician states are two examples of this, and today there are states with very strong commercial cliques within them.

3. The financial state

This is a state basing itself upon money-power. Switzerland is an example of this. More importantly though, if we call the last global era of capitalism the age of finance, we can say that the financial cliques or monopolies have grown extremely strong in all the states to the extent that it has a decisive influence on the administration.

4. The industrial state

There are many states that can be called industrial states due to the industrial production that played a leading role in economy since the Industrial Revolution. To be an industrial state was the ideal in the beginning of the 19th century. Industrialization equaled becoming wealthy. The main aim of all the states was to become industrialized as quickly as possible. Therefore, the strongest state clique consisted of industrialists. The fundamental monopolist cliques that nested within the state were the large merchants (mercantilism) in the eighteenth century, industrialists (industrialism) in the nineteenth century, and the financiers from the twentieth century up until today. They are the ones who really manage the web of relations called the state.

Fake designation of state distinctions in order to disguise the capitalist state monopolies:

These designations make the concept of *state* unrecognizable. Therefore, it may be instructive to re-consider the various models of such states that are nothing but ideological constructions. This is also necessary since our daily lives are bombarded by such concepts.

1. The liberal state

This is the favorite ideological concept of the political-economists. It can be translated as the free state but there is nothing in common between freedom and state. Instead, there is a total contrast between these two concepts. State in its essence represents the restriction of freedoms. The biggest problem of all throughout history has been to defend an individual's or group's freedom against the state. This has been one of the fundamental political and legal battles. It is also defined as the state that interferes least with economy. But a state can only exist if it is an economic monopoly. Therefore, the proclamation that it is a state that interferes least is nothing but a fallacy. It is against the essence and identity of being a state. It just may be that through such a concept capitalist economic monopolies wish their paths to be paved and their share multiplied.

2. The socialist state

This concept, used a lot in the real-socialist camp, is a fallacy as much as the liberal state is. For one thing, true socialism has nothing to do with the state. The state is in contrast with socialism at least as much as it is with democracy. It is the biggest sin of opportunism to confuse the state, which is the sum of all the big historical economic monopolist cliques, with that of socialism, which is an egalitarian regime. Socialist state is the present day equivalent of the phenomenon conceptualized as the *Pharaoh socialism*. It is capitalism's most obvious form of state and therefore very much related to proto-fascism. The counterpart of real socialism is nation-state (fascism). Nation-state is the real characteristic of both liberalism and real socialism (in terms of being state socialism). Thus, it is important to evaluate its relationship with fascism (in terms of authoritarianism and totalitarianism). It would be quite instructive to evaluate the liberal and social or socialist state to be proto-fascism in the path to fascism itself.

Those who are supporters of socialism must know that the state is the main institution through which surplus product and value has been appropriated throughout the five-thousand-year-old tradition of civilization, not simply the four hundred years of capitalist tradition. To deliberately defend the construction of socialism with the use of state is fascism but to be an instrument of it unknowingly is nothing but negligence and betrayal. I hope to discuss these topics in depth in my next book called *The Sociology of Freedom*.

3. The fascist state

It is a concept with not much meaning. Nation-state and fascism are similar in their essence. To define fascism to be an exception that has externally imposed itself on capitalism is the biggest misery of the liberal and socialist intellectuals. Capitalism, in terms of being the civilization and state, is the systematic expression of keeping the nation-state, and therefore fascism, at hand at all times. Fascism is the norm. What is an exception is reaching a compromise with democratic structures.

4. The democratic state

I have repeatedly explained why the state cannot be democratic. There can be no democratic state because the mentality, social structure, and manner of functioning in both are essentially different. However, due to the crisis inherent in the structures of civilization, but more so during the presently intensifying crisis in the structures of capitalist civilization, the necessity for the state to find a compromise with the system of democratic civilization has emerged. The state can no longer rule on its own. It has come to a position where it is compelled to a shared governance with the democratic forces, making it possible to find a compromise. There have been such examples in history. If the state (no matter what type) seeks and establishes a partnership with democratic principles and structures it may be meaningful to have a concept such as democratic state, provided this means the susceptibility of state to democracy. To me the best definition would be state plus democracy. I had already proposed that the most urgent duty of political philosophy is to focus on different state modes. This is because it is no longer possible to rule today's societies with the classical state mentality. This is why NGO's have come into play but they are quite insufficient. It does not seem possible for the moment that these organizations shall be able to fulfill the administrative vacuum and share governance.

The only way out seems to be the finding of a compromise between the structures of democratic society that are more radically organized and the state institutions that are more productive. At this current historical stage (no one can presume how long it shall take), neither capitalist civilization nor democratic civilization nor socialist system alone can bring about the desired results. What we are losing is the society, and the only achievement is to prolong the exploitation, spilling of blood, and pain.

There are other concepts in relation to state, such as the state of law. The state, being the economic monopoly, can only exist if it appropriates surplus product. Therefore, essentially it can neither be fair nor juridical. But it is called the state with rules or the state of law because it treats its members and citizens according to predetermined and equal rules. Although this is obviously more positive than the despotic states in which the rules change each day, its essence does not however constitute a separate definition of a state. For example, a religious state is also not very meaningful. The state has always been presented under the cover of sacredness because of the existence of priest-state. Religion, mythology, philosophy, and even scientism are the state's ideological tools of propaganda. Secular state is thought to be the opposite of religious state but they mean the same. These kinds of definitions carry no serious meaning other than being used for propaganda.

In conclusion, the state has multiplied and carried itself to date as the nucleus of civilization and of the history of civilization. It has continuously intersected with numerous modes in order to disguise itself. In capitalist civilization, it has obtained the chance to be truly defined for the first time despite all the ideological counter-efforts. The chance to truly define the state is the most meaningful gain of the struggle against capitalism and is the end result of intellectual and practical efforts. However, the burning question is how to raise the efforts, in terms of organization and action, to enhance the development and success of democratic civilization in regards to its content and forms, and to make it permanent.

The Ideology of the Capitalist Civilization and its Religionization

Civilizations are formed over a long period of time and on the basis of ideological constructions. Questions such as "did the material culture exist before the immaterial culture?" have no meaning. They only create confusion. Let me clarify this point with an example. For a long time, there was much debate over whether the constituents of matter and light are wave-like or particle-like, especially to the question as to which aspect is primary. It is now generally accepted that the constituents are wave-like and particle-like at the same time. This is known as the wave-particle duality. It is also widely accepted that the universe essentially developed through a fundamental dialectic of the wave-particle duality. In this dialectic, we don't see destruction but development. Although its nature may be different, the material/immaterial duality plays a similar role. They do not oppose one another: they are constituent factors that complement one another. They generate one another through differentiation. Just as there is a wave or factor of immaterial culture that is triggered or caused by each particle or material culture, there is also particle or factor of material culture formed by each wave or immaterial culture. There is a general aberration of analytical intelligence within the civilizational system which is due to the advantageous system that it has formed: They wish to systematize and perpetuate their interests by building absolutes, such as immutable rules, absolute laws that all must comply with, precedence of gods, the state's divinity and perpetuity, as well as dichotomies like the perfection of Forms and temporality of phenomena, unchanging substance, and volatility of form. This is contrary to the universal dialectic of existence.

The discussion that human society consists of two parts, base and superstructure, is closely related to these constructed aberrations of civilization. In Hegel's system, he gives precedence to superstructure, state, and law, just as he gives precedence to Geist (or Reason or Spirit) in terms of the universal system. However, Marx gives precedence to the base—forces and means of production and the social relations of the production whereby he claimed he "placed Hegel on his feet."[3] But I think he shares the same mentality as Hegel. And what is that? Where for one something is a fundamental element, for the other it is secondary or the determined. This is falling into the vulgar logic of subject-object distinction. Although they claim the opposite, they have maintained the mentality of the former civilization. The answer to why Marx's socialism was not successful is hidden in this logic. Not only does his definition in relation to economy consist of great complexity, he also uses all of classical civilization's tools of conception. Despite the heroism and the truth that has been spoken, the result shows us that the reality is not what it was interpreted to be.

The ideological construction of capitalist civilization (or modernity) was so masterful that it surpassed that of the Sumerian priests and has been systematized. It may even be said that at first the state made a great headway with ideology. All civilizations avoid the impression of having been created by the same God. This is really important. For example, let's examine the Prophet Muhammad. The contents of the first and the last verses of the Quran are very different. The concept of God is continuously developed. The God that said "read" at the beginning later develops a system. These verses, piece by piece, have formed the system or, more precisely, have laid the foundation of the system. Later a huge ideological corpus was formed, but the construction of the system has taken many centuries.

Without truly understanding all the aspects of capitalist modernity's systematics we cannot really construe its mental tools. Capitalist modernity has not constructed all of its concepts, hypothesis, and implementations on its own. It has inherited a legacy over thousands of years. Through this inheritance it achieves a new architectural layout and content. Its own class, and later the one or two state classes constructed just like it, are all integrated together via an ideological construction. This integration is then completed with the addition of a spectrum of things such as fashion to philosophy, together with the control of production and consumption, as well as the control over politics. It then does the same thing by spreading it over the continent and globally.

People who develop ideologies, especially Descartes and Francis Bacon, constructed the new principles of reason and utopias required by formations that made themselves felt in the sixteenth century. It may sound simple but by putting the dichotomy of body and soul on the agenda this led to the dichotomy of subject and object. As if in a chain reaction thoughts that are later constructed shall be escalated to the extent that they spearhead "capitalism and bourgeoisie." There is not only a break away from feudal reason, but a new reason is being constructed. All this is done for the benefit of a new class and all its various acts. Moreover, and more importantly, the new ruling class achieves its supremacy over the new and old classes through these ideological constructs, a very ancient game, renewed time and again. The new priest class is now called the philosophers and scientists. New concepts and theories are continuously taken but renewed from the feudal and even the slave-owning ideologies. Depending on the situation they are either patched or a completely new model is created (but with the same principles).

An evaluation of Descartes alone will highlight the striking elements of the ideological construction. Initially, he doubts everything. If we decrypt his message: The feudal class's ideological armor, and therefore rule, must be overcome. If he talked openly he would have had to face the Inquisition. He was obviously afraid of being burnt alive. Therefore, he resorts to an abstract philosophy. Later, he concludes "I think therefore I am." This signals that all ideological preparations are completed and its elements shall be put into action one after another. He tells all to "doubt everything and the only way to prove one's existence is to have powerful thoughts." It is not that hard to decrypt what is being said: The lifestyle imposed by feudalism has no value at all. You could construct a new life with your powerful thoughts! Through the dichotomy of body and soul the importance of this world is reminded to God and the world beyond.

After God's initial push, the universe is set into a continuous mechanical motion. If we decrypt this sentence we find that although the creators of the old world are fundamental, there is now a new civilization that is set into motion. Thus, a new civilization can be constructed. If we interpret what is being said in term of class, it heralds the emergence of a new class. It has the power to think. It can arrange its own world through its own laws of motion and action.

If we try the same thing with Francis Bacon, then we shall see that experimentation is essential in his reasoning. If experiments verify a certain thing, then that certain thing can be generalized. Any thought that is not experimental cannot be scientific and hence of any value. Meaning that "everything shall be learned through implementation and action. Don't believe in the old fallacies. Science is power. Thoughts that are acquired through your actions and trials can only strengthen you." Its decryption in terms of class: It calls on the new powers that have formed over the surplus value using the methods of capitalist monopoly, "Not according to the old dogmatic reason but under the guidance of your own acquisitions you should try out everything, develop their results and then generalize them; you shall as a result be empowered with knowledge and hence construct your own home and worlds."

It is of course incorrect to view the increasingly growing army of scientists and philosophers with the onset of the sixteenth century as the leading proponents of capitalist monopoly. We are aware that the majority of those who took their places in the three important historical movements (Renaissance, Reformation, and Enlightenment) were people of profound wisdom and morals who had a free mentality. They hated capitalism—a system whose consequences were apparent even in its early days, with its ruling clique and their way of life. It is, on the other hand, without a doubt that the revolution in mindset which appeared in Europe is also of value to humanity in general. Leaders of this revolution were mainly humanists. They kept away from religion and nationalism. Indeed, the work on science and philosophy itself is a revolution in its own. If they must absolutely be associated with a social section, then it is not the section that is affiliated with the values of the classical civilization but with those who are most in need of democracy, freedom, and equality. We are of course grateful to them even as I write these lines. But this is not the problem. The appropriated surplus product was used by the new social class in their construction of themselves as rulers. This new social class similarly appropriated the surplus products and values of this mentality in order to use them in the construction of their own mindset. Such an action can easily be called the theft of mentality. The bourgeoisie knew how to construct the new modernity in terms of their own class interests. It is of vital importance to know the following characteristics of the monopolist state cliques: They shall "throw a sprat to catch a whale." They knew how to exploit the pioneers of the new mindset by skillfully playing with the difficulties endured by them (economic, social, and political), just as they exploited those at the bottom who created economy. They realized this exploitation by placing so many craftspeople, scientists, and philosophers under their own control and even integrating them into their tools of power. They also knew how to neutralize those who resisted: through the use of the same economic, social, and political means. We are all aware of what happened to people such as Erasmus, Galileo, and Bruno.

Just as it was possible to renew control over economy using state monopoly, the ideological monopolist movement had similar influences. Rebellions were quashed through extensive action in the political, ideological, and economic fields. By the end of the eighteenth century it was not just a victory won in the economic monopoly front (industry), but also in the political (French Revolution) and ideological front (nationalism and nation-state) as well. Those that lost were Christian Catholicism, classical monarchies, empires, and humanism. Just as economy was absorbed by its counterpart monopolists, the democratic movements and nations were also taken under the process of being absorbed by the nation-state and nationalism. Thus, the aristocracy and Catholic Church, as well as all Christianity—not preserving their former reputation—sought to renew their alliance with the new masters in return for the protection of their interests, and they sought to reconcile under the most favorable terms. Therefore, as the nineteenth century begins, it is not only the victory of the new economic monopolies (commercial, industrial, and financial). The ideological victory was just as important and it was won.

The way religions were constructed by the feudal civilization had also become undone. Protestantism was the end result. The Catholic Church lost its magnificent position. Max Weber has already shown us in his splendid presentation how compatible Protestant morals were with that of capitalism. Secularism, a concept in need of analysis, was one of the ideological successes of this period. The Christian world assaulted European people's mentality with much dogmatism whilst they still were mostly free tribes. Its conflict with the world was visible. It was not difficult to guess that when it lost its political and economic influence it would be very quickly ideologically surpassed. What was more important was the monstrosity called secularism. It is still quite an ambiguous matter to determine whether it is encompassed by religion or not. The bourgeoisie embraced the phenomenon called positivism. But since positivism declared itself the new world religion, how can secularism be outside the boundaries of religion? What then does a new religion mean?

Positivism's religious nature is due to its reliance on empirical facts. For positivism, essentially, an empirical fact is the most fundamental truth. There is no truth if it is not factual. However, research and philosophy (as a whole) show that facts and perception are the same. Perception, on the other hand, is a simple mental process, a method to coarsely inform (not scientifically and in a very deceptive way) oneself through the most superficial observation of the object. To make the shift from facts to positivism is to grant an object the role of being a fundamental reality. A similar approach forms the basis of paganism: the object is worshiped. Thus, positivism may attack metaphysics, especially religion, as much as it likes; it has itself become the most vulgar materialist religion because it takes the object to be the truth. That is, it is a new derivative of object-paganism in modernity, and positivism, as its representative, is metaphysics. Actually, it is more superficial. Nietzsche is of the same opinion. But let's discuss this in more detail in my next book, *The Sociology of Freedom.*

Positivism damaged the mentalities at least as much as the medieval theologies did. It was not even aware of the great immaterial world of human societies. It declared the end of the metaphysical world and threw all the human sanctities, the accumulation of millions of years, into the garbage bin. It was a movement of total ignorance. The title ascribed by the Prophet Muhammad to Amr Ibn Hisham was Abu Jahl (the Father of Ignorance). This title is best fitted to these positivists. They are the modern Abu Jahls in terms of the social sciences. It is important to understand that the ideological mesh of irreligiousness (or laicism, from the Greek *laïkós*, layman) and positivism (positivist philosophy or religion), together with vulgar materialism, are closely related to capitalist monopolies. It has been exactly four hundred years since the destruction and terrorization of this new society and its immaterial world was achieved through the usage of these three ideological versions.

The victory of capitalism's material culture would not have been possible if the society that preserved its existence with the influence of immaterial culture (morals) had not dissolved. This is why there was a need for an ideological conquest. Their anti-religiousness was due to its moral dimension. These three philosophies were quite effective in the destruction of society's morals. Societies whose morals are drained can easily go either off the track or surrender. This is exactly what happened. Secularism through its irreligiousness destroyed the moral virtue inherent in religion. Positivism, because it is based on empiricism, paved the way for the new idolatry (the present stage of consumption, that is, the passion to own things). Thus, an enormous moral decline also occurred in this way.

Positivism's anti-metaphysical stance is one of its most ignorant attacks. Metaphysics has been a human need since the formation of humanity, not only for civilizations who are built around states but for all humans. No single person past or present is able to survive with information, science, or even, as positivists put it, with scientism alone. This is not impossible but our intellectual power is as yet insufficient. If you take away or destroy the metaphysical world, then you will either end up with a lifeless body or crazy people who will not abide by any laws. This is indeed what happened. In any case, facts only constitute a portion of the truth.

Quantum and cosmology have not had their final words. Life on the other hand has not been analyzed yet; we have not even become aware of its greatest mystery. This is the reason why positivism deserves to be designated as modern ignorance. Vulgar materialism is not all that different. The questions associated with life and mind cannot be explained through mirror image theories: even science itself stumbles upon a related new miracle each day. Social life is even more complicated than life and the mind. Once it had become clear that these were movements of ignorance and could become a meaningful center of attention, a more disguised synthesis of these three philosophies stepped in: bourgeois internationalism and nationalism. They appear to be paradoxical but they actually complement one another.

Internationalism of the bourgeoisie or its globalism: In the history of civilization, people who constructed ideologies were careful about two things: those sitting at the top floor and the common symbolic values. They are symbolic expressions of the common interests. Ideologies always have a symbolic quality but it is important to understand whose interests are symbolized. The council of gods at the top floor of the Ziggurat was a symbol. En, Enlil, and Marduk represented the supreme council of the hierarchy that was newly emerging and institutionalizing. We will probably never know whether this symbolization was intentional or spontaneous. But the tradition is an ancient one and has some general traits. This very symbolization became more complicated and continuously transformed but was nevertheless carried through to the present. For those at the lowest floor, symbols of enslavement and servitude are formed. Sharp and clearly defined lines are drawn between the council of sacred gods and them. The servant must meet the requirements of being a servant and must leave the duties of the gods to them. One may well ask "what did society lose or gain with such stories?"

The present-day council of the upper floor meets regularly in Davos, whether openly or in secrecy. However, this one thing is for certain: Those who constitute the present day upper layers—the unmasked and naked versions of the ones that sat in the upper floor of the Ziggurats—at times appear in human society. In these meetings, the priests on duty continuously preach that there is no reason for humans to be scared, the situation is under total control, there are enough war preparations and stocks, and that their defeat should not even be contemplated. The necessary conclusions are drawn by all concerned. The distinguished priests enforce this internationalist ideology on the minds and emotions of people with saturated coverage on advanced media channels. The universities, mosques, and churches now lag behind. The age of communication is at the same time the age of globalism. Consumption and entertainment is in line with the final stages of all past civilizations. Even though the ecology is truly being destroyed for the first time they do not allow any criticism of themselves. Although societies, cities, rural areas, and demography continuously signal unsustainability they do not hear or see in line with their internationalist ideology. It is as if there is no community that can resist being drugged with sex, sports, and arts as well as having their value content being drained.

Nationalism: Although it may look to be the opposite of internationalism, it is indeed the strategic tool of the new "divide and conquer" religion used by the upper floor internationalists to drug the lower floors of the society. Positivism is the most effective ideological tool that capitalism can't do without. It enables capitalism to overcome the insufficiencies and problems created by secularism, vulgar materialism, and scientism. Above all, it is the only effective religion of the nation-state. Each civilizational era has its own effective beliefs without which they would not have been successful. Nationalism is the most effective pattern of belief of modernity. Its construction is quite simple: Each factor that constitutes the nation must be turned into a sacred belief.

The next step is to equate all these with honor and to penetrate them so much during all activities at school, in the barracks, mosques, family, and other places that even the most insensitive individual shall be awakened and turned aggressive. You have just been successful at creating the most effective religion. Contrary to widespread belief, religions are not constructed to prepare us for the afterlife or the world beyond. They are political programs and strategies. In terms of worshiping they are daily educational tools.

It is a fundamental function of sociology to evaluate religion in such a way despite the severe disguise. If this is not done, there will be no escape from being a sub-branch of scientism. Moreover, religions have sanctities and they are of great importance. It is also a serious task to bring them out into the open. If religion, through the betrayal of its sanctities, has been turned into a vulgar ideological tool, then it has been pushed to hypocrisy by its own preachers. In short, religion is also a tool much used by today's nationalism: the tool of a tool. I shall only define it here since I will be discussing the formation and use of religion in more detail in the next two topics.

It may be really difficult to free the mind, thought, and therefore free action, not only from capitalist modernity's economic monopoly but also from the influence of the centuries old ideological tools. However, it is the fundamental duty of democratic modernity.

The reason why I have directed such harsh criticism against social-democrats, national liberationists, as well as anarchists, utopists, various fraternity orders, and even Marx and Marxists, is because there has not been an effective ideological construction of democratic modernity. It is quite clear that Marx and the Marxists tried to adopt a stance and resist against the emerging capitalist monopoly. The democratic tendencies of the others should not be belittled either. But in comparison to the present situation of capitalist modernity, it is going through its most comfortable period. Despite the presence of profound and continuous crisis, despite being anti-social, despite environmental disasters, unemployment, and poverty that it has caused. It becomes clear how insufficient, wrong, and passive they are.

Therefore, the democratic civilizational front must re-examine the heritage of all the past ages in order to pick out what it needs to successfully complete its ideological move forward and to complete the missing parts from its analysis of today's concrete situation. There is no other duty that is more urgent and sacred.

In Memory of the Victims of the Jewish Genocide

It may be unexpected that I would include such a separate section but I felt that it was essential. My exodus abroad, my abduction, and the link between Jewish genocide with nationalism (capitalism's modern religion) are the reasons why it is so important to include this story in this book. The fact that intellectuals have not explained the Jewish genocide in a satisfactory manner and the absence of sincere self-criticism concerning the Jewish ideology—or, if they have, I have not seen it—compel me to delve into this subject as an important part of my defense.[4]

The Jews and Civilization

Any scholar who has even the slightest interest in the history of civilization will easily notice that a thorough analysis cannot be prepared if the role of the Jews is not included. Because of my limited knowledge of the issue, I had only slightly touched on it in my previous defenses.

All the indications point to the identity described as Abraham to have entered into a paradigmatic conflict (this is how it is portrayed) with one of the Babylonian Nimrods (around contemporary Urfa).[5] Abraham destroyed the idolized statues at the pantheon in order to show that they cannot be gods. Nimrod then threw Abraham into the fire which then turned into the Pool of Abraham that still exists today along with its mythological story.

Most probably the Urfa-Jerusalem route had the status of being a buffer zone between the two majestic powers of its time: The New Dynasty of Egypt and the Babylonian Dynasty with Sumerian roots. Trade had, for the first time in history, become a rising economic sector. Trade between the two civilizational powers played a more superior role than politics. There was an increase in merchant's traveling in and out. The magnificent trade period of the Assyrians also coincided with this phase. Besides, the Urfa-Aleppo-Damascus-Jerusalem route had been the most important route for migration and trade, as well as invasions, occupation and, most importantly, the exchange of religions since the early ages (since the Neolithic times and the initial cities). It is not a coincidence that this is where the prophet Abraham made his moves and also migrated to. It is also widely accepted that it is the initial route where both Christianity and Islam were formed. Abraham (this name is thought to probably be a title given by the Egyptians. Egyptians used to call those coming from the Sinai Apiru or Habiru because of the dust and dirt on them. It is quite possible that this could later have evolved into Hebrew and Abraham) wanted to first reside around what is today contemporary Jerusalem. The local rulers did not easily give their permission. It is said that he bought a small tract of land and later died there. Those who wish can follow the story that began with Sarah, Hagar, Ishmael, Isaac, Jacob, and continued with that of Prophet Moses, Jesus, and Muhammad and in between many more connecting links of prophets from the Sacred Books

(The Old Testament, the New Testament, and the Quran). History books can also be quite instructive. I shall find it sufficient for my own purposes to outline the history of the Jews under a few periods:

— The story of Abraham in Urfa and his emergence between 1,700-1,600 BCE. He is the chief of a tribe and a merchant.
— Captivity in Egypt: 1,600-1,300 BCE.
— The exodus led by Prophet Moses: 1,300-1,250 BCE.
— Settlement in the "Promised Land": 1,250-1,200 BCE during the period of commander and prophet Joshua.
— The period of judges: 1,200-1,000 BCE. These secular and religious leaders had not yet become kings or prophets; the period up until King Saul.
— The period of Kings of Judah and Israel: 1,000-700 BCE. This period starts with Saul, David, Solomon, and ends with Ezekiel (Assyrian occupation).
— The period of occupation, invasion, resistance and diaspora: 700 BCE–70 CE (the period that marks the occupation and rule by the Assyrians, Babylonians, Alexander, and the Romans).

During this period the Kingdoms of Judah and Israel fell. In its place two groups come to the fore: one of resistance and the other a collaborator group. The collaborators appear as two main groups depending on whether they are pro-Greek or pro-Persian. Their third exile (after Urfa and Egypt) is the infamous Babylonian exile during the period of Babylonian King Nebuchadnezzar. This lasted for forty years (between 535-495 BCE). The passages in the Bible that clearly have a Zoroastrian influence have been conveyed from this period. There was much admiration of the Persians because they ended the forty-year-old exile. The first written copies of the Torah were most probably compiled in this period after 700 BCE. Hence, for around 600 years (1,300-700 BCE) there were no written copies of the Holy Book. This means that the relevant section in all three Holy Books rely on verbal accounts after 600 years had passed. Homer's *Iliad* and Hesiod's *Theogony* are also the written forms of such narratives and were penned around the same time. The destruction of Solomon's Temple by the Romans (around 70 BCE and again 70 CE) resulted in a great resistance. Christianity is the tradition of resistance for the poorest sections of society, although there are cases where resistance was led by the upper classes, such as that of the Maccabees.

The dispersion of the tribe or people intensified after 70 CE with the onset of diaspora. They concentrated in two regions, the Roman and the Persian empire, living in those places where Assurian, Armenian, and Greek culture existed. This long period is also called the era of scribes. There was a continuous compilation and interpretation of the Torah, and while many prophets emerged being a scribe became more important. The high intellectual level in Jewish culture rests upon this very important historical tradition. The other important profession must be money and trade. This is because they did not have the chance to work comfortably in their own land. As a result, they focused intensely on trade and its effective tool, money. Hence, it is possible to say that they overtook the Assyrians in trade and controlled the monetary and trade monopoly in the Middle East. This status later led them to very influential and profitable positions in the medieval cities, as well as in the cradles of capitalism: London and Amsterdam. This also indicates that there is a long historical tradition of them becoming owners of big capital. It is believed that many had dispersed in the diaspora and only a small number stayed behind around Jerusalem. As they became dispersed, two important cultural traditions were formed: The Eastern and Western Diaspora.

We can say that the Jews can be defined as "an ethnic people" after the Diaspora. The regions where they specifically gathered were: Arabia, Iran, Kurdistan, Egypt, and ancient Greece. They became Jewish groups based on local culture. And so they became a bi-cultural people: their original, Hebrew, culture and the culture of the society where they settled. This situation had a very important and positive influence on their intellectual abilities, especially as this made it possible for the Jews to have contact with all the ancient cultures of history.

A new tragic period begins with the emergence of Islam. Islam made it possible for the Arabs to switch to a trade civilization although, at the time, trade and monetary monopoly was mostly in the hands of Jewish merchants and moneylenders in the many regions of Arabia. Therefore, the *hadith*, that "the Jews should not remain in Arabia," attributed to Prophet Muhammad may be doubtful but it is suggestive. The animosity between Arabs and Jews is very old. The story about Hagar and her son Ishmael being expelled to present day Mecca (like an unwanted duo) is in fact related to the conflict between the then Jewish and Arabic tribes. The conflict of interests between Jews and Arabic sheikhs and merchants which began then has continued until today, and it had escalated into a conflict between Arabs and Israel, and Palestine and Israel. This conflict, having started around 3,500 years ago, has now turned into a conflict between civilizations.

It is quite normal for intense competition to develop between trade monopolies in the region. Thus, we can well understand why Islam views trade as so important. Also, the relationship between Khadijah and the Prophet Muhammad can be better understood. In conclusion, the Jews have had to accept both assimilation and collaboration if they wished to stay in the area with the alternative being deportation to different regions. Both of these situations have materialized. Even in the time of the Roman Empire, significant groups of Jews left for Europe while those who remained became converts and remained in the region as half-slaves paying their tributes. The Jews developed their historical roles (as clerks, moneylenders, and being in trade) during medieval times and in the Islamic civilization (especially in Iran and Andalusia in Spain), for which they became renowned. They interacted with many political powers and became known as a people of intellectuals and merchants and moneylenders. Consequently, they incurred the wrath of the intellectuals and merchants in the areas in which they had settled. Therefore, there seem to be material, cultural, and historical motives at the heart of Antisemitism throughout the ages.

At the start of the modern era the hatred towards the Jews increased greatly due to the aforementioned motives, with the concomitant escalation of threats and banishment. This was because capitalism is a civilization that grows out of trade and monetary monopoly. Hence, anyone who has an interest or faces losses in trade and money will point to the Jewish intellectuals, merchants, and moneylenders as being the obstacle that bars their access. The Jews face a dangerous paradox. The merchant's and moneylender's monopolies of other nations who have an interest in capitalistic developments will regard Jewish elements as obstacle to themselves. Traditional agriculturalists and craftspeople whose interests clash with the development of capitalist monopolies can also easily show the Jews to be a mystical danger. One the other hand, the intellectuals, fueled by their devotion to the system (and thus its interests), have shown the Jews to be Pandora's Box with all of its evils inside. Under these circumstances, the fifteenth and sixteenth centuries heralded a new civilizational period where banishment and pogroms were renewed and intensified against the Jews.

What is really interesting is that Jewish intellectuals, merchants, and moneylenders would not only be the most important factor in the construction of this new civilization, but that they were also the greatest victims of this civilization's wrath. This is the paradox. In 1492 it was not just Muslims who were thrown out of Spain: the Jews were also thrown out. The justification was ready and effective: were they not the ones who crucified Jesus? But the true reasons are as I have tried to explain. There was a similar situation in Poland and Tsarist Russia. Thus, the Jews gathered in new countries, above all the Netherlands and England. All the influential Jewish merchants, moneylenders, and intellectuals went to those countries. Some migrated to the Ottoman Empire, which was at war with the European monarchs. They were not only taken in but actually invited by the empire to take on an effective role in the Sultan's monopoly of trade and money exchange. Gradually, the migration to the American continent also began. As new German cities developed they strengthened their position in various intellectual fields, as well as in merchant and moneylender monopolies. The Jews settled in Germany and integrated into that society.

Some scholars link capitalism to Judaism. I think this is an exaggerated claim although I do believe Judaism influences capitalism. But it is clear that the conditions and characteristics of sedentary society is the decisive factor that made capitalism possible. Nevertheless, we must not underestimate the triggering role of minorities. The influence of Jewish bankers, merchants, and philosophers in the rise of capitalism as the hegemon of the new system and the development of the intellectual environment in the Netherlands and England is extremely important. Spinoza is the most important intellectual at the start of the modern era. He is one of the early Jewish secularists (in terms of the people who have come out of the synagogue). He is also one of the greatest thinkers of freedom. The recognition that "to understand is to be free" owes much to Spinoza.[6] The money lent to England and the Netherlands by Jewish bankers and merchants was very important in helping them win wars and become strong states. They would later play a similar role, especially in Northern America, during the war of independence by the English states. Everyone is aware (and if not they should be) that Jewish intellectuals, merchants, and bankers are amongst the most important factors in the formation of the USA.

The Jewish Ideology

I must clearly point out something from the beginning: The worldwide ideological leadership is still in the hands of Jewish intellectuals. This leadership also has deep historical roots.

In the initial formation of the Jewish culture there are extensive traces of two major cultures, the Sumerian and Egyptian. The Old Testament (Torah) is the reflection of what the Hebrew tribe absorbed from these two tribes in terms of tribal language and conscience. The reflection is quite clear. It is the early version of these two cultures and this can be seen in the stories on Adam and Eve, the creation of the world in seven days, and in the concepts of God and prophet. Let us not forget that the story of Noah is a Sumerian legend and, for that matter, so are the legends of the prophets Enoch and Job! The first attempt at monotheistic religion was during the period of Pharaoh Akhenaton in Egypt. Remember also that Urfa was the main ancient center of Neolithic culture and therefore we should not neglect the transformed influence of Neolithic ideology, another important source to be considered. There are two major language and cultural groups behind the Jewish ideology: The Aryans and the Semitics. The role that these two played in Hebrew tribal culture cannot be denied either.

At the time of the first exile the influence of Babylonian and Zoroastrian (Persian and Medean) cultures are also visible. Many stories originated from this culture.

The Greco-Roman culture is the third largest source, especially in the development of religious philosophy. The foundations of the philosophization of religion and the religionization of philosophy that can be found in Christianity and Islam go way back to Aristotle, Plato, and especially to philosophical schools such as the Stoics.

It is clear that Christianity and Islam are like two denominations of the Hebrew religion, adapted to the requirements of Greco-Roman and Arabic societies. Clearly they both benefited from the same source. The conflict between these two denominations and Judaism is due to Judaism's profound tribal characteristics. Judaism had been shaped as the national religion of Hebrew tribal society at the beginning, but later (with the onset of Diaspora) evolved into being that of the Jewish people. In fact, we have identicalness: The Hebrew tribe equals the Hebrew religion which in turn equates with that of Hebrew or Jewish people. From very early on Jewish ideology had a religious context which in turn was totally tribal and later ethnic. Islam and Christianity on the other hand were constructed in relation to the material and moral needs of ethnic communities close to the Jews but who had deep-rooted relations and conflicts with them. As a result, they both have been extensively influenced by Judaism and have been in frequent conflict with it.

Jewish ideology is at the same time an ideology shaped by a profound material culture. We observed how such a material culture defined the various civilizations. Therefore, Jewish ideology is a civilizational ideology shaped in a close relationship with all the civilizations formed in the Middle East since the Sumerians. The following formulation might be useful: The Jewish ideology contains the essence of the synthesis of all civilizations and it derives its power from this essence. The role of Jewish prophets and scholars throughout history is decisive. Thus, just as relevant societies have relations and conflicts with their own civilizations, they would also have relations and conflict with Judaism. Another conclusion that can be drawn from all this is that Judaism is not just a religion and ethnicity but a civilization which is a synthesis (or a junction) of civilizations. If we take into consideration the role of Jewish ideology in the strengthening of intellectual structures of civilizations, then we understand why they continue to play a worldwide leading role today.

Jewish ideology fragmented with the modern era and divided into two main channels, one religious and the other secular. Spinoza (1632-1677) was the leader of the secular wing and many other similar philosophers of Jewish origins continuously reinforced this secular channel. It is of course contestable whether secularism is a new religion or is anti-religious. Frankly, I do not find the generation of religious or anti-religious thought to be meaningful social or ideological work. This is not the distinction that should be made: it is not very enlightening or instructive but rather diverts and distorts. All the various knowledge types, such as mythological, religious, philosophical, and scientific, have a social counterpart. Their role, relationships, and conflict together with their social and political foundations can only be understood through sociological study.

The secular wing of Judaism had a great influence on the ideology of Enlightenment. This ideology, which we can also call "scientism," is the same as positivism from a philosophical point of view. This ideological trend that left its stamp on the modern era gradually became the religious belief of capitalist modernity under the name of positivism or scientism. I must emphasize: Positivism is the old religion with some differences; it is the same as religion but turned upside down. There is a mental unity between the law making of scientism and that of religions. Contrary to widespread belief, while religion is not an "ethereal" or "spiritual" concept, secularism and being secular are not "worldly" concepts either. This is an artificial distinction. All religions are related to worldliness and linked to sociality. And those that are said to be worldly, too, are above all related to sociality. The concepts of etherealism and worldliness not only disguise a serious conflict that pertains to sociality, but also serve to continue the conflict covertly. As the enlightenment ideology became systemized as scientism and positivism it became the official ideology of the new nation-state. This in turn meant a rapid transformation into nationalist ideology.

Jewish Nationalism

The traditional Jewish merchants and moneylenders became known by the more visible and modern title of bourgeoisie within the capitalist system. It is understandable why the bourgeoisie as the new social class would be ideologically positivist, and in turn why the concept of state would give way to nationalism. Through the strength of its new ideology the bourgeoisie reinforced its position as the creator of the nation. First, all factors that made up the nation were nationalized. Thereafter, it was not difficult to transfer them to the economic monopolies through the channels of state monopolies. The monopolization that rapidly developed in all the nations of Europe could only have been passed off to the whole nation by making use of nationalism. This is a similar formation to the ideology that gained success by the Sumerians. The nation is declared the supreme unit (the oldest god or something to take its place), and the state within the nation puts the material life under its monopoly. It becomes the biggest power of society. When they unite, the nation-state becomes the new version of the old god-king state. In order for society to embrace it there is a need for mythology (or philosophy and all its vulgar forms during the capitalist era). Nationalism fulfills this need perfectly and European societies finally attain an official representation for their four-hundred-year-old ideological quest: national societies. Nationalism reinforces the nation and the nation reinforces nationalism, and both reinforce the state. The state, on the other hand, reinforces the economic monopoly and so the modern era becomes certain (although, of course, only within its own temporary period). When the era of the enormous distinction between nationalities and passionate nationalism occur, everywhere Jewish ideology of course both influences and is influenced by it.

It can be easily understood that Jewish ideology had, from its earliest days, a link with tribe and ethnicity and thus with the assertion of tribalism and ethnicity. The oldest nationalism, in terms of tribe and ethnicity, is certainly a fundamental and natural characteristic of Jewish ideology. As ideologies go, Jewish ideology was most easily transformed during the phase of turning into the bourgeoisie. We face another paradox: It is the founding father of the ideology of nationalism, but later it would be rejected by its own new versions. Just as this paradox developed materially it also developed morally and ideologically. All nationalisms began to grind their teeth against their founders. All the nationalists of each European nation began to hold the Jew (ideologically, in terms of material culture and nation-ethnicity) responsible for the problems and obstacles before them. The same is true for Christianity and Islam: although they are of Judaic roots they consider Judaism to be the fundamental obstacle. Here is an issue which confirms my thesis and that has played a major role in the foundation of the civilization. This is the fact that the state, which is the nucleus of the civilization, is itself an economic monopoly. When a new state is formed anywhere it is inevitable that there will be conflicts or wars between the old and the new monopolies. The war must continue until one of them is annihilated, surrenders, or becomes insignificant.

The 3,500 year old proposition of the "Promised Land" for the Jewish tribe once again becomes important as this need is felt intensely in the era of the nation and nationalism in Europe. A new Jewish nation means a new territory. Since Europe is always opposing them, the trend of back to the "Promised Land" is inevitable. This is how the Jewish bourgeois nationalism called Zionism was born. It is a powerful example of nationalism of the nineteenth century, the age of nationalism.

The story continues. But what needs to be discussed briefly is that two strong nations at the time were needed to solve the need for homeland: Germany and England. France had become the third most important state. The Jewish nationalists worked on both these countries. It is widely known how they gave strength to the states of England and the Netherlands, and the Jewish owners of capital had a similar function in Germany. The Jewish intellectuals had made great contributions to the formation of the intellectual capital (German ideology). The German Emperor, in return for their support, visited Jerusalem twice to show his interest in the new homeland movement. Had Germany won World War I, Judaism would have returned to Palestine or its ancient territory earlier and much stronger under the protection of the Germans and Ottomans (the strongest wing of the Progress and Union Committee were pro-German and they were linked to the Thessaloniki Jews and owners of capital).[7] They also had a traditional influence on London as well.

Let us put aside the political history as it is a broad topic. Hitler definitely blamed the Jews for the defeat of Germany: "The superiority of London is not independent of Jewish ideology and nationalism. Germany has been betrayed terribly. The Jews are responsible for it." This is how anti-Jewishness develops in each nation with similar problems (like the Dreyfus Affair in France). But it can of course be proved that this is not the truth. But how can we then explain the existence of such claims worldwide even today? This is indeed related to the function of Jewish ideology and nationalism worldwide. It is still the leading ideology just as it is in the monopolies of capital.

No doubt Hitler cannot be defended. Genocide is the biggest crime against humanity. These are unquestionable and nonnegotiable social and human realities.

The status of Jewish intellectuals in the noble struggles for freedom, as well as an egalitarian and democratic society cannot be belittled. If we leave the prophets aside, we know many of those in the long list of intellectuals and revolutionaries of the modern era, namely Spinoza, Marx, Freud, Rosa Luxemburg, Trotsky, Adorno, Hannah Arendt, and Einstein. I am aware that the democratic socialist dimension of the Jewish intellectuals is quite strong. I will not repeat Adorno's decree but when will they make the necessary criticism and self-criticism of Judaism's material and moral aspects so that objective analytic and political conclusions can be drawn and implemented? If there is no true analysis of Jewish nationalism, both in terms of it being an ideological power and in terms of its leadership, then there can be no true commemoration of the Holocaust and new ones cannot be prevented. Jewish nationalism is not the nationalism of a small nation but world nationalism. It is the father of all nationalisms and nation-statism. Unfortunately, the biggest and unique victim of nationalism in history has also been the Jews. Judaism has been discussed much by the leading Jewish intellectuals such as Marx and Freud. But the question of how we came to the point of genocide is not asked. The commemoration of genocides is closely linked to the prevention of other genocides. But how are we to achieve this? Let me formulate all the conclusions I arrived at on the basis of the Jewish example:

The Jewish tribe wanted to emulate the Sumerian and Egyptian civilizations but in response they were exiled. The persistent small tribe (as if to lead what all the other tribes wanted to really do) constructed its own tribal ideology (religion) out of jealousy. They established the Kingdom of Jerusalem only to see it destroyed. They became even more persistent and spread all over the world. They then began to look for a place to settle first as tribe then as a people. Nobody would give them land and they were once again forced into exile. In order not to be defeated they turned to the atom and space. This tribe now aspired to the leadership of the civilization with its small nation-state. Although the Jews midwifed the Middle East and even the world civilization, these may destroy the Jewish civilization and state. But that would be their own end as well, because the small Jewish civilization is indeed the essence of world civilization. Without world civilization, there would have been no Jewish civilization and indeed without Jewish civilization there would not have been a world civilization. This is the conclusion at which I arrive when I think about the genocide.

Just as I often think about similar incidents, I always think about this incident as well. It is of great importance. The sages have always said that fire cannot be extinguished by fire. One cannot attain liberation by lighting small fires of civilization (nation-states, and in general, monopolies) from the civilizational fire. The leaders of all the poor people of the tribes, ethnicities as well as the oppressed and slaves who fought against the powers of the civilization throughout the history were either killed or they were victorious. The memory of those who died shall never be forgotten. But the very first thing the winners did was to set themselves up as a civilization. This is because they knew no better. Even the victorious leaders of scientific socialism could not but establish a system similar to that of capitalist modernity's iron cage. Those who were subjects of genocides never thought they would be subjects of such things. But it did happen.

At this point I understand the victims of the genocide much better than those who are against genocide. Why do I understand it much better than even the Jews? This is because the very same system has placed me under the very same machinery. But at the same time, it was the Jewish elite power that was behind this machinery. If it was not for the power struggle of that ideology and its power to create a civilization, could there have ever been anything like Christianity? And if there was no Christianity would Hitler exist? German nationalism generated Hitler, but its roots go back to the German ideology and therefore to Enlightenment ideology (that is positivism and biologism). Jewish ideology and Jewish nationalism have played their role in the Enlightenment. Thus, German nationalism is in a dialectical relationship with the Jewish ideology and nationalism (the common root is Enlightenment). Just as Jewish tribalism and ethnicity forms the roots of Jewish nationalism, German tribalism and ethnicity forms the roots of German nationalism. Their intertwined development in Germany (German nationalism and Jewish nationalism) have resulted in intricate relations between them because of the economic and political monopolies. All these historical and social developments clearly reveal the link between the two nationalisms. If both nationalisms are not overcome, then the victims of Holocaust cannot be meaningfully commemorated and new versions of genocides cannot be avoided.

Similarly, we can compare Arabic ideology and nationalism to Jewish ideology and nationalism. The conclusions drawn will be striking and dialectical. If Jewish ideology and nationalism had not existed, would Islam? And if there were no Islam, would there be Muhammad the prophet? Had he not existed would there be the Ba'ath Party and, accordingly, Saddam Hussein? I may be accused of tautology but my statements have come through the filter of my analysis of civilization. The USA is a world power, a hegemon. It may even turn into an empire. It is now fighting in the Middle East for Israel. It may even fight with Iran later. Once again there is the threat of genocide, but this time it will be perpetrated with nuclear weapons. To prevent a nuclear war with a nuclear war! No one can deny that this is the imminent danger, but one Hiroshima was more than enough! I stand by my analysis: When civilization was constructed, it was said to be under the protection of the heavenly gods. As the civilization collapses it takes refuge in nuclear bombs. The forged one is more preferable than the real one. I am talking about the naked kings and their unmasked god walking on earth and its nuclear thunderstorm.

I am one of those who want the Jews—a people with great awareness— to take their place in the Middle East. The Leviathan, which has become a global monster, cannot resolve issues such as the democratization of the Middle Eastern culture, as well as the formation of a democratic confederative Israel and Palestine. This monster, named by the Jews, is the real source of genocide.[8]

The solution lies with democratic Middle Eastern civilization. Just as the Middle East would be in ruins without the Jews, the Jews are always subjected to genocides and exiles without the Middle East. History is full of lessons. The Jewish intellectual becomes increasingly aware that their problem is the world's problem. However, the solution to the problem must be sought in the Middle East. Let us not forget that a Democratic Middle East is not a dream: it is as important as the air we breathe. The Jews should be aware that the only way to commemorate the victims of the genocide and to never fall into new ones depends on the construction of a democratic Middle East civilization, whereas all the Middle Eastern people should be aware that there cannot be a democratic Middle East without the Jews. Hence, we should all be aware that a historical democratic compromise is the only solution and all involved should put their hearts and souls into the construction of the democratic society.

Power in Capitalist Modernity

Concepts such as civilization, power, and state are the most difficult categories of social relations to resolve both in terms of their interrelatedness and in their own right. Civilization is a subject where discussion in relation to its description continues through the present. Any attempt to describe where power began and where it might end, when and how it was formed and should terminate, is even more complex. Although people readily talk about these matters they cannot really reach consensus on their definition. Why is that? This is not only because these are very complex, riddled matters but also because there is a desire to leave them that way. There is much ideological activity aimed at leaving them in the dark. If one wishes to make a topic the subject of fear, then there is a need to leave it in mystery and complexity. If their true faces are revealed, then they will be ridiculed by all and they shall no longer be a factor of fear. As a result, the aspirations of the whitewashed interest groups shall be annulled. Ordinary people can tell many stories about this.

Civilization starts off with its own mythological tales. Interest groups or surplus-product monopolies would only have been able to plunder successfully once or twice if it were not for these stories. For them to be permanent and acceptable there is a definite need for mythologies, religion, and law. Today, however, there is an attempt to seal their permanency and acceptability by making additional use of sex, sports, and arts with the help of media in order to mentally and emotionally condition communities.

I tried to divide civilization into three main periods and characterize each of these periods. I do not hold the method of scientism in high esteem. I have at every opportunity underlined the fact that they could be useful provided that they are limited. If, however, they are dogmatized, then they shall threaten the chance for free life. I took care to implement the method of sociological interpretation without dogmatizing it (with scientism and positivism). The guidelines of my interpretations together with several examples have been presented in such a way that they are open for discussion. I know that I have repeated things at times: I shall try not to do that unless there is a need.

Although I have tried to analyze capitalist modernity (civilization) as the official and victorious modernity (contemporariness) of the new era (from sixteenth century to the present), I have also been very critical of the approaches that attribute our era totally to capitalism and have made comprehensive criticisms in relation to its anti-modernity. I also indicated that although I agree with the definition of modernity made by the sociologist Anthony Giddens, I do not totally share his interpretations when it comes to the "three discontinuities" which are capitalism, nation-state, and industrialism. I presented my analysis of these through extensive interpretations and examples: all three have roots in the early days of civilization and they have attained their strongest position in capitalist modernity. In this section I will try to expose how official modernity has shaped power and state relations more concretely. I make the distinction between official and unofficial modernity (contemporariness), with the latter denoting democratic modernity (civilization or contemporariness).

The positivist sociologists (like Giddens and others like him) think that they make a sociological analysis at each period of the civilizational history when they interpret their civilization to be unique. This can be seen in the case of the English civilization and state. There has been a great deal of research in order to classify this state and civilization as one of its kind. In fact, all they are doing is a very refined distortion, that is, by blurring the forest through focusing on the trees. We cannot effectively define the forest by only evaluating the millions of trees. It is clear that such a method will not give accurate results. But it is not a very bad policy to use thousands of young people in such research to disregard the real characteristic of the system in the name of realizing social sciences. This is how the contents of social sciences or sociology in general are rendered meaningless and drained of its substance.

However, the correct interpretation would be to link the English state, power, and civilization with a development like the state (as class-city-economic monopoly) whose fundamental categorical features are evident for the past five thousand years. The classes that developed around the cities which have revived since the tenth century first became economic state monopolies in the form of kings and aristocrats, and since the sixteenth century in the form of bourgeoisie. They came to power and consolidated their power by making themselves invisible under various ideological patterns or adorned themselves with symbolic values in order to render themselves unrecognizable. One of the early examples of this development is the English state and civilization. The English state and civilization is one of the hegemonic representatives of the main ongoing civilization. I am sure that this definition alone makes more sense than the vast research done on the English web of relations. In terms of substance (disguising fundamental interest groups), there are no real differences between the Sumerian priest's interpretations of society based on the movements of stars and the interpretations made by the thousands of priests of scientism of capitalist modernity. The only difference lies in their method, time, and location.

The difference in time and location means change and development (called universal formation). Societies, too, develop and change in accordance with differences in time and location. At times, it is also possible to go backward. I am not criticizing its state of being unique: there is no development and change in the universe that is not unique. Each change means a uniqueness. "Exactness and repetition" is only a dogmatic belief value. Such words are nothing but a meaningless play of words when it comes to natural developments.

Hence, of course, capitalist modernity has many important uniquenesses. These have been realized in the three important areas that Anthony Giddens has defined them. It may be instructive to conceptualize them as "discontinuities" in this sense. I shall not dwell on capitalism for the moment as I have interpreted it already, but I believe there is a need to summarize what power and the nation-state—the concrete and juridical definition of power—are.

Power has been much talked about in social sciences but it is also a topic that has been heavily distorted. I am not talking about only intentional distortions here. One of the more important uniqueness of capitalist modernity is to make each individual think that they hold power. No other civilization was able to achieve a success with such scope and features in rendering the individual as such.

The sociology of political power still awaits analysis. This is a topic Michel Foucault dealt with greatly, but he was not able to completely expose it. Lenin wanted to define the state in his work called *State and Revolution*. But even while he was alive it became clear that the state was the one point where he was the most mistaken. Moreover, he did not even want to understand what power is. He did not understand that by employing this magical stone (carried by the strong and cunning man by putting on various civilizational masks throughout the ages), he was invalidating socialism from the start in the name of "socialist power." This is because socialism must be built through democratic modernity.

I find the following saying by Mikhail Bakunin to be very meaningful: "If you took the most ardent revolutionary, vested him in absolute power, within a year he would be worse than the Tsar himself." The sociology of power awaits a necessary analysis. It is not only the topic of what power is that awaits analysis, but also whether and to what extent it is needed. According to some mentalities and the interest groups that are disguised under them, absolute power is the ultimate solution. This must have been the historic Assyrian way of thinking: to completely take the life of the target. There are also those, especially the anarchists and pacifists, who view power as the complete state of disorder. According to them one should distance oneself from all kinds of power and authority. Such an understanding is indeed another way of surrendering to power.

The definition and solution proposed by the system of democratic civilization has qualitative differences. The right of each social group to defend itself is sacred. To defend oneself against each attack which aims to destroy the existence of a group or any of its values related to its existence is not just an irrevocable right, it is the basis of the group's existence. I believe that one could not call such a defensive force *power* in its classical meaning. It may be more appropriate to call it the democratic defense force or authority. A rose defends itself through its thorns; let us then call this democratic authority paradigm the "rose theory."

I think it would be most appropriate to define power in relation to civilization as a variety of societal activities aimed at the acquisition, increase, and seizure of surplus-product. If ideological and military activities, deceptive tales, genocides, games of entertainment, and religious rituals are used to squeeze out the surplus-product and value, then it is possible to call all of them activities of power. Hence, power is a very comprehensive area of societal activity. Power, especially in the civilizational societies, has the inclination to continuously grow both in depth and scope in proportion to the increase of surplus-product.

We need to clarify what we mean by surplus-product and value in order to better understand the composition of power. When we analyze the act of seizing the material and immaterial creations and gains of an individual or a group or, indeed, their cultural values in general, then "the thing seized" and "the one who seized it" shall be more concrete. Power is the act and art of seizing things that are not one's own through the use of force, assimilation, and possession. If unsuccessful then it is the art and act of dumping, expelling, and, in general, making it insignificant both materially and immaterially. It would be a narrow approach to limit this to economic surplus-product and value. Here the important thing is to seize it. But, of course, in the process different values are seized and hence it may be more realistic to call the sum of all of them power.

The fundamental function of democratic authority on the other hand is to defend the material and immaterial values which are directly or indirectly linked to the relevant person's or group's existence and not to overlook their seizure; if they are seized they must be claimed back. Hence, it is related to rightful and irrevocable situations. Democratic authority is the art of taking action as described in this context. It may be more correct to call it the power of preventing seizure and its artful action. There is an ontological difference between the use or art of force (army and war) to seize someone's homeland and the prevention of such a seizure. These are antagonistic notions. Society describes such situations through dichotomies such as good and bad, sin and deed, right and wrong, just and unjust, and beautiful and ugly.

It is possible to classify power from various perspectives:

1. Political Power

It is the most used form of power. It denotes the administrative and executive functions of state and its projections (such as political parties and NGOs that are dependent on state). It is the most significant and most used form of power throughout history.

2. Economic Power

It defines the monopolist forces that carry out the seizure of surplus-product and values. Throughout history such seizure has taken place in different forms.

3. Societal Power

It defines the tradition or act of force established by the fundamental societal sections over another. It is distinguished through many important divisions such as family, class, gender, and ethnicity. In a family, it is the father; in class, it is the one who seizes the surplus-value; in terms of gender, it is the male; and, in ethnicity, it is the oppressor who represents the power.

4. Ideological Power

This relates to the mentality of rulers. The individuals and groups who are advanced in science and culture have the status of being the ideological power.

5. Military Power

It is the foremost institution that is identical with power. It is the most excessive, anti-societal, and anti-human form of power. It is the source of all power.

6. National Power

It describes the central power exercised nation-wide. It takes care to depict itself as one and indivisible. This can also be called national sovereignty.

7. Global Power

It describes the hegemony or empire of the dominant civilization and modernity. At present, capitalist modernity makes use of such power under the leadership of USA and together with global economic monopolies and nation-states.

Power is the sum of historical, societal, and institutional relations. Historically, it tries to position and traditionalize itself on the most vital issues and areas of societal development. Traditionalization also means institutionalization. Power is the most institutionalized and elaborate area of societal relations. It is rendered very much functional by those concerned with it. This is why it is vital to ground its institutionalization and formation to some rules of conduct so that it is best represented and its continuity is ensured. For example, the construction, transfer, and handing over and seizure of a sultanate's power are arranged through magnificent symbols, protocols, and ceremonies. From their clothing to food, marriage to death, each relationship has forms that became traditional thousands of years ago. That is the reason why one cannot just become a power through the use of any force: one would be called a bandit or tyrant. But, indeed, the most clear and true essence of power is banditry and despotism. Hence, the exalted and blessed institutions of power find it compulsory to intensely oppose these clear forms of power so that the truth is not understood, and to ensure its own continuity and prestige. It is aware that its legitimacy is secured significantly through these traditions and symbols.

I must remind you of the metaphor I previously mentioned. Power (the knot of interest monopolies that have gained historical quality) may be likened to a snowball that grows and becomes stronger as it falls from the peak of a mountain. This was its course throughout history.

Power may be better understood if we liken it to an infectious disease. Power is contagious. In the beginning this societal disease was exercised over hunted animals, and later over the mother-woman with accumulated knowledge by the *strong and crafty male*. But later this was institutionalized by the trinity of priest (the person who holds the meaning), administrator (the one who administrates the society due to his experience), and military commander to be the hierarchic patriarchal order. With the construction of class and the city it became statist. I must quickly point out that with the construction of state power the hierarchic patriarchal order of the strong and crafty man has not been abolished. The formula for power has changed to equal the total of *strong and crafty man* plus the *hierarchical patriarch* and the *state*. These three fundamental institutions define the *society of power*.

As a general categorization, we call this order civilization with all its multiple upper and lower floors. On the ground floor is the economy and on the upper most floor is the council of gods. This is how the Sumerians built the civilization. Its form has changed but its essence grew whilst preserving its meaning. Throughout time the ground floor belonged to the human material that has been used for the purpose of attaining surplus product, especially the slave, serf, and worker. The craftspeople, farmer, and all the other professions too mainly perform their activities on this floor. The top floor belongs to the mythological gods, the gods of the monotheistic religions (and sometimes their shadows, the sultans, or their messengers, the prophets; the shaman and priests, too). To this floor belongs the ideas and laws (Plato's theory of Forms) that rule.

During antiquity and the Middle Ages, power was often established primarily in the form of these fundamental institutions and especially in the form of the state. However, during capitalist modernity, the whole society became contaminated with power. If we put it another way, the whole society is infected with the idea that they have power. What's more important is that, although power becoming widespread through the use of institutions (called "discontinuities" by Anthony Giddens) is a state of illness, it is essentially unique to capitalist modernity. Some ideologies and institutions play a decisive role in this. In the next section I will set out my thoughts in more detail.

Just because the whole of society gets contaminated with power does not mean that it has become very strong. It also means that it has become desperate, miserable, and approaching the final state and speed of its dissolution process. When anything reaches its end two things can happen: Either the relevant people do something about it, or if not, then that thing shall rot. It may be a coarse analogy but when an apple reaches its most mature stage it should be picked from its tree. If this is not done, eventually the apple will rot and decay. This is also the case with power. The phenomenon of power was already a state of illness when established but now it is just about at the decaying phase in capitalist modernity. Just as Bakunin had pointed out; power has decayed so badly that it will make the most ardent and morally strong person ill. He is right, even if the most oppressed of all, the woman, was vested in such decaying power she, too, would turn to a dictator within 24 hours. The only way to avoid such a decay or illness is to build democratic modernity as a system.

Capitalist Modernity and Nation-State

The notion of nation-state has not only been left in obscurity but it has also more often than not been distorted. Any effort to determine its main role and real function is resolutely avoided. It can be said that it is mainly used for propaganda. Special effort is made to disguise the ontological link between fascism and nationalism especially. This is similar to the omission of the subsidiary link between fascism and nationalism with that of official modernity. This is not unique to bourgeois liberals. The socialists, too, are either defensive when it comes to the nation-state or evade it by making it sound as if it is trivial. But nation-state is indeed one of the key concepts to understand and change our era. I found Antony Giddens to be quite illuminating because he put forth the importance of the nation-state, albeit inadequately.

The issues I tried to set out thus far may also be viewed as preparation to define nation-state and elucidate its function. Without defining the factors influencing the birth of capitalism, modernity, power, nation and state, at least a little, it would not have been possible to determine the role of nation-state. There was also within this framework a need to present the Jewish question under some main topics. Just as the analysis of nation-state is a key concept in the resolution of present societal problems, in order to resolve the question of the nation-state, it is quite instructive to analyze the Jewish question in the context of civilizations both historically and societally. If we do not understand the Jewish question and nation-state, then any meaning and commemoration given to the victims of the Holocaust will be incomplete and inaccurate and that is quite wrong. The current tragedy of the Middle East confirms these evaluations many times over.

The nation-state is the form in which capitalist monopolism comes true. Even during the sixteenth century, the necessary state form needed in Netherlands and England to destroy the Spanish and French empire's aspirations was a sort of proto nation-state. The Princedom of the Netherlands and the English Kingdom tried to attain superiority by evolving into nation-states. When in 1648 the Peace of Westphalia was signed amongst the states the nationality factor gained prominence and this in turn accelerated the development of the nation-state. The states based themselves on mercantilism as their political economy. This was another factor that sped up, enhanced, and gave prominence to the national market. National language, arts, and historical research were increasingly put under the monopoly of the state. Various disagreements and wars between nations could no longer be carried out without power in the form of nationalism and nation-state. The Napoleonic wars played a leading role in this regard. Napoleon could not have waged war if France had not been turned into a nation-state. The German ideologists who were following the developments closely found in the personage of Napoleon all that they needed for the creation of German nationalism and a nation-state. The rapidly developing German nationalism would now provide the leverage needed to unite Germany and create the state sought by modernity. The process that would later breed Hitler would begin at the onset of the nineteenth century.

In fact, these issues are of course much deeper. They are linked to the roots of capitalist modernity (civilization). This movement, which harbored the economic monopoly's quest for success at its core, did not just distort the national development but it had to nationalize all the factors that would constitute a nation. In the absence of the nationalization of religion, the economic monopoly would not have easily dominated the market. The nationalization of culture and arts is linked to the similar monopolist position. The nationalization of wars will constitute the last but most important factor. The nationalization of all these factors gives birth to the national spirit that results in nationalism. The work of ideologists on nation and state had long ago prepared the intellectual ground for them. Obviously, all these factors were the work of national markets and the monopolist capitalism that fought over these markets and imposes itself to the very end.

The Industrial Revolution accelerated all these processes. Industrialization gradually produced more surplus-value than trade and as a result it began to constitute the fundamental issue that would be subjected to nationalization. The national industry meant the most profit for capitalists in a certain nation. The nineteenth century was significant because of this. Industrialism, as an ideology, is closely linked to having a nationality. It is not possible to distinguish nationalism from that of industrialism as it becomes the favorite ideology and power of political action of the nineteenth century. The trade bourgeoisie does not have the capacity to sustain a nation on its own and mercantilism is far from forming an economic monopoly that could lead a nation on its own. The bourgeoisie, which expanded its capacity quite a lot because of industrial monopolies, began to feel that it had the right to represent the whole nation. It re-wrote its own history and clarified its philosophical tendencies. It made national culture part of its own history. It left its mark on the national army and national education. Capitalism's nationwide victory and concomitant domination was here to stay, especially through the national industrial bourgeoisie.

The concept of bourgeois revolution can only be meaningful if all such processes are included. Despite the contrary belief, the singular English, French, and similar revolutions cannot be considered to be planned bourgeois revolutions. What the bourgeoisie did was to exploit it to serve its own interests. It is also wrong to think that the Industrial Revolution is a victory for the bourgeoisie. This revolution, too, is the consequence of a huge historical accumulation.

What we have here is simply the appropriation of this area, just as was the case with other areas, by the selfish and monopolist bourgeoisie imposing its interests. Just as economy is a social area that does not require the bourgeoisie, the industry is also an economic area that does not require an industrial bourgeoisie in advance. What the trade monopolists did was to appropriate this area that brought in more profits than commerce had. None of the real revolutionaries were bourgeois. The bourgeoisie is not to be found in either the theoretical or practical preparations of the Industrial Revolution. It was the most important leap by economy within the rhythm of historical and social development. It may be compared to the agricultural revolution of the Neolithic period. The economic production, which develops at every stage of history, turns the state (in essence economic monopoly) and its collaborators into new monopolies that impose themselves over the new productive area. These new monopolies do not hesitate to use force when necessary and are most ambitious and reckless. The material basis of the nation-state is indeed found in these monopolies, and if they are not they are to be created.

The mid-nineteenth century was a turning point in history: There would either be a victory for the centralist nation-state of the bourgeoisie or the democratic confederate movement of all sections of the society that were left outside of that new monopoly and aristocracy. These two inclinations were essential to the 1640 and 1688 English Revolutions, and to the 1789 French Revolution (although there was no obvious distinction between the revolutionary forces). The Levellers in the English Revolution and the communards in the French Revolution were the representatives of the democratic tendency. But they were later eliminated. The 1848 revolutions were totally popular revolutions and the work of Marx and Engels on the Communist League and Manifesto were significant and historical. The very first strategic loss was the defeat of the revolutions as a result of the betrayal by the bourgeoisie who had compromised with all kinds of reactionary forces. Therefore, the people's spring was short lived and once again the gloomy winter came. The extent to which the bourgeoisie would be revolutionary is linked to its immediate interests. If it were successful, it would have turned its political power into economic monopoly as soon as possible. But instead of losing everything it knew how to protect what it had and to be satisfied with limited gains. The expectations of the old pro-monarchists and aristocracy were also not met. The nation-state, like a sort of balance of power, would strengthen itself even more in this period. The alliance of the economic and political monopolies over the centralist nation-state would determine the period to emerge. The Italian and German nation-states officially declared themselves in 1861 and 1870. The turn of other nation-states would follow.

When the new wave of revolutions was not as expected, Marx stepped aside in London and began his examination of capital. At the time, he also became involved in the First International which was an association. The German communists objectively acknowledged their defeat by basing themselves on (including Marx and Engels) the centralist nation-state. Formation of a program, establishing an organization, development of a strategy and tactics were all taken up through theories of depression and according to the decline of capitalism. Gradually, it ended up reconciling with capitalism against the society under the same patterns of modernity (considering industrialism and nation-state legitimate). It finally turned into a movement that demanded its share from the monopoly called economism. Economism is the acceptance of economic and nation-state programs of the industrial monopolies. The Soviet Revolution, like those before it, could not escape becoming an instrument of the monopolist state capitalism and its nation-state program. The Chinese Revolution, too, after a long period of turmoil, followed the same path to a Chinese nation-state and Chinese monopolist capitalism, and global monopoly reached a compromise.

National liberation revolutions are revolutions with a more superficial modernist mindset having readily accepted industrialization and nation-state as their ultimate program. Although there may be many examples of real-socialist attempts amongst them, their mutual program was the same. The fundamental reason for the failure of the one hundred and fifty year old movement in the name of scientific socialism was its inability to surpass the Enlightenment's modernity and to show the strength to form and implement the theoretical, programmatic, strategic and tactical aspects of democratic modernity. In fact, it has not even shown such an intention. All these indicators unite in determining this movement's bourgeois characteristics, restricted horizons, and its ease in surrendering to the system.

On the other hand, the anarchists had raised their protests in that period. Bakunin, Proudhon, and Kropotkin especially had significant criticisms and program proposals. But because they could not organize themselves, had ideological shortfalls, a superficial knowledge of the society, and a pro individual action stance, they could not become a political alternative. Their intervention in the historical process that was going on at the time did not achieve the required success. The real weakness of both tendencies was their total embrace of the Enlightenment philosophy and dogmatic devotion to positivist scientism. Failure was more dependent on ideological reasons than anything else. Murray Bookchin seems to make a better diagnosis in relation to the developments in the societal arena when he says that although the democratic confederation tendency of the urban and rural laborers of Europe up until 1850s was strong, this chance was lost altogether as socialists surrendered to the idea of centralist nation-state.

The great philosopher Nietzsche (it would be right to call him the strongest oppositional prophet of the capitalist era) was the first to notice the dangers associated with the 1870 declaration of the German nation-state. As everyone, including the social-democrats, was applauding he could see the great loss of humanity in this. If I am not mistaken, the substance of his analysis amounts to this: as the state becomes a god, the laborers and individuals become ant-like, and this in turn results in a castrated and housewifized society.

Critique of citizenship by Proudhon is even more striking: it is as if he was able to predict the present-day individual. Max Weber defines the society under the influence of modernity as "the society enclosed in iron cage." There are other grislier descriptions made by the world of literature. As society is squeezed under the nation-state trap similar interpretations will increase. But all these criticisms and projections are far removed from being a concrete analysis of society and its freedom program. The resistance of peoples and intellectuals from the sixteenth to the end of twentieth century cannot be compared to any other time in history. They had many temporary successes. But if the global hegemony of capitalism in the era of financial monopoly is up on its feet with all its might, then this means the democratic modernity tendency has not rid itself of its deficiencies and the faults in its analysis, program, strategy, organization, and line of action.

The three main factors of modernity should be analyzed giving equal wait to each. The important and un-postponable task is to carry out the main factors of democratic modernity with great intellectual enlightenment and all types of societal movements on this basis and as an alternative. The critique of capitalism, albeit with inadequacies, has been done excessively. This is why we should point the tip of the arrow to the nation-state and complete it with a critique of industrialism. This continues to be an important task presently in the monopolist financial era and preserves its importance in the struggle for a democratic, free, and egalitarian society. And I am trying to accomplish what befalls our share.

We see quite clearly now that all kinds of nationalism act as bonding agents in the formation and sustaining of nation-states. I would like point out that I define nationalism as an ideological element with a unique role. It may be more appropriate to call it religionization of positivist-secular ideology. In the early stages of the system, positivism and secularism played a positive role in overcoming the traditional dogmatism although they are far removed from the mentality of democratic modernity. They have contributed to the development of scientific interpretation. But the system since mid-nineteenth century, as with all civilizations, ideologically slipped into religiousness because on the one hand it had attained its political and economic victory, and on the other there was the continuous threat of democratic action. Such a need was fulfilled by nationalism.

It may be more instructive and essential to try to make a more concrete and detailed analysis of nation-state after such introductory remarks:

A more comprehensive definition of nation-state would be the combination of tools of power which have been spread across the whole of society with that of individuals (citizens) within a legal framework. The determinative concept here is "power that has been spread across the whole of society." The legitimacy of all the prior states was limited to their own cadres and institutions. With the nation-state, such a restriction is surpassed. The essence of nation-state is to incorporate the citizens or the individuals it wishes to create in terms of its own ideological, institutional, and economic interests into the state as if they were members of the state with rights and duties. The formation of the citizen is a priority for the nation-state. In order to achieve such a citizen many factors are used and from which benefits are drawn, such as ideology, politics, economics, law, culture, gender, military, religion, education, and media.

The most influential tool is nationalism. It has the value of being a new religion. Nationalism attributes a sacredness of "the image of God on earth" to the nation-state. The requirements of this new religion include being devoted to the state to the death, and to embrace it as the most valuable thing.

In order to turn the individual into a citizen, the appeal and influence of political power is used intensely. Political parties specifically work towards this end. Entering the services of power and to say "the state is mine" is the shortcut for security and reputation of the individual.

The state's economic monopoly characteristic became more widespread with the Industrial Revolution and as a result industrial monopolism also developed further. Thus, nearly half of society is employed as workers or state servants within the state institutions. This situation alone pushes the majority of society to compete with one another in order to be a member or citizen of the nation-state. It is really difficult to distinguish the so-called private monopolies from those of the nation-state. Both form a very close unity and partnership. It is really hard to distinguish where the state and private monopoly begin and end. As the private monopolies give some of their profits to the state, the state in turn provides them with unlimited conveniences in the form of modern tax farming. Therefore, at times the turning of an individual into a citizen by the private monopolies can be more backward than that done by the state. This is because it becomes easier to mold the individual as desired when they are threatened with unemployment. These are some reasons why unions have lately become so conservative and pro nation-state. Laborers have almost been turned into being the militants of nation-state with the practice of real-socialism.

The bond between citizenship and law is quite clear. Each individual wishing to take care of his or her own needs must have an identification card. This in itself means being a citizen of a state, the symbolic expression of being a member of a state.

The consciousness or tradition of state and power kept alive throughout history clearly makes significant contributions to the formation of citizenship.

The influence of sexism is also due to the perception of the father as the representative of state at home. At home, each man equals the state before the women. Such a perception is also true in terms of the whole of society. The nation-state tries to further educate and adapt this perception to suit itself.

The military institution is at the top of the list of those state institutions where the nation-state is engraved as the most fundamental value upon the emotions and consciousness of the individual. Each institution of the nation-state has a similar function but none of them can attain the role played by the military institution.

Religion has been used most often by nationalism during the process of becoming a nation-state and is a tool that has been turned into a nation-state religion. Religion has been both nationalized and made nationalistic. Thus, religion has become a societal institution in conflict with its moral essence during the nation-state period. The religion of sections of the society that are left outside the influence of secular nationalism is integrated with nationalism; so the individual has become reintegrated with the new form of the ancient God, as its conscious or unconscious servant. This is a kind of internal betrayal for religion. The conflict between religion and secularism is closely related to this betrayal.

The most influential institution of modernity for turning the individual into a citizen is education. It competes with the military institutions in this respect. The historical society continues its development and change by becoming different. The values formed by historical society are put through the filter first of religionism and then nationalism for the benefit of capitalist modernity. The educational institution's main target is to use these to mold the most stupefied citizen within its pot of official ideology. In this way, a citizen is created; fanatical adherence has superseded the medieval scholastics.

Media is the most influential brain washing and heart winning tool. The apparatus of the media makes it much easier for the nation-state to create the desired citizen. The media is at its the best when presenting sex, sports, and arts, removing all its substance and thereby creating a very stupid, dull and lethargic citizen.

Through the use of these methods and tools the type of citizen created is incomparable to any other period in history. This citizen's real aim in life is to have a car, a family (to find a husband or a wife, to have one or two children), and to own a house; in other words, to become a daily standard consumer. The meaning of sociality can be easily brushed aside for menial selfish ambitions. The citizen's memory is wiped out and consequently it is detached from history as well. History is thought to be nothing but all about chauvinistic national clichés. The citizen has no philosophy and does not believe in the existence of any other philosophy of happiness than narrow pragmatism. In appearance, the citizen looks modern. However, at issue is the individual of the "herd of citizens," "mass society," or, indeed, lack of individuality that has been created and prepared to work for the most obscure aspirations (such as fascism) which are hollow and devoid of substance.

Many excellent novels and many famous authors tell of the role played by this type of citizen as fascism arises. Such novels which analyze genocides are very instructive indeed. The more recent critique made under the influence of postmodernism on "citizenship" is also quite enlightening.

The main obstacles facing democratic modernity are the nation-state and its society as they generate this type of citizen. Therefore, the most important duty of democratization is to analyze the nation-state and the society that produces such a lack of individuality (where the individual is considered non-existent) and to raise egalitarian, free, and democratic individuals (free citizens) who can construct the democratic civilization.

It is important to see the ontological tie between the nation-state and fascism. One of the most fundamental errors made in relation to fascism is not seeing or explaining its relationship with the nation-state systematics or avoiding it even when it is most obvious. But even this draft analysis shows fascism's fundamental relationship with the Enlightenment ideology (including positivist secularist ideologies). The main power form of official modernity is nation-state and its new religion is nationalism. Societies that have gone through the filter of nation-state nationalism are societies that are constantly ready to produce fascism. It is not possible to imagine fascism without the nation-state. In turn, it is not possible to envisage nation-state in the absence of economic monopolism (that is, trade, industry, and finance).

It is not so difficult to find the roots of Hitler's fascism in German ideology. The only way for the German bourgeoisie to advance was to concentrate on becoming a monopoly on the basis of a nation-state. The most important work and success of the German bourgeoisie and ideologists were to produce this type of state both ideologically and materially throughout the nineteenth century. But this is a long story which I am not about to tell. The contribution made by Jewish capital and ideologists to this cannot be belittled either.

The German model later was to become a source of inspiration for all other nationalisms and nation-state movements. The most important weakness of all the anti-fascists, but especially that of socialists, was their inability to notice the systematic bond between nation-state, monopolies (state and private monopolies), and fascism. Moreover, the ontological bond between capitalist modernity in general and fascism had not been determined.

Another topic which preserves its significance and awaits an analysis is the question of nation-state and the Soviet Union. The source of all problems was the German centralist nation-state but it had come to be seen as the fundamental framework of struggle for the working class even during the period of Marx and Engels. Marx and Engels held the view that the democratic confederative formations based on strong urban and rural rebellions in Germany up until the mid-nineteenth century were backward, and that instead of supporting them the centralist nation-state should be supported. I think the criticism and views of Bakunin and Kropotkin on this matter are still topical. This finding by Marx and Engels is the fundamental reason behind the miscarriage-like birth of the First and Second International. There is an objective alliance established with German industrial bourgeoisie, a matter openly written about. The consequence was to dissolve within the nation-state. The one hundred and fifty years old story of Marxism is the story of being a victim of such an error.

The proofs to this are the Soviet experience and today's China. The democratic structure of the Soviet Union had been terminated before the onset of 1920. Hence, all they were left to do was to build a socialist construction in a single country using the nation-state model. In order to achieve this all opposition was eliminated, peasants who were a democratic force were destroyed and intellectuals were silenced. The system constructed was nothing but a modern *Pharaoh Socialism*.

They did not even think of democratic modernity, moreover, they prevented it. Such a democracy also had a miscarriage-like birth and came on the agenda only after the 1990s. I would not find it appropriate to call Stalin's practice fascism compared to Hitler's fascism which existed at the same time. These are movements that originated from different approaches. However, history shows us that the Soviet experiment was not socialism and that if socialism is to be realized it must be based on democratic civilization. Mao did have an interest in democracy and his criticism of the Soviet Union is of importance. The Cultural Revolution in China is a proof that something went wrong. However, neither his knowledge nor tools and methods were strong enough to surpass the Marxist error or the Soviet experience. Today's China clarifies many things.

Many of the national liberation movements evolved with real-socialist political intention and had accepted the aim of nation-state in their programs. The realized model can only stand on its two feet if there is an alliance with the main capitalist monopolies such as the USA, EU, IMF, and the World Bank. Therefore, it should not surprise us to see their structures to be increasingly anti-democratic and conservative.

One of the most tragic examples is the Ba'ath socialism of Saddam Hussein: it is the perfect example. The "welfare state" of the social democrats is no different to the nation-state. The German social-democrats, who are also the leaders in the world when it comes to this, continue to secure their strong positions by attaining huge profits through their economism in contrast to the damage done by Hitler to their nation-state. But this was in exchange for emasculating the world democratic movement and turning it into a backup of their own bourgeoisie!

Another grave consequence of the nation-state is the destruction, elimination, and assimilation of cultural heritage incomparable to any other period in history. One of the more distinguishing characteristics of the nation-state is that it basis itself on a dominant nation-ethnicity and ignores all the other ethnicities together with their thousands of years old cultures (one language, one nation, one land, and one state was Hitler's main slogan), and then to destroy, eliminate, and assimilate it. Its main cultural policy is to create citizens and institutions that are alike. There was also an attempt to practice Darwinism or biologism, which was intended to be applied to the society. Here we have one of the gravest sins of positivism: It considers the strongest culture's dissolution of all the other cultures a rule of evolution. But this is only possible if you eliminate or ignore millions of years of evolution of the human being!

Nowadays culture has become shallower than ever before and it has lost all its fascination, revelation, and inspiration. This is due to the damage done by the nation-state. Thousands of languages, tens of thousands of tribes, clans, peoples, archaeological heritage, different lifestyles, and indeed many cultures have all but become the victim of this policy of cultural genocide. It is as yet not clear if and when the nation-state will stop this. The nation-state, nation-individual, and nation-society (which represent nothing but uniformity) do not just generate fascism but also take the productivity out of life. It enters into a process of behaving like a beast that continuously seeks new targets to fight with. The consequence of all this is the complicated ethnic, religious, linguistic, and other cultural wars. The present time is wracked by such wars. Hitler is the symbolic value and beginning of this culture of war, and this symbolism is at this moment turning into reality. For those who wish to know, the situation in Iraq is a golden opportunity to learn from.

The nation-state cannot be evaluated just as a political and military war movement, as seen during the Second World War period against states and prominent cultures. It is a massive social war movement against all historical and societal tradition and other promising things, as well as all new formations that are different. Single nation, single state, single language, single homeland, and the existence of many other "single" concepts are engraved within the logic of its establishment. Hence, this is nothing but a continuous, albeit at times open and at other times disguised, state of war on all fronts.

The nation-state is also careful to develop uniformity when it comes to politics. Just as there is no room for different national identities, there is also no room for different political formations either. What is meant by centralized state, or indeed unitary structure, is to render it impossible to participate in politics on the basis of their differences (a fundamental condition of democratization). It considers this a threat to the integrity of the state. It is even suspicious of giving minimum authority to the local governments. The central bureaucracy constitutes its main power base and bulk, as the nation-state is the state that is created by the modern bureaucracy. The whole society is kept under surveillance, in an iron cage. The fundamental provision laid for all the parties and NGOs is to act in accordance with state policies. Therefore, different political, social, cultural, and economic organizations and their development (pluralism—an essential principle of democracy) are seen as a source of threat and are constantly monitored. Hence, they are not allowed to form an alternative and take their place within the governance. The nation-state, because of how it is structured, is against political plurality and is therefore anti-democratic. The reason that democratic and socialist (real socialism and others) concepts do not develop and are being eliminated is because they either defend the nation-state or surrender to it. If the nation-state and democracy, as two separate units, can reach a compromise based on principles then one can talk about the presence of a structure that is open to democracy.

The nation-state does not create a uniform mentality and emotions on the individual alone but also instills them on all the societal structures. As a result, it is able to spread its power to the whole of society but it can also create a uniform society: the nation-state society. It aims to form a corporatist (fascism's model) society. One should not misunderstand their concept of society's hold of power. The opposite is true. The nation-state positions its agent individuals and institutions into all the pores of the society in order to multiply its power in depth and width. Herding society can only be realized through such a method. Indeed, the spread of power in society means war against the society. This does not mean that the society holds the power. Foucault finds this issue important. The dominant male plays this role, as agent institution, against the woman. And, thus, societal sexism is spread all over society like a plague through the use of sexual policies. A war against society is waged in this manner. Especially women are thoroughly enslaved. For women to think that becoming a man is to become free is nothing but a defeated womanhood and a very profound one indeed!

Sports and arts, in terms of their function in society, also serve the nation-state and they have been turned into effective agent institutions in the war against society. I refer specifically here to popular cultural and sports programs as these are widely used to serve this purpose. The essence of sex, sports, and arts is drained deliberately by global capital so that they can be turned into effective instruments of war against society. This analysis is not about the existence of sex, sports, and arts. On the contrary, democratic civilization should, as a fundamental task, ensure that these, as the greatest ethical values, serve to benefit society.

Although sport was a tool of education for a healthy society it has now been reduced to being the state's tool for honor and reputation. It has become trapped in an impasse of triumph and defeat as if in a war and hence turned into a tool of war in the hands of power. Football specifically is used in such a way, as a power monopoly, by nation-states. Sports have become nation-statist and turned into an effective arena of war against society.

Art is the second most important area for both state and private monopolies to wage societal war. Entertainment, especially through the use of pop and arabesque culture, is effectively used to capture society, as if there is an attack by an army of stars against society. Classical arts have been disgraced, folk culture has been removed from its real function by being popularized and now playing a totally opposite role, that is, a role in its own elimination. Sex or sexuality has been turned into an object of war against society like never before in human history. Sex is the most effective tool in the war against society.

I hope to have an in-depth discussion on this topic in my next volume, *The Sociology of Freedom*. But let me just say that for each male the sexual act has been turned into an act of power. The sexual act has been distorted or detached from having a biological function, an act for the continuation of life and its own species and has been turned into having a function of unlimited reproduction and spread of dominant male power in both the societal and political arena. The sexual act has been transformed into an act of power. In all homo, hetero, and other kinds of sexual relationships, such a relationship of power plays a determinant role. Although sexuality has a prevalent historical background, there has been no other form of society and state than the nation-state and its society where sex has been reproduced in depth and scope and implemented so systematically and widespread for the purposes of attaining power and hence for the purposes of enslavement. Societal sexism is in fact the relations and a phenomenon of societal and political power.

The nation-state has perverted power because of the policies implemented in relation to sexuality both within and outside the family. Women see themselves as a commodity of sex and men make themselves tools of sexual power. Not only does this lead society into a moral crisis, but they turn both themselves and to the society victims of the power struggle.

The most effective tool of waging a war in these three areas (sports, art, and sex) is the media. No other tool than the media (which is under the control of the monopolies) have played such a destructive role in the war waged against the society. On the other hand, it is without doubt that it has the capacity to be a very effective tool of democratization if it is utilized by democratic civilization.

The nation-state has diligently created policies in respect to prisons and hospitals, and these play an important role for the strengthening of its power and to capture society. Those who end up in prisons and hospitals face losing much of their material and immaterial values in the face of such power.

Indeed, as the nation-state imposes its power on the whole of society, even down to the smallest detail, it at the same time admits that it has come to the end. A power that has attained such scope and size cannot escape crashing. What is needed is to spread and implement the concepts of effective democratization, organization, and action of the democratic civilization to all areas of society.

The nation-state indeed backs the middle class and is based on the middle class. It is theoretically but not practically possible for it to develop any another way. The nation-state is the modern God of the middle class. It lives in its own mentality and passion with the dream of reuniting (through attainment of task and benefit) with this God. Just as society would worship the ancient gods without really knowing what they were, today's modern middle class too does not really know its own god (in terms of capitalist modernity). But it is also aware that it has no other alternative. A position within its bureaucracy or monopolies means salvation. It thinks society is merely made up of itself. It is a very selfish class. Liberals view the middle class as a fundamental pre-condition for democracy. But the contrary is true. Middle classes are a reservoir from which fascism, not democracy, compiles its ingredients from. Just as the relationship between fascism and the nation-state is structural, the relationship between fascism and middle class is also structural. The judgment about the middle class cannot change just because fascism has structural relations with capitalist monopoly. The presence of exceptions just verifies the main trend.

Liberal democracy aims to drain the substance of democracy by trying to attain supremacy over the real democratic forces of society by supporting the middle class in this great game called democracy. The liberal bourgeoisie and liberal democrats can only play a positive role, as left-wing, if there is a strong democratic development but one must guard against the perversion of the middle class. Capitalism is quite experienced in using the middle class against the democratization struggle of society. It continuously frightens the middle class by pointing at the lower sections of society, as well as gives concessions and awakens the imagination in its execution of internal policies. We can thus say that the nation-state is an intensified war of the middle-class. The nation-state, within this context, is also the god of war of the middle-class which understands, envisages, and worships the nation-state as such. The democratic forces have no other option but to create their own mindset and action against this god and the war it has intensified. The only option and most sacred alternative against this god is free life itself!

It may be enlightening to compare the nation-state to other forms of state in order to understand the possible different models. The nation-state must not be equated to a republic either as a concept or as an institution. Not all republics are nation-states and even monarchies can also be nation-states. Some republics can turn into nation-states. But republics are more receptive to democracy. Its relationship with society is not the same as that of nation-state and there is more of a distance between itself and monopolies. A republic is a regime of alliance and compromise, whereas nation-state is a regime of one-sided imposition and formation of society. Republic is aware and careful about its alliances and society's equilibrium. But the nation-state disrupts all alliances and equilibriums, thus becoming unrivaled and maximizing the central authority. It also aims to dissolve all the different political, social, economic, and cultural values and perspectives. A republic can be shared by many; different views, cultures, ethnicities, political institutions, local and regional governments can exist under the roof of a republic. But the mindset and structure of nation-state are against these differences and their unity.

There are three models that are talked about most when it comes to nation-states. The French example is the initial nation-state model. The birth place of nation-state is France and its creator and god, Napoleon. It is based on a political identity. By strengthening the political and juridical arenas they form a traditional approach which prevents them slipping into German-type fascism. They are not so narrow-minded when it comes to race and dominant ethnicity. Anyone who participates in the French language and culture can take part in the French nation-state. It has followers all over the world and the Turks have been inspired by this model.

The German model is based on the culture unique to the German nation and this is the underlying precondition both for citizenship and nation-state. The fact that it is more prone to descend into fascism is closely related to the way in which the German nation-state developed. The German nation-state has influenced the world, including the Turks. The Germans are trying to make this model prevail.

The English example is the more flexible one. They do not base themselves on a political unity like the French or on cultural unity like the Germans. The English state is an example of a nation-state that is more receptive to different political formations and cultures.

Probing into the nation-state in terms of its timeline is important in order to understand the changes and development that it underwent. Although I have constantly emphasized that it is the main state form of capitalist modernity, we will not fully understand its role unless we look at its historical development.

The nation-state came on the agenda because the Netherlands and England embarked on a quest for a more effective state in order to shatter the imperial ambitions of Spain and France. The nation-state increasingly proved its financial and political superiority over the former political and military structures. This was especially true for military innovation. First, they achieved naval superiority. By the end of the sixteenth century, the Spanish hegemony at sea, had passed over to the Netherlands and England. In the early 1700s, these countries also proved their superiority on land after the battles with France and Spain. But the French and Austrian dynasties would not abandon their imperial ambitions. They paid dearly for it. They were losing their chance to be a nation-state. In addition, their state structures were financially more costly.

The Netherlands and England politically supported the construction of nation-states against imperial ambitions. In particular, it was an effective policy to put the Prussian state as a strong nation-state up against Austria and France. Another effective policy was to continuously support all of the opposing forces in Europe, as well as all those seeking a nation-state, to wear their rivals out. It looked quite impossible for their rivals to deal with the emerging nation-states. The Peace of Westphalia was the result of such developments. The Europe of nation-states was gaining ground and having an edge over the imperial Europe. The aim of England during the French Revolution was to topple the king who would refuse a compromise and back his opponents. England supported anyone that had a conflict with the king. Therefore, in this sense (but of course not totally), the French Revolution was a conspiracy by England. But the transition from monarchy to republic, and under Napoleon to a nation-state, thwarted their plans. England narrowly escaped from the hands of Napoleon. Moreover, its Prussian policy also faced a similar result.

A construction similar to that of the Napoleonic model is seen in the Republic of Turkey. When England supported the pro-English opposition against the pro-German faction of the Committee of Unity and Progress, Mustafa Kemal came out as the winner in what was almost a repeat of the Napoleonic example. Both the pro-German and pro-English opponents lost. This, like other similar English political experiments, requires careful examination.

The triumph of the nation-state became clear with the unification of Italy in 1861 and Germany in 1871. The hegemonic war became the war between England and Germany. The forty-five years from 1870 to 1914 were a period in which both sides tried to establish an alliance. The First World War dealt a serious blow to the hegemonic aspirations of Germany, but the Second World War was more like a war of revenge with the consequentially severe destruction of the German nation-state.

With the October Revolution of 1917 Russia wanted to fill the hegemonic vacuum left by Germany. To succeed in doing this the Soviets were rapidly turned into a nation-state. But the alliance of the experienced England with that of the USA quickly annulled the hegemonic desires of Russia, just like it did with France and Germany. The official dissolution of the USSR in 1991 meant the end of its hegemonic claims. The three-hundred-year-old English hegemony was turned over to the USA in 1945 in return for remaining its smaller ally. The policy of support for national liberation struggles by the Soviets against the hegemony of the USA was the result of Cold War from 1949 to 1989. The Cold War between the USA and USSR was the golden age for nation-states as the tension between them prepared the ground for the birth of many nation-states. The period of nation-states was completed by 1914 in Europe and by 1970 all over the world. The Second World War was the first serious crisis of the European nation-states. The EU was born as the product of this crisis.

It may be appropriate to add another reason for capitalist modernity developing the nation-state as a model. This model does not easily allow for empire-like formations. If empires had triumphed the chances of the capitalist monopolies would have been as that of medieval times. That is why they declared an all-out war against the four big imperial ambitions; the imperial ambitions of Spain (1500–1600), France (1600–1870), Germany (1871–1945), and Russia (1945–1990), while the Ottoman and Austrian empires can also be added here. They could only be defeated with nation-state policies.

Although nation-states are called national bourgeois, the reality is that it is a product of capitalist monopolies that are after an international world-system. Even Turkey, which thinks it is a strict nationalist state, could only come into being after the approval of England and in alliance with the USA. Without the international capitalist system, the birth of the nation-state and its development cannot be envisaged. The Soviet and Chinese nation-states are also included in this. The main reason for their formation and development is because they were the best political counterpart for the guaranteed profits of the capital. When they lost these characteristics, they were slowly transformed and they tried to continue their existence under English and later US hegemony. No nation-state can exist for long if it does not comply with the policies of the world-system (capitalist modernity and the hegemon's). The contrary would be against the mentality of the state. Such systems would really struggle to exist or they would collapse, as can be seen from Soviets and China. Even they needed to make compromises in order to exist.

We may therefore now understand the tragic end of Saddam Hussein. He did not or did not want to understand the system. His only chance to exist lay in his transforming Iraq into a comprehensive democratic system. He could not make use of this chance because of his very strong belief in the nation-state god. As he was to be executed, he held the Quran which had the words of the ancient god, and he tragically realized that it did not have the strength to rescue him from the new god of the system. But the god of the system, the Leviathan, is now stuck in the Iraqi swamp. It is in a difficult situation in the whole of the Middle East.

Europe is searching for a new god. Most probably it will build itself a god that is more peaceful and that leaves room for law. The efforts to develop the EU is a reaction to the militant past of Europe, especially that of the Second World War which is the last of the terrible wars experienced during its four hundred years of nationalization and nation-state history. They are trying to correct those exposed destructive aspects of nation-state through evolutionary methods. As a result, a new European citizenship with new thoughts, beliefs and institutions in economic, social, political, and historical areas is being developed. It is a bit like self-criticism. This development needs to be closely followed as we cannot predict the end result. On the other hand, the US showed a radical stance to the nation-state that no longer suits it by destroying Saddam (he can be likened to Louis 16th in terms of the nation-state civilization) and his regime. It may try to re-construct the nation-state more through a federative model (which is the structure of US itself).

The fact that USA is stuck between being a hegemon and an empire shows how difficult of a period it is going through. It is difficult to manage nation-states with a weak hegemony, as we see from its relationship with Turkey. It may isolate itself if it decides on being an empire but the memory of the collapse of Rome is still fresh. Then again, it may be lucky because there is no other power that dares to become an empire. All indicators point to a deadlock. The classical nation-state just barely made it to the twenty-first century through hegemony. The EU on the other hand is a step which is still under formation with a future which is not that clear. The UN, as if a reflection of the nation-state, also points to the nation-state's deadlock. Instead of being a place to resolve matters it seems to be a place to aggravate them. It is not expected that other regional or continental alliances will be able to overcome the nation-state obstacle. It looks as if they do not have the ability to resolve matters either. The nation-state model has long ago ceased to be the solution for both internal and external societal problems. Besides, although during its formation it may have been the most appropriate model against occupations and for initial capital accumulation it is now understood that it does not have the power to resolve anything. This can be seen from the resurfacing of issues with historical, societal, cultural, ethnic, environmental, feminist, and political dimensions that were suppressed. In addition, it has been exposed many times that it is an obstructive model in relation to international disagreements too.

Much can be learned from the Israel-Palestine question. Both are devoted to the very strict nation-state model. In order to be able to solve the problem of Jerusalem they either have to tear it into pieces or eliminate each another. It is perhaps difficult to find another example that exposes the deadlock of the system as clearly. Indeed, the situation of Iraq, Afghanistan, and Lebanon is now before us all. It may one day be Iran's turn and there may also be others in line. It becomes clearer with each passing day that since the model is not just and humane, nor political and democratic, it will not be able to keep itself going.

The nation-state, after reaching its peak around the 1970s, entered into a deep crisis especially with the disintegration of the USSR. Its crisis, with its inability to respond to the problems of the system and increasingly itself becoming an obstacle, has led the nation-state to lose its former esteem with the capitalist monopoly. Overcoming this crisis through evolution as proclaimed by the EU model does not really offer hope, linked as it is to the general global crisis of capitalist modernity. The Middle East, on the other hand, is where the crisis has turned into chaos: it virtually has the dimensions of a Third World War. A second EU or Greater Middle East Project is unable to respond to the realities of the region and thus the chaos may remain for a long time. The system may try to re-construct the nation-state under the disguise of democracy. The best response of those forces that favor equality, freedom, and democracy is to develop the democratic civilization.

In volume four I shall try to discuss the project of Democratic Confederation for the region.

It is a serious mistake not to discuss the epistemology of the nation-state as it is a deep-rooted paradigm. All the descriptions thus far show that it rests on a totally different paradigm than any other state. The works of Thomas Kuhn in relation to epistemology have laid down the importance of paradigms in general. What I am trying to say about paradigms in relation to this topic is that the nation-state has a tremendous power to distort. The scientific perspective of anyone raised in the nation-state's societal environment is ninety percent opposite to the truth. The fundamental reason for this lies in the way citizenship is formed and how the nation-statist paradigm that is practiced on all layers of society constructs its own historical and collective consciousness and then prevails them. The history of nation and state it especially forms (constructing them both interrelatedly) not only denies the general history but also mostly denies the history of other nations, states, and societies. It also distorts and makes use of them in the construction of its own history.

Therefore, it is really difficult for a citizen who has not passed through such a paradigm to become a scientist because he won't be able to advance meaningful interpretations. Such a scientist can only evaluate things from the perspective of the nation-state; thus, above all he is a fanatic. All facts are meaningless unless they are tested by his nationalistic templates. It is not possible for him to understand social sciences because the chauvinist nation perspective has limited his chances to do scientific work: he can only understand when it coincides with his own terms of reference. No other fact, relationship, or event can change this perspective. This is exactly where the damage done by nationalism as a religion surfaces. The reality of anything that does not serve nationalism does not have any meaning for him. He is not interested and his state of mind and thought-processes are set and unchangeable. Any social reality that falls outside the boundaries of the nation-state appears contradictory to him because social reality must be evaluated using the nation-state as the frame of reference. This frame-work cannot evaluate history and philosophy objectively and is also not suitable in order to understand science. The fixation of the mind is an obstacle in its own right.

Apart from its nation-state society it does not contemplate on the well-being of other societies. This fixation either distorts objective observation or drags it to a disinterested point of view. Viewing everything from such a fanatical paradigm, more fanatical than the fundamentalists, one would either not see the other or, when one would, the other would be seen as an enemy. This is the reason why the world of nation-states continuously generates wars. In this regard Hitler and Nazi-Germany are striking examples. Europe and the world will be as he sees them or not at all, in which case they are to be banished or eliminated. It is not too difficult to show how this paradigm turns into a factor of violence.

The wars of religion are clearly related to different paradigms. The increase in wars originating from nationalism is related to the nation-state paradigm, that is, with the fundamental perspective the nation-state imposes. Indeed, if the information is not understood correctly then it shall lead to misinformation. And that will be followed by wrong decisions and wrong implementations.

No scientist who is so deeply rooted in the paradigm of the nation-state can be expected to be able to meaningfully interpret especially social sciences or any other scientific areas.

This mindset that tries to turn everything into his own possession ("my borders," "my society," "my country") is submersed into a massive egoism and makes himself grand through exaggeration. Therefore, it is understandable that because of this, no sound decisions, relations, and actions can be expected from such a person. There can be no expectations of peace and solidarity (nationally or internationally) whilst such a person identifies himself or herself so intimately with the state and its society, history, and horizon together with its interests and passion.

Therefore, if we do not step outside this paradigm, the nation-state point of view, we cannot begin to obtain correct science, and therefore the chance to make right decisions and relations. All indicators show that a democratic atmosphere creates the most fertile ground for scientific revolution. Examples are the period between 6,000–4,000 BCE (Fertile Crescent), in Ionia and Athens between 600–400 BCE, as well Europe's Renaissance, Reformation, and Enlightenment since the fifteenth century. They all show us that science develops fastest when the level of societie's freedom is at its highest. If Europe is still being criticized world-wide, despite the great values it contributed to humanity, this is definitely because of the nation-state's selfish interests. The reason why modernity is unable to solve present problems is that it bases itself on the nation-state system. This is also the reason for the unprecedented important wars of the last four hundred years.

The perspective of democratic civilization provides a tremendous opportunity for scientific production. The need for new science can only be satisfied under the presence of a democratic society paradigm. This is especially so where there is an atmosphere of crisis and chaos which needs to be transcended. It is not possible to develop practical solutions without resolving epistemological questions. Therefore, the destruction of the nation-state paradigm and the achievement of the democratic modernity paradigm will provide the ability to reach the needed solution of power.

The Time of Capitalist Modernity

It is not wrong to divide the history of civilization into three sections: Antiquity, the Middle Ages, and the New Era. Often the substance of the definitions rather than the divisions themselves is disputed. I hope that my explanation of them is understandable and the content is enlightening. I have discussed whether capitalism can be considered a civilization or not. I see civilization as a whole, having a flow similar to that of a "main stream," and this view forms the essence of my discourse on civilization. The advance of this civilization is dependent on the triangle formed by the city, class, and the state. The form of the triangle also determines the form of the civilization. We may, therefore, regard the Sumerian and Egyptian Civilizations as the initial classical form; the Greco-Roman, Islamic, and Christian Civilizations as the period of maturity; and, the European Civilization as the period of disintegration and chaos.

I must also distinguish from all of this the Democratic Civilization. Although it is included within the central civilization, it cannot be equated with it. Indeed, civilization itself is quite a contradictory whole.

The fundamental contradiction is between the civilization with state monopoly and the democratic civilization of stateless society. This difference between the state civilization and civilization with democracy can best be seen in the two ancient Greek cities of Sparta, administered by monarchy, and Athens, administered by democracy. As the European civilization developed, there was an intense contradiction similar to this. The conflicts experienced between the state and the city democracies between the fourteenth and the mid-nineteenth centuries were in essence conflicts between state civilizations and democratic civilizations.

An important short-coming of Marxism is its narrow class-centered perspective in evaluating this conflict. The direct conflict between classes is an abstraction. The concrete conflict occurs between societal blocks: the society of the state and democratic societies. We are all aware of the consequences of a narrow class perspective. For classes, whose strict borders can never be drawn and where there is an ongoing mobility between them, the important thing is their consciousness and the culture that they are in. A class that cannot identify its own civilization or is unable to create one already has a non-existent status. In the absence of civilization there can be no class struggle. The Soviet experience showed us what a terrible error the thesis of the struggle of two classes in a single civilization is. A unique Soviet civilization could not be established because the molds of European state civilization could not be transcended and it largely based itself on capitalist modernity's moulds— and as a result could not avoid being like them. Many similar examples can be found in history. If you fight with others' weapons (civilization's lifestyle), then you shall be like them. Such a situation arises only because revolutions fall short in determining their own forms of civilization.

It is from this perspective that we can see that *capitalist civilization* is a very narrow concept. However, it would also be quite wrong to view European civilization as the joint civilization of two classes (workers and capitalists). This is because there are very strong democratic elements within European civilization. It may be more instructive to distinguish between a democratic and a capitalist Europe, instead of taking the view that there is a single European civilization. The current EU model is one that is trying to be developed into a Europe of civilizations that have reached a compromise.

It is an interesting experiment and certainly worth examining. The need for Europe to counterbalance its strict state civilization with very strong democratic traditions, as well as that of softer forces such as reason and law, is in line with our definition (the interrelatedness of civilization and crisis) of the final period of state civilization. The four hundred years of intense warfare is another proof of the inherent crisis in the structure. The Soviet system may also be seen as a supportive example. The discussions on the structure and future of the EU alone is enough to reflect that the modernity is undecided and unable to escape the crisis.

The structure of capitalist monopoly has led me to such a judgment. Marx proved in his monumental work, *Das Kapital*, that the crisis is related to capital, that is, it is structural where a monopoly is concerned. Profit and accumulation of capital cannot be achieved without crisis. Therefore, since capital cannot be content with no profit there must also be crisis. The reason why revolutions, struggles for democratization, and human rights are continuously on the agenda is not only due to the need to find solutions to the crisis, but also due to its internal problems. This is because the world is ungovernable. Global capital did not always rule the world: it fought with the world. Because of the inherent crisis in its nature, wars became wide-spread around the world. Since the birth of the civilization there have always been professional armies and wars. State civilization cannot advance, in accordance with its essence, without establishing its domination over the society. Domination is power and power cannot be achieved without establishing its control, which in turn cannot be achieved without force. This is why Hegel likened history to a bloody "slaughterhouse."

The difference between capitalism and the two preceding civilizations relates to the relative size of the structures of class, city, and state. Cities were small, classes were limited, and there were only a few states and they were small. Therefore, there were fewer wars and they were of a limited duration. In any case, violence is inherent in the civilization's structural character. In capitalism, the city, class, and state engulf not only the society but also the environment, as well as the wealth above and below the ground. The chaotic situations envelope not only the society but also the environment. Immanuel Wallerstein writes that capitalism entered its structural crisis after the 1970's and predicts that such a crisis may continue for the next 25 to 50 years. As he points out, that outcome is to be determined by the nature of science, organization, and action, he is partially correctly describing their relationship. I think he still has not rid himself of the Marxist concept of *cyclical crisis*. I believe it to be more correct to assume the existence of crisis at all times in capitalism. In this section I will attempt to divide capitalism into several parts in order to briefly discuss its structure, its state of crisis, and problems associated with the changes it has gone through.

Monopolist Merchant Capitalism

The oldest domain of capital is trade. From archaeological evidence, we know that the city of Uruk was the center of a well-established trade network around 4,000 to 3,000 BCE. We also know that the Assyrians established trade colonies from Anatolia all the way to India, and that the Phoenicians were the first people who had the ability to establish trade colonies throughout the Mediterranean. The expansion of the Persian Empire and the safety it offered led to the most widespread globalization in terms of trade. During the Greco-Roman civilization trade maintained its effectiveness. Without trade, big cities cannot sustain themselves and big cities means large scale trade. The Islamic civilization, which was the global power during the Middle Ages, is the last major stage in the development of Western trade. Almost all of the required traditions for trade were formed. Money, credit, banks, bonds, markets, and other elements such as transportation constituted the most important sectors within Islamic civilization. The Italian trade cities essentially took over the traditions of the eastern Mediterranean, Islamic, and Byzantine trade.

In the thirteenth century, the supremacy in trade shifted to the European continent via Italy. The Italian trade cities maintained their superiority between the thirteenth and sixteenth centuries, but this superiority was passed on to the city monopolies of the Netherlands and England at the onset of sixteenth century. The triumph of merchant capitalism was mainly achieved via the capital cities of these two countries, namely London and Amsterdam. The discovery and incorporation of the Americas and Southeast Asia into trade routes via the Atlantic and the Cape of Good

Hope constitutes one of the biggest commercial revolutions. The Middle East's control over the traditional East-West and North-South trade routes received a serious blow and lost its previous significance. The fact that the Middle Eastern civilization entered into a process of continuous regression with the onset of the sixteenth century was closely related to these newly opened trade routes. The Industrial Revolution, however, dealt the Middle East civilization the most strategic blow; it has not, to date, caught the opportunity and found the strength to recover.

The first big capital accumulation of Europe played a leading role between the fifteenth and the eighteenth centuries. It established its first hegemony over the urban craftsmanship and agriculture that had been on the rise since the tenth century. The monopolization and expansion of manufacture, which was the first serious industrial action, as well as its growth in volume, were all formed in close connection with the commercial monopoly's hegemony. The Netherlands and England maintained their leadership positions with their various East and West India Companies, the biggest trade firms at the time, for centuries. Banks, bonds, credit, paper money, accountancy, and their organization of affairs, all became strong institutions during this time, as the most effective tools of capital.

We witness yet again that there was a strong unity between private trade monopolies and state monopolies. Without the existence of the state as a monopoly, trade monopolies would not be able to exist on their own. From the first trade age until the European trade age, state monopolism was always the pioneer. Liberalism cannot exist against the will of state: the contrary is nothing but nonsense. Liberalism's true purpose is to ensure that the state is totally at the service economic monopolism and to turn the political state into an economic state. Liberalism without a state is like an abandoned garden. At the time trade had a significant weight over the state, or rather the state's relations with trade monopolism have had more significance.

And so the period between the fifteenth and eighteenth centuries is also called the mercantilist period. Essentially, it is the recovery of the state through trade. We may also call it commercial nationalism. (The most effective way of becoming a superior state is for the state to sell more than it buys!) This was also the period where the national state and monarchy were on the rise, when, on the social level, the aristocracy turned to trade and became intertwined with the merchant's entrance into a process of aristocritization, and the new modern class or bourgeoisie became firmly established. Radical reforms took place in many areas: from the bourgeois ideology, lifestyle, and sense of fashion to urban architecture.

This was also the Age of Reformation and Enlightenment. It would be a grave mistake to regard the Reformation and the Enlightenment as bourgeois movements. The Reformation had no causal connection to the bourgeoisie: it was essentially the nationalization of religion and the opening of its national branches. Under the new conditions of the time it aimed to renew religious thought which had been inundated with obsolete dogmas. It was the movement that adapted religion to keep up with the times. It, too, was part of the revolution of thought. The Enlightenment was an even more comprehensive thought revolution. It was to a great extent the surpassing of the old paradigms of thought and the establishment of a new paradigm. It was a renewal in the ways of thinking in all respects. The developments in these two important areas are also closely related to the scientific and philosophical revolutions. It is mere coincidence that they occurred during the commercial era. However, because of the bourgeoisie's class characteristics it appropriated them. It turned these two areas into its intellectual capital. Such a move was very important because in return it attained, as a class, the title of legitimacy. The thinkers of the Enlightenment played an important role in obfuscating the fact that monopolism is at least as parasitical as aristocracy and absolutism. Because the bourgeoisie constituted a new class formation its consequences were not thought through, and all the problems were attributed to the old classes. The bourgeoisie has played an important role in the qualities of middle class, making their mark on the era.

The reason for the bourgeoisie's support for nationalism as an ideology is to establish its monopoly over the national market. Nationalism was very effective in eliminating its rivals. The exclusion of commercial capital owners from other nations and nationalities fueled the reciprocal development of nationalism and became the basis for all sorts of racism, as well as for national, ethnic, and religious animosity. The Jews became the most significant obstacle to this growing malice and national ambitions. This was the reason behind the world-wide rise in hatred for Judaism. To counter this, some Jews turned to Freemasonry in order to build some kind of international defense, strengthen their friends, and eliminate their enemies. Although Freemasonry has its roots in the Middle Ages, its role became important in this period. It has had an important contribution in several revolutionary movements.

Considering how colonialism was closely linked to trade ever since its birth, the advance of colonialism during the period of mercantilism was to be expected. In this period, exploitation through colonies appears in the form of classical colonialism. Two continents, America and Australia, together with thousands of small islands were colonized for the first time during this period. All the continents of the world, especially Africa and Asia, were rediscovered in order to be colonized. To this end, the disciplines of orientalism and anthropology were instituted—a good example of the relation between science and the new society. Superior race theories, too, had the opportunity to develop during this period. There were even attempts to apply Darwinism to the society. To this end, geographic and historical work was taken up under the new paradigm. It is as if exploratory work for opening the world up to capitalism was undertaken.

Colonization or colonialism, which has more systematic consequences, is essentially the expansionist policies of the trade monopolies, but it has more systematic consequences. They are a more modern form of plunder. Europe's merchant capitalism has mostly been established on the basis of colonial plunder. The plunder of American silver and gold was achieved by the selling of cheap fabrics at extraordinary prices. Trade not only went through periods of unstable price formation, but also periods where prices were determined unilaterally. Colonization played a dominant role in trade monopolies imposing their own prices and in taking exorbitant gains. In any case, behind the merchant's gains lies the utilization of price differences at different markets, or in fact forcing a difference in price through methods like the stocking of goods or creating scarcity.

Fernand Braudel says that the speculative movements of large trade play a decisive role in the formation of capitalism. He adds that ordinary exchanges in the market do not have a role in this and that they are normal economic activities. The production of goods for use cannot be considered economy either. When the threshold of the exchange period is reached, economy has begun. At this point we cannot really talk about profits, only of gains in exchanging. There can be no speculation here. The real speculating is done in the area of large trade. Differences in price can be attained by directly fluctuating prices. Large trade is defined as the home of capitalism. Hence, Braudel does not consider this to be economy but sees it as a *thing* that is imposed from the outside and it is as if he does not want to expose it. He does not really define much after this point, leaving us puzzled as to why.

Braudel is well-aware of the difference between state and power. Although he does not accord the same degree of insignificance to the function of state and power as Marx does, he also does not determine the true degree of their effectiveness. When *state* is defined in Marxism as "personification of the economy," it comes closer to the truth than any other definition.[1] But it is a very abstract generalization. Power and state are in fact *economy which is not economy.* That is, state and power view economy as an area where the produced surplus product and values can be squeezed out, and where they establish their monopoly. In this sense, they are in the area just above economy. They are very much interested in economy. All their mechanisms are to ensure that the surplus product and values are seized by various methods. Agriculture, trade, and industry are the main areas in which the state establishes its monopoly. Its main method is taxation. For example, indirect taxes are the state's link to acting as a direct merchant monopoly. Here the state acts purely as a merchant: it is not just the merchant's personified expression but the merchant itself. The contributions made by the taxes constitute more than half the state's revenue.

The state is also a total economic monopoly because it determines the agricultural markets and prices. In the European economic literature, the relationship between economy/state and power is always ambiguous. Although both the socialists and liberals have published thousands of books on this issue it has still not been clarified. Marx's neglect to deal with this area is a severe short-coming (or maybe he did not live long enough to work on this) and has contributed to this great confusion.

No matter how we look at it, we have to admit that the fundamental role played by non-economic mechanisms led to the victory of the age of trade between fifteenth and eighteenth centuries. Thus, if these mechanisms are not economy what are they? In general, it is very difficult (though not impossible) for any force other than the ruling power or state, as its legal expression, to use this non-economic area as they wish. It may be possible to mention various cliques of monopolist forces but these forces must have some kind of relationship with either the ruling power or the state as its concrete expression. This area may at times also be called the monetary area. When money is no longer a mere medium of exchange, it can be at least as powerful as the sword. It was not in vain that Napoleon talked about money when it came to discussion on the army. But what money is this? It is certainly not the money that is the medium of exchange, but the money that is *not* economy. It is the large trade money and the money that is the medium of speculation. Money becomes the absolute commander in these areas. It is the ruler. The bourgeoisie has grasped this reality quite well and this is the reason why it has assigned such a major role to money. To ensure that money is the continuous commanding power of society, society has been shattered to pieces. Society, and even the state, has been maneuvered into a situation where it cannot continue living without money.

The fact that money has attained such a position may be considered the real revolution of the bourgeoisie. A society and state that are dependent on money are a society and state under the command of the bourgeoisie. Such a state of affairs, which we may call the monetary revolution, has been comprehensively attained for the very first time in history during this period in Europe. No longer is there a need to treat a worker as a slave or a serf because if he does not receive his wages then he will starve. Hunger condemns him to money. The worker has been put into such a position that he has no way out but to surrender to money. Therefore, there is no longer a need to be a classical slave owner or feudal landlord in order to acquire and manage the worker. This will only require more responsibility and will be more expensive. The capitalist, on the other hand, acquires and uses the worker as it wishes by just showing the power of money.

Similar issues can be raised in the case of commodities. Commodities, as goods, have been reduced to a position where they cannot move without the assistance of money. All movements of commodities are linked to money. It is not possible to produce, transport, or consume them without money. And this is also capitalism's biggest revolution: to put the economy under the absolute command of money. Economy is now a toy in the hands of money. In no other era has economy been dependent on money to this extent. Money is now like a state. Indeed, it *is* the state! Even the state itself is dependent on money in the same manner. A moneyless state or worker has been moved into the category of a good. It may sound paradoxical, but the state of the state is money. This new position of state is the sixteenth century invention of the Netherlands and England. A powerful state has been created. But it is a state that has been made dependent on money. Historians say that because France could not acquire this success it lost the hegemonic war against England and the Netherlands.

A comprehensive discussion of the effects of the trade bourgeoisie's appearance in society is called for, as this group is the most important actor in civilizational development between the fifteenth and eighteenth centuries. The characteristics of the commercial society are clear. Their place in society's memory is quite negative: they are excessively fond of money, obtain excessive interest rates, and are loan sharks and bankers. Art, especially literature, mentions the great blow to morality dealt by these elements. It is as if a virus has infected society. It eats into society. Money, which is held responsible for the general degeneration of society, freezes the old affectionate and humane relations in its cold face. Those without money are seen as having lost the struggle for survival. Furthermore, there is no longer a need for golden crowns, silver plates, palaces, magnificence, a show of brute force, fabulous costumes, and luxurious meals. You only need a place to hide your money. You are now the greatest. This position reached by humanity cannot be regarded as ascension. Although it is called the new or modern era, there is nothing new about it. But it may be the beginning of the civilizational crisis. For anyone who has not lost its respect for society there can be no situation that is more critical and derogatory.

The commercial capital does not seem to be willing to do anything in other areas during this period. The profit rates offered in these other areas do not seem to satisfy it. They cannot match the profit made in large trade. The areas of agriculture and manufacture are sectors that are turned to only when they offer profits close to that of large trade. They have therefore had limited opportunity for development.

In terms of political history, this period saw great upheavals. Spain, France, and Austria competed intensely to become the inheritor of the Western Roman Empire. However, their imperial inclinations inevitably caused them to lose. The relationship between money and state played an important role in this: the commanding power of large trade money led to the hegemony of the Netherlands and England, one after another. As they strengthened their states with merchant credit, they forced the states to act as merchants as well. Here we are talking about the emergence of a state and politics that make profit. They proved the commanding power of money as they developed new armies and fleets.

The triumph of capitalism in its economy is its attainment of cheap production. Cheap production means the superiority of trade. This in turn means the loss of their rivals (states which are brought to their knees) in the international arena. And, in fact, these states mostly lost in the military arena as well. The conspiracy-like revolutionary interventions of the Netherlands and England proved their political superiority, too. Their superiority in all these areas over their rivals inevitably led to their hegemonic superiority. This superiority had previously already been proven as Spanish and Portuguese colonies changed hands, and similar situations took place in Asia and Africa, resulting in commercial superiority. The alliances secured on the European continent meant that France was neutralized, Austria's aspirations to establish a German Empire were destroyed, and the Russian Czar could be used as they pleased. They also succeeded in the semi-colonization of the Ottoman Empire, one of the strongest empires at the time. Just like the other dynastical empires, the Ottoman Empire also came to the end of its term in the face of the capitalist production and state forms. The fate awaiting the Chinese and Indian Empires were full and semi-colonization. The elimination of old civilizations was rapid. What was new? Everything in relation to progress without actually knowing what they are. As with all new religions having faith was most important. Their religion was trade and their god money.

Industrial Revolution and the Age of Industrialism

The industrial period is most often equated with Industrial Revolution. But industry has existed throughout history. The very first hewn stone was an instance of industry. The discovery of agriculture was an industrial revolution specific to itself. Craftsmanship is also an industry and each new tool, knowledge, and method related to production constitutes a development in industry. The human species is the only entity to produce its food, clothing, and shelter through the use of tools. Industry, production with the help of tools, is unique to human beings.

The phenomenon led by England, the hegemonic country in Europe at the end of eighteenth century, was an important part of the ongoing innovations. The rotation of an engine through the energy obtained from steam has become symbolic of the industrial period, but in fact the power of steam and engines had been known and used long before this time. The leading position in agriculture and manufacture had already been seized by the Netherlands and England. Cheap, mass production (that in fact can also be regarded as an industrial revolution) had already been achieved. Initially, France and Italy were industrially quite advanced. But the huge advantage of low cost and mass production laid the foundations for England's hegemony. The importance of industry which took off with the onset of the nineteenth century was due to the profits (that is, the gain from the invested capital) that put it in the lead. What made it revolutionary was the fact that the profit generated through industrial production was not only much higher than the profit obtained from trade and agriculture but also had exponential growth. Industrial production took the lead for the first time in history. This is essentially why the Industrial Period constitutes a revolution. Previously, agriculture and the textile industry were the traditional areas of production. Trade was seen as commodity exchange of the excess production in these two areas, and it was the essence of economic activity.

If viewed solely from a production perspective, we cannot really understand the Industrial Revolution. Humanity has always known periods of diverse and abundant production. One could even say that no revolution has yet matched the agricultural and social revolutions either in terms of significance or in terms of duration.

Therefore, the importance of the Industrial Revolution lies elsewhere; indeed, it may lie in multiple places:

For the very first time, urban production was bigger than rural production. For many thousands of years, the craftsman, as a city-based producer, was a subsidiary producer to the rural. While the city was dependent on rural production, the rural area could sustain itself without urban production. The nineteenth century's Industrial Revolution reversed this process. If we consider the fifteenth to nineteenth centuries as a period of equilibrium between rural and urban production, then we can say that the nineteenth century turned the balance completely in favor of the city. This was an innovation that would bear many important consequences.

A more important innovation relates to the societal area. From now on, urban society moved ahead of the rural society. While previously cities were merely supplementing the rural society, the Industrial Revolution increased the power of the urban society extraordinarily. From now on rural society, with all its infra- and superstructures, would be dominated by urban society—in some way, the establishment of colonial dialectics of the city over the village. The colonization of village society by urban society had begun. An indisputable colonial domination of the village by the city was established, visible in the ideological area, production tools, morality and arts. The revolution of the mindset rapidly paved the way for the superiority of the city.

There were also historical transformations with regard to social classes. With the onset of the Industrial Revolution the bourgeoisie attained a position where it could declare its superiority over all other social classes and layers. It turned the working class into its reserve force and presented itself as the most progressive, as the only ones to posses the truth, to live in a modern way, and with a paradigm. They imposed themselves against those sections still representing the feudal era and craftsmanship. Through the use of mythology, religion, philosophy, and science it became *the* society, nation, and history. The rest belonged to the past.

During the Industrial Revolution, for the first time, there was a planned participation of science in production. Formerly, science and production techniques developed separately via their own channels. Now for the first time they joined forces. Science itself was no longer the aim: it was reduced to being an instrument. The instrumentalization of science would play a significant role in the downfall of society.

Industrial profit was much larger than the profit obtained from all the other areas. The new actors of society were the industrialists. Industry meant a strategic superiority in all areas. Those utilizing this weapon most effectively could never be defeated. Even trade lost its superiority. Those who made a living through agriculture were reduced to being pariahs.

The political consequences of the Industrial Revolution are even more significant. While internally it paved the way for the nation-state, externally it initiated the process of imperialism. Compared with colonialism, imperialism meant a more systematic domination of the world. The key industrial nations were now in a position to impose the second biggest move for global hegemony, across the world. Capitalism's initial move towards world domination was colonialism, but the inherent difficulties meant that it was not a very productive method of domination. Colonialism could only be reinforced with capital outflow and with the help of local collaborators. The imperialism capitalism needed only became possible due to the Industrial Revolution.

Clearly, the consequences of the Industrial Revolution are profound. The social and political consequences of the revolution had as much effect as the economic consequences. The nineteenth century industrial moves finalized the triumph of the European civilization. It is, however, important to criticize some approaches in this respect.

First, the Industrial Revolution cannot be equated to capitalism. It is generally viewed as a direct result of capitalism. This is a view that needs to be shattered. Just like the Renaissance, Reformation, and Enlightenment, the Industrial Revolution also has an historical and societal process unique to itself. It is the result of a long historical and social accumulation.

In general, state monopolies, but especially capitalist monopolies, are institutions that focus on surplus product and values. They immediately identify the places where surplus accumulation is gathered. It is inconceivable that they would not have noticed the existence of energy and self-operating machines and that their effect on production would lead to tremendous source of profits. What capital managed to do with regard to industry was to connect these two (energy and machines) to the most profitable area.

Energy, for the first time, was not dependent on manual labor. Machines possessed an engine design that removed most of the need for manual labor. Energy sources underwent a real revolution when, in addition to steam coal, petrol, electricity, and water were transformed into new sources of power. The production boom resulted from the design of the self-operating machine combined with the new forms of energy. The consequences for both nature and society of these new forms of energy and machinery, with millions of different varieties, are not yet fully known, but are mostly negative. Already nature and society were disintegrating, shattered and disrupted. Capital, on the other hand, viewed this as the greatest opportunity in its history, and hence constructed and implemented forms of power in society and nature unmatched in any other time. Society and nature were facing unprecedented attacks from capital. Therefore, the defense of society and nature was no longer a class or even a social struggle: it became an ontological question. I will now give some concrete examples to support my hypothesis.

The towns have become cancerous and the countryside is collapsing. In the towns and countryside as well as between them, life is no longer balanced between society and nature. We hence face a situation of a diseased society and an unsustainable ecology. Society is being turned into an extension or component of the machinery of the tyrannical and exploitative system, instead of being a form of existence that one lives in. For the first time in civilizational history society, the individual, and nature have been made to confront one another. This in turn has put individualism and nature (with a deteriorated ecological balance) into such a situation that it takes revenge on the society and environment. The society is no longer the framework for life.

The biggest threat of industrialism (the view that regards industry only as a source of profit) is that it has reached anti-social dimensions. Marxism views the industrial society as an ideal phenomenon due to its positivist structure. It even deifies it. This is due to Marxism's supposition that the working class cannot be formed and cannot continue to exist in the absence of the industrial society. This is the essence of its theoretical content. A case can be made that Marxism's contribution to the formation of the religion called industrialism is as effective as that of the capitalists since, while there is no criticism of the industry, the factory assembly is highly glorified. The truth is that industrialism has long since become a global Leviathan comparable to that of the nation-state Leviathan.

The town constitutes the core of societal carcinogenicity. Although I have often remarked on the history of its establishment and its function, there is also a need to discuss its relationship with societal development. The town is not only a form of society; it is also the setting where class division is created and the headquarters for state formation. It is generally accepted that these three phenomena are fundamental to becoming civilized (class, urban, and state societies). The Arabic equivalent of *civilized* means "unique to towns, town-like or town life." The literary meaning of the word *civilization* is close to this.

On the other hand, it may be a very narrow perspective to view the town only as a civilizational phenomenon. The town does not have to be the location of becoming civilized. Just as the establishment of villages is a historical phenomenon of social life, the town can also be interpreted as such. There is no reason why society should not have progressed beyond living in caves or villages. When the need developed for a way of life and a setting that surpassed cave and village life, the town took up this position. The role of the town is quite important in the development of analytical intelligence. The town, which is the location of a society that has become complex, requires intelligence to work analytically. It forces this development. The increase in social problems compels the brain to search for answers and solutions. Hence, the mind develops in a way conducive to analytical thought. Though the nature of the society itself requires this kind of intelligence, the town pushes this development to a higher level. Besides, the town can also be seen as the location where the mutual needs of different village groups are centered.

This is an important point. The reason for establishing the town lies in this phenomenon. The establishment of towns cannot be envisaged without villages. This widespread view, which has not been pronounced, but can be called urbanization in fact positions the village in opposition to the town. This is where the disaster begins. It is more than just a point of view: it is a well-known tendency seen throughout the historiography of development that the town is regarded to be in opposition to the village and countryside. In fact, this trend *cannot* be seen in the founding philosophy and historical basis of the town, but reflects a narrow class and statist point of view. This position, much to the detriment of the village (which means more surplus product and power), has kept its ground in the depths of civilization. The belittlement and vilification of the village and countryside originate from this archaic attitude. It seems as if the state and town have established a historical alliance against the countryside and village, hence against the tribes and clans that mostly live there. The conflict between the village and town societies has unjustly distorted and distanced the town from its true founding philosophy and has channeled this wrong understanding of the town to the present day.

But, of course, town and village-countryside could have been seen as locations that nurture one another (symbiotic) and, thus, as the societal life's living quarters, can be built in a balanced and coherent manner. The most ideal thing would have been to find an ecological equilibrium or a ratio between the population of the village and town. This would have been the ideal way of living. One of the most serious damages caused by civilization is the enlargement of the town as against the countryside and using it as a location of domination and exploitation. The town's role has been distorted and they have lost their original functions. The restoration of the real founding philosophy of this area alone will require serious societal acts.

Another conclusion that can be drawn from the history of the town is that its excessive growth happened without any regard to its relationship with the environment. There is no answer to the question as to where its borders should lie. The distorted city logic and the civilizations that have developed according to this logic are not monuments of intelligence, but the work of analytical intelligence that has lost all ties with the emotions and life. The dimensions of the disasters and the irrevocable damage they have done can now be understood better. The towns were magnificent structures in Antiquity. Common sense was still prevalent. During the Sumerian and Egyptian civilizations, the conflict between nature and village-countryside was not that deep-rooted and the equilibrium was still in favor of the countryside. The towns growing inside and outside of the castles were still in harmony with agriculture: their population seldom more than a few hundred thousand, with possibly only a few capital cities reaching this mark. Environmental pollution had not reached problematic levels. The architecture was substantive and all together they formed an organic whole. The temples, markets and forums, the arenas and gymnasiums of the Greco-Roman civilization were all based on a proportional and magnificent architecture. The terraces and gardens combined with the layout of the houses to form a unified, organic whole. Their remnants are still breathtaking. These were places with a certain philosophical meaning and a sanctity attached to them.

This wholeness constituted between town and countryside continued—though deteriorating considerably as trade increased— during the Middle Ages. Although the growing influence of the immaterial culture led to an increase in religious architecture, towns never reached threatening dimensions—they were more in balance with the countryside. Constituting a whole was still more likely. The importance of the agricultural sector stimulated development in the sector of urban craftsmanship: the craftsman needed the peasant and the peasant needed the craftsman. Far from being in conflict they were an organic whole. The only risks they faced were natural disasters and wars. The city walls and castles were magnificent. Large trade had not yet reached the dimensions needed to absorb the craftsman and village. Trade functioned normally as a sector of economy. The Italian towns of the thirteenth to the sixteenth centuries were the last representatives of this era to be influenced by the Renaissance. Venice, Genoa, and Florence were in a position to unite the classical civilization with that of the Modern Age.

Urbanization began to take on different meanings with the onset of the Modern Age. Market domination appeared on the horizon with trade beginning to outweigh all else. The historical equilibrium began to deteriorate, with the countryside and village being the losers. A town architecture based on the needs of the merchant began to emerge. The connection between life and environment was being lost and the mentality of profit-making began to shape everything. Some towns— especially Paris, London, Amsterdam, and Hamburg—carried the mark of the new period, that of mercantilism. The towns of the trade era opened a gulf between themselves and the classical towns, and very soon showed themselves to be in conflict with rural society and nature. The town, which is the home base of the Leviathan, had begun to extend its claws into the entire society and environment around it. The Industrial Age would be the death of the town. Interestingly, biological cancer is also mostly an illness of the town. Cancer is most definitely related to the town turning its society into a sick society.

The Industrial Revolution, growing rapidly with the onset of nineteenth century, first struck society in its places of birth. The rapid growth of the industrial establishments in the cities did not originate from the requirements of life, but that of profit. The shanty houses and suburbs that the modern slaves, the proletariat, were placed in were not something the towns were familiar with. They represented the colonization of the countryside. These shanty houses and suburbs were developed as an internal colonization movement worse than the colonization movement of the trade era. These areas were a depot of labor for industry. Shanty houses and slums mean to industry what a depot means to trade. This had many additional side effects. For sustaining factories, many smaller factories were invading the town. No one could remember the model of the Classical Age any longer. The towns became the centers where society was absorbed. By the end of the nineteenth century, the towns were barely alive under the town policies of industrialism. For the first time in history towns were emerging with the population of millions. It is clear that a town that surpasses the half million mark cannot be functional. More than a million shows the critical dimensions of its sickness.

The phenomenon of being cancerous is the growth of a cell in such a manner that it covers the entire body. Under such conditions, because the other organs cannot function, the patient dies. The growth of the town means similar consequences for the society. There are several dimensions to the historical and societal phenomena. If only one of these dimensions has excessively grown, then cancerous growth has begun. Once a town has a population that numbers more than a million or, worse, ten million, its inhabitants can no longer be classified as a society: it has become a herd society, constituting the masses. Just as herds are put into barns, the humans are turned into herds and placed in towns. There, long ago, they were convinced to become mere consumers. This is no different from the herd placed in the barn. In addition, there is a herd of unemployed placed in there. They are appeased by the unemployed. On the other hand, the government centers, villas, or houses with gardens do not require the town either: they can be built anywhere.

So, what is left of the town? The temple, theater, parliament, gymnasium, and the market place have long ago become mere copies of the original. It is more accurate to call them places of artificial life. The future of the city, in a position like this, is ambiguous. To feed a city with ten million people is the death of a region as an ecological society and would require the massacre of the society and the environment. In order to eradicate a country, it is enough to have a couple of cities with a population of five to ten million. The traffic pollution alone is enough for the death of a city. The town has lost its meaning by growing way out of proportion. In the absence of meaning there can be no life—that is, of course, if living is not defined to be merely breathing.

Towns were places where the truth was discovered and philosophy constructed. But now, in the collapsing towns of industrialism, we can only talk about stock farms where herd-like behavior is made possible through the usage of sex, sports, and arts that are drained of their contents. If this is not the death of the town, what is?

Another destructive dimension of industrialism is its attack on the relationship between life and environment. Where the town makes society cancerous internally, industrialism attacks the living environment as a whole. Industrialism, the policy of the nation-state that has not yet lost its significance, requires all the resources of the nation and society to be subordinated to the industry. The nation-state views this as a development path. However, this policy has really nothing to do with the nation's wealth and development or, indeed, with growing stronger. The fundamental reason for this policy is that the industry achieves its highest "profit" in this area. Industrialism is an operation to manage profit. Concepts such as *investment* or *development* are covers disguising the real aim. If there is profit to be gained there will be investment and development, otherwise they do not apply. Industrialism is a bigger theft than ownership of property: *it is* theft from the people as a whole and from nature.

Let me just say that I am not condemning investment or production based on factories per se. There can also be appropriate models of investment and factories based on the well-being of society and environment. They are not harmful on their own. However, in the service of profit they become cancerous. Industry is for profits, not for social needs. The rule of maximum profits does not stem from needs. It has its own logic. If the needy areas bring profits, then industry will be interested in them. If not, they will be left to die. If the present technologies are developed and implemented properly, unemployment, poverty, disease, and education will no longer be social problems and, more importantly, there will be no need to destroy the environment for extracting resources.

Many areas that are not seen as profitable but are able to provide many vital necessities are left inactive just because there will be no profit made. On the other hand, just for the sake of profit, resources resulting from millions of years of evolution are consumed in a very short time without any regard as to the consequences. Petrol, sea, forest, and mine policies have devastated the environment for the sake of high profit. The brutal aspect of profit can best be seen in the environmental genocide. If this rate is kept up for a few more decades, not millennia, the environmental disaster will be irreversible.

Industrialism is a super victory for analytical intelligence but a disastrous defeat for emotional intelligence. Industrialism is the renewed rise of the ancient divine revelation that has put all living beings of the world at the services of the human. It may be wrong to say "at the service of the humans," as all living beings are sacrificed to the aspirations of a handful of greedy profiteers, the capitalists. Therefore, it is just a matter of time before the human being will be offered as a sacrifice. All the examples of evil given in the Sacred Books do not represent evil as purely as industrialism does.

Industrialism should not be seen as a production related problem. Its true meaning will be better understood if viewed as the monopoly of profit or capital built upon production. Having production (and thus an investment policy) based on social needs, as well as scientific and technological resources, is quite feasible provided that industry is not in the service of the profit monopolists. Essentially, it does not really matter whether there are machines involved or not, the one method of production is just faster than the other. The determinant factor should be compatibility with social needs, the environment, and ecology. Fast or slow production is not an end in itself and thus automation cannot be considered good or bad in itself. But if the only intention of production is profit—and this has been the mark left on the phenomenon of industrialism since the nineteenth century—it is inevitable that every aspect thereof, all investment, production, and consumption processes, becomes a problem and gangrenous whether automated or not, fast or slow. This is why towns have grown abnormally big, why horrific weapons have been developed, and gigantic armies are constructed. Dreadful world-wide wars have occurred. Environmental massacres are being committed. The nation-state monster has been invented. Life has been drained of all substance. Politics has been totally destroyed. When capitalism as a monopoly made its mark on automated production the industrialist monster was created. This is the crucial issue.

The state monopoly first seized the surplus-product in agriculture and then in trade. With the discoveries of energy and machinery in the nineteenth century a monopoly on industrial production was established. This led to unprecedented profits or capital in return for surplus-product. When profit is imposed on industrialization everything gets out of hand. Therefore, industry and industrialism (which is based on making profit), are two different concepts. Industrialism also cannot be considered economy—it is an economic *monopoly* imposed on the industrial production. It does not really matter whether it is a state or private monopoly. I am not talking about areas of production or economic activity that society carried out for thousands of years such as manufacture, agriculture, shops, and factories running on their own labor. The source of the problem is not the production attained from these areas. It is also not due to their exchange in the market. Serious economic and social problems arise when these areas, which are there for the needs of the people, are controlled externally either directly by the state or in its name in order to steal the surplus by means of taxation, plunder, and other profit-making methods. Production has become an area of abnormal profits after the Industrial Revolution of the nineteenth century. This has resulted in terrible class and national wars; the imposition of monopolies has led to the deepening of conflict between communities within a society, between societies, and with nature. Society is placed under the domination of the rulers like never before. Everyone is fighting with everyone else. In a way Hobbes' monster, the Leviathan, is not ending "the war of everyone against everybody else." On the contrary, it is turning the war against society and against oneself. This is the final phase to which the monster has brought society.

The concept *industrial society* is not really meaningful seen in isolation. When industrial monopolies are established, society is put under control of commodification and production, whereas production is put under control of industry. Monopolist industrial capitalism is the stage where the other production areas become dependent on the monopolist industry. Hence, it may be meaningful to view the industrial society as a different phase of the civilization. Saying that such a civilizational phase left its mark on the nineteenth century will be more realistic. We may call it the "magnificent age of capitalism" as it allowed for the highest profits of all times. The entire society was immersed in a passion for profit. Becoming a capitalist was held to be a goal in its own right and a natural way of living. Because of this the industrial society is a first: it is the utmost capitalist society. This is how the king became naked: that is, now, for the first time, prominent capitalists turned into a group of kings that represented themselves as normal citizens with normal clothes. The kings have multiplied and can only exist if they are stripped off their old pompous, decorated clothes. The industrial society can hence be called "the society of the naked kings."

The situation of the worker that is dependent on wages became widespread in this society. In this sense, this represents a class severed from society. The only difference with classical slavery is that this slavery bounds with wages. Ethically, judging which of the two is better would be wrong. One of the most serious mistakes made by the Marxists was declaring the industrial bourgeoisie and working class as progressive and the rest of the society as backward. The opposite is true. The co-occurrence of industry and the working class may be a characteristic of modernity, but from the perspective of equality, freedom, and democratization they are part of the monopolist state. Their position is closer to that of anti-socialism. The engagement of intellectuals with this class alliance is the most unfortunate deviation for socialism. The society of industrial monopolies are essentially societies of continuous war. It is not for nothing that the nation-state has become *the* state form of this period.

The politics and state form of industrial monopolism is the nation-state, which is the product of combining the national society with the most intense nationalism and state. Idealization of the nation-state reached its peak during the Age of Industrialism and most instances of realizing this ideal occurred in this period. The fundamental reason for this is the widespread and excessive profit of capital. Such an increase in profit requires the dependency of the entire society on the industrial monopolies; this, in turn, means civil war. This civil war can only be suppressed through intense nationalism and the nation-state, where power is most strongly concentrated. This is how you secure a scheme that ensures maximum profits. During this period the gradual development of fascism as a system is not a unique event. A herd-like society and the spread of power in all its layers is possible only through the religionization of nationalism.

Western modernity has acquired its quality of being the bloodiest civilization in history because it consists of industrialism, nation-statism, and capitalism. This modernity, that is based on this intertwined trilogy, constitutes a state of civil war (fascism), and amongst states national, regional, and world wars. I know I keep repeating this, but the factor underlying these wars is the way in which profit is created and shared. When the nation-state declares industrialization as its main goal, it is really stating its capitalist character or desire. When capitalists name the formation of a nation-state as their political aim, they know that the nation-state is possible only by gluing nationalism with that of nation, and that this is the most required state form for setting up their profit scheme. When industry became the main goal both of the state and capitalism the fate of the nineteenth and twentieth centuries were determined. Industry, just as it was for agriculture and manufacture, is a production era. It rests on the heritage of the civilization. But none of the other production eras has given the state and capitalist monopoly the power to multiply profits and power. This is the reason why both the state and the capitalists compete to industrialize. They are not driven by concern for society or the individual or by respect for the nation, but by "the chance of a lifetime" for a historic profit.

The industrial society is historically and closely related to the ideals of war and hegemony. As the alliance of England and the Netherlands was hard pressed by France, they found refuge in cheap production so as not to lose their hegemonic position. History indicates that had England not taken the lead in the Industrial Revolution, it probably would have lost its hegemony at the beginning of the nineteenth century, specifically to Napoleon. It is said that the United States and czarist Russia also had a chance for hegemony. Later, Germany would also enter the race. England's chance, and maybe it's only way out, was the Industrial Revolution. This once again proves that necessity compels creativity. Steam engines and weaving machines turned the wheels of history to England's advantage— once again. Political and military inventions gained speed and power with the new industrial production. This in turn brought about military success.

Once this chain reaction is established it is very difficult to break up. In addition to all the other factors, the real reason for Napoleon's defeat is most probably the Industrial Revolution. The English hegemony progressed to the nineteenth century world empire due to the Industrial Revolution. The nineteenth century was England's most spectacular century. England was the first to win the label of "an empire on which the sun never sets." This is not a classical empire organized, for example, like that of Rome or the Ottomans. The existence of many political formations represented at state level does not harm its empire. Although it has become quite weak as a model of empire with multiple political formations, it still lives in the form of the Commonwealth of Nations, formerly the British Commonwealth.

The way in which England exported the Industrial Revolution to the world was similar to all the other forms of civilization. Once it had proven itself, it first completed its expansion into Western Europe and then continued its expansion into Europe at the end of nineteenth century. At the beginning of the twentieth century, its expansion into the world accelerated. At this time, England and Germany were the front runners in the competition between industrial monopolies. The imbalance caused by this development meant two big world wars and many regional and local wars. Once again we are faced with the fact that industrial profits mean monopoly, monopoly means the nation-state, and the nation-state means war. If we consider that no nation-state has ever been established without war, we will soon understand the bloodied and profiteering history of seizing regions for industrialization and industry export through these wars. Clearly, profit is the factor underlying all wars and nation-states.

The reason why the industrial period is equated with imperialism lies in these external exports. The limited degree of industrialization in colonies, semi-colonies, and dependent territories—as expected—would mean the start of internal and external wars. The national liberation struggles, a prominent feature of the twentieth century, were related to the industrialization programs of the colonized and semi-colonized regions. Regardless of the leadership position of these national liberation movements they all adopted the nation-state as priority. But the nation-state prioritizes industrialization. This constituted the cornerstone of the establishment of world capitalism. In this respect, the Russian and Chinese Revolutions were, in the final analysis, nation-state and industrial revolutions, as confirmed by later developments. Thus, the twentieth century was the era when industrialization outside of Europe was secured through national liberation wars or other methods.

This era continued until the last quarter of the twentieth century. Europe then began exporting to the world the industry that no longer brought in high profits and was a burden to itself (in terms of environmental pollution and high costs). Thus, the goods were first exported; then, in the nineteenth century, the goods and the capital; and in the twentieth century, the goods, capital, and industry were conveyed to the world. We now have a situation where there is no longer any region that has not met industrialization. Hence, we can conclude that the Industrial Age has lost its true significance, or rather, industry has been replaced with financial capital. The European civilization that began its initial age with trade and its second age with the Industrial Revolution is now in its third and last phase, which is the global age of finance. The age of finance took up the leading role after the 1970s. This will be my topic of discussion in the next section.

An age does not erase its predecessor but relegates it to a position of secondary importance. Thus, trade continued in the nineteenth century, but in comparison to the profits made by industry it lost its former position of strength and became of secondary importance. The age of finance laid its foundations a long time ago. The Italian city republics were actually closer to being finance republics. They made many kingdoms dependent on themselves by handing out finance. During the Age of Trade, they also quite busily borrowed and handed out money. In this age, credit became a serious means of profit. But this sector yielded only the third highest profits.

The number of those critical of industry started to increase as the dangers of environmental destruction began to threaten our planet. Methods of combating the disasters caused by industrialism are a hot topic of debate: it's irresponsible use of science and technology is predicted to result in a doomsday situation.

The relationship between profit and industry is the underlying factor of all these problems. An unrestricted combining of the two has created a web of problems instead of development. The industrial domination of all social areas, the fact that all social areas have been turned into commodities, has escalated the social problems to unprecedented levels. Many developments based on industry are not only a threat to the society's nature, but also to the environment. We have just begun to face the problems resulting from urban areas being engulfed by the town. The consequences of towns being turned into what they were not intended to be are also just starting to surface. We have not progressed any further than mere discussion of what the alternatives should be. Clearly, society cannot survive without industry, but it cannot be expected to agree with what is being done in the name of industry. Anti-industrialism may gradually become stronger. Urban and environmental work has embraced many such tendencies. Slowly, they are being represented in the political arena as well. These efforts cannot be more than reforms, and expecting them to re-achieve the equilibrium between the two natures is nothing but being naive. As long as we remain in the present paradigm of the civilization we cannot expect substantial changes.

The view agreed upon by all observers is that the problems of the five thousand year old civilization have been multiplied by the Industrial Age. Climate warming is only one such example. The destruction is more profound and comprehensive than we can imagine. Therefore, there is a need for a comprehensive critique of the entire civilization, not only of the Industrial Age in isolation. There are benefits resulting from the attempts by Marxists and other oppositional groups, although they categorize the problems into narrow class economism, environmentalism, culturalism or feminism. But the fact that they have not been able to arrive at nor to implement a serious political program must be related to their fundamental failures.

The more I focus on the option of democratic civilization, the clearer it becomes to me that this is the best option of all. However, the choices that we will have to make to build a profoundly democratic civilization will require comprehensive critique and programs. Moreover, implementing these choices will require an organization and a course of action. This is the only way to view nature and life from the paradigm of a free, egalitarian, and democratic society; our only hope for making headway.

The Age of Finance

Undoubtedly, money becoming a power of societal command is an important development. In the absence of a thorough analysis of this phenomenon, society cannot be completely understood. Money is a value that allows mobility in economic life. What it is and the way in which it attained such a position make it the most serious societal phenomenon that needs to be understood. It cannot be denied that this instrument carries an awful amount of dirt with it. But which historical and societal factors have led to the attainment of such a position? What does it really accomplish within society? Who are the individuals and groups that gain or lose because of it? Can one do without it and what could be put in its place? There are more questions that can be asked.

Money as instrument of exchange (that is, as the instrument of a simple process) can be understood well. Nevertheless, one should still be careful. What is being exchanged? Can money be a tool that provides a fair measurement of the value of two things to be exchanged? It is clear from the start that the question entails many difficulties. Let us assume that we are exchanging apples and pears—quite a simple transaction. Let's say that we exchange one apple for two pears and presume that money functions in this transaction. We may ask why it is not a one for one exchange or a one for three. Our answer may entail the inclusion of labor-value. But other questions may follow: What is it that gives value to the labor? Thus, it becomes clear that money can hardly ensure a fair measurement in transactions. What gave money its power and reputation is, most probably, the fact that it offered new options. It is useless to look for dimensions such as justice, value, and labor in the foundations of money. Money acts as a mediator so that transactions can be done with ease. But the mediator we are faced with is making a big mess: instead of playing its assigned role it takes on other roles. In my opinion this mediator was used to ease things confined to a certain time and space. Consequently, it spread over time and place although it was never meant as such. This is an incident of grave misuse. The society may have resisted against such a widespread use but there was nothing that could stop it now. How did it attain such a position? Let us continue to probe into it.

Although it is not so meaningful to initiate economy with exchange, exchange itself is an important economic factor. Two things exchanged are called goods or commodities. For a long time, society did not know any value other than the use value, and it did not find it morally appropriate to exchange things. Society adhered to a system called the gift economy. Produced or obtained objects of value would be given as gifts to those they valued. The gift culture denotes honoring the other. Anyone to be honored would be given a gift. This meant that those who were precious were honored and their value proven. The remaining objects would then be used in daily life. Accumulation of things was also not appreciated. Human societies were able to live this way, that is, without exchanging goods, for tens of thousands of years. Society's consciousness and morals could not consent to the exchange of goods or exchanging goods for money. This was because they did not think that there could be an equivalent for the value they produced. To them, thinking like this would be morally wrong; possibly their common sense or moral consciousness would even consider this to be fraudulent.

If the threshold of exchange is the threshold of economy, such a start to economy cannot be considered a good one because it ran contrary to tradition. It may be a hypothesis to consider exchange as the fundamental value of economic relations. However, I believe it would be wrong not to consider other hypotheses as well. It is possible to scientize economy with factors other than exchange. Or, rather, it can be other forms of exchange where the exchange is not reliant on a mediator such as money but on consensus. In theory and in practice different and creative forms of exchange should be developed. A more important issue than exchange is how products are turned into goods. Commodification is described as the exchange of use value. Commodity appeared for the first time at about the start of civilization. Commodity was the fundamental factor behind the acceptance of trade. A product becoming a commodity coincides with the initial owner parting with it. Acceptance of parting with the product is the start of the product becoming a commodity. And if someone else obtains it in exchange for something else, then the process of commodification is completed. Let's think of a gazelle and a goat being exchanged after being looked after for many years. No one can ever prove that such an exchange is a fair and just one. This is due both to the amount of labor put into their care and the goat and gazelle being two different things. This analogy should make clear the paradox in the reason for exchange.

If we now return to the issue of money on the basis of seeing these contradictions, we will perhaps be more aware of its deceptiveness. It is important to better understand another point when studying societies: Societal phenomena are not the same as physical phenomena. Under the conditions of this world, two hydrogen atoms combined with one oxygen atom will always form the water molecule. It can never form any other chemical structure. Society, on the other hand, is a package of phenomena constructed by the human being. Although there are many obscurities involved with it, the human can change what it has constructed and make new constructions. Hence, we seem to end up with this rule: *Societal realities are constructed realities.* They are not natural or god-created realities. Money can easily be said to be a constructed reality. Exchange and commodities are also social realities that are constructed and not natural or god-created.

The biggest sin of positivism is placing social realities in the same category as physical realities. If we equate societal phenomena with constant realities, we will be paving the way for societal paradigms containing serious flaws. Understanding this makes it impossible not to see the drawbacks of viewing economy from such a positivist point of view. Similarly, if you see nationalism as an expression of objective reality, you will end up in the same position as Hitler and Stalin who are from a philosophical point of view the same (albeit they arrived at these positions from different angles). Neither of them, nor any of the other positivists and vulgar materialists, can escape rendering the realities they accept within the society the value of absolute phenomenon. So, another factor that makes the issue of money so delicate stems from the positivist approach to society: to assume that money is completely real. Therefore, commodities changing hands through the mediation of money gradually gives rise to the perception that money is real.

Our topic is not how money entered the economy alongside exchange and how it developed in the course of history. But we have to understand that money gradually established itself as an indispensable part of the economy, thus increasing the drawbacks inherent in itself. If we compare the underlying paradox in one instance of exchange alone, we will understand the undesirable situation money leads to when it gains limitless exchange power. Money has become the embodiment of thousands of contradictions. As money made its way through economy, society gradually arrived at the age of finance. But without understanding the gravity of the situation claiming to understand society would be false. What makes the situation so serious is the fact that money has reached its most sophisticated era yet, together with the enormous contradictions inherent in itself. It is like appointing a tyrant with a poor record as the commander in chief of a very big army. The momentary acceptance of money by some in the society elevates the temporary status of this suspicious instrument to that of a god, giving into its grip the most effective power of command.

It would be really interesting to examine the historical development of money. King Croesus of Lydia is said to have issued the first gold coin in history. He is said to have lived in the city of Sardis, present day Manisa, Turkey, where the search for gold is still creating problems. Croesus also experienced many problems as a result of his hunt for riches. We know from the hundreds of different coins that have been found that the use of money was wide-spread during the Persian and Greco-Roman Civilizations. Together commodities, exchange, and monetarization rapidly developed and thus seized the prime position in the economy. Money became something that you could neither do with nor without.

In the Islamic Civilization, the rial attained as esteemed a position as the sultans. The throne of money was quite robust in the cities and the Jewish money agents became especially important. The Jewish and Armenian money agents and merchants established a money and trade monopoly route parallel to that of the trade routes between Europe and India. This route of capital, in parallel with political domination, was very powerful. The sultans and the emirs were made dependent on them. These agents' influence in Europe and Asia increased continuously, a fact that might have contributed to the increasing reaction of the communities towards the Jews and Armenians as peoples. When researching the Jewish and Armenian pogroms one should also research this issue.

Toward the middle of the thirteenth century, the Italian towns took over the leading position in money and trade from the Islamic world. Especially Venice, Genoa, and Florence came into being as the miracle of money and trade. Until the sixteenth century, these towns led Europe in all aspects. They not only brought about the unfolding of the Renaissance, they also were the architects of a monetary revolution. Although the precursors to this change came from the Islamic world, these towns made enormous contributions: they developed and institutionalized all of the indispensable financial instruments of modernity such as banks, bonds, paper money, credit, and accountancy. These developments played a crucial role in the history of money, constituting a revolution in the development of market and trade. Thus, the speed of commodification and monetarization was a manifold increase. They were milestones in the development of the rule of money.

Society was gradually prepared for the domination of these instruments. From the outset, they were presented as nothing more than tools for a simple technical transaction. The banks were going to be the places where money would be accumulated. Bonds were pieces of paper that corresponded to money. Paper money was in a way like a bond. It was light and made transactions smoother and faster. Credit was the money lent to customers who were short of money in return for an appropriate interest rate. This sped things up and prevented waiting around with nothing to do. Those interested would take the credit and continue with their work and make the payment of the debt with the profits attained. Accountancy enabled one to clarify the profit and deficit, as well as inventory of the income and expenses for the work done.; It reflected the financial situation of the individual or firm. These financial inventions were simple revolutions with great consequences. Cities such as Seville, Lisbon, London, Amsterdam, Hamburg, Lyon, Antwerp, and Paris quickly passed on Italy's products of revolution to their own countries and it spread and expanded over the continent.

Above, I gave an overview of how, with the onset of the sixteenth century, the Netherlands and England were able to turn into a general capitalistic revolution the revolutions that were achieved for the first time in agriculture, then in trade and later in industry. Capital, capitalist, and capitalism were the first steps toward money's sultanate. Each, who had skipped all these steps, were a true king: Naked kings. The Age of Trade owed its profits that grew with its high speed to monetarization and monetary instruments. The rule of money advanced silently but profoundly. It did not just try to attain a kingdom for itself but tried to become divine without, for the first time, hiding behind a mask; by openly showing its true self. The Industrial Age owes much to the Age of Trade and the great opportunities that it passed on. Without the existence of marketization, urbanization, commodification, and the concentration of trade in society the Industrial Revolution would not have been possible. And none of these processes would have been achieved without money. The increased speed of monetarization and the flow of money gave it a role similar to that of blood circulation in the body. If it was interrupted even just for a moment the organs could no longer function. This would mean their death.

An analysis of the relationship between the factory and worker will clarify things. It is not possible for the factory to function on the labor of the old slave, peasant, or serf. Becoming a worker without breaking your ties with the master, seigneur, and the land is impossible. The state of becoming a complete worker can only occur if an absolute wage is obtained. Wage is not a value that can be paid in the absence of money. Hence, the worker is doomed to depend on money. Money has reached a position from where it can put the new slave under its own absolute domination without the need for master or seigneur. This was a huge step towards assuming total power. The newly formed industrial society was the first big societal form confronted with the hegemony of money. None of the other civilizational societies had known such domination by money. With the arrival of the industrial society money has become a culture. Things obtain meaning only in relation to money. Although money leads to many great dreams, if there is no money no great project can be started. Each and every family, from the rural settlements to the urban dwellings, is aware of the absolute necessity of money in order to buy a pair of shoes for a child, to be able to turn on the light in the house. There was no plan or endeavor that would not be taken up in order to acquire it. Everyone was compelled to offer whatever was necessary to please their new god in order to obtain money.

From the outset, people have believed what they are selling is labor, the sacred value. This is the most typical delusion created by money. What is sold off in return for money is not only labor itself. To be able to work you need a healthy body: to have a healthy body you need an endless list of things including, and especially, the woman. On top of this, labor is needed to acquire skill. In the absence of skill, labor would not be bought. This in turn needed the craftsman and the shop assistant who were also based on thousands of years of work experience and the laborers of their times. Hence, a simple wage—a bit more than what was needed to be sustained—meant all these sacred values were being sold off. History and society were being sold off. This was how the human being was instrumentalized. No other societal god had ever before established such domination over its subjects.

Breaking its ties with gold, silver, and other precious metals was another important milestone in the history of money. This big revolution—the black money revolution—occurred in the 1970s. From then on, money became totally "free." The initial step towards this freedom was secured by the Italian cities by linking money to instruments such as paper tokens, bonds and credit. The second big revolution was achieved when the US dollar officially freed itself from its to gold and silver.

This is how the age of finance was officially entered. This is what lies behind the historical development called the third big globalization move. The first big globalization move of capitalism was the continental colonization and semi-colonization of the Age of Trade in the fifteenth to eighteenth centuries. Its second big globalization movement was the imperialism move of the Industrial Age, resulting in a period of wars based on class and nationality. It is indisputable that one of the master builders of this period that continued for about four hundred years was money. It may not be wrong to call the sum of all these periods the Age of Money. Capitalist modernity's great god is the nation-state (Zeus-Jupiter), its power and war god (Ares-Mars) is money, which is the rising new god of the modern era, a god that has no antecedent in economy or history: The god that suppresses all the other gods and establishes its own hegemony!

The main characteristic of the age of finance is that of the institution of money (with all its instruments) obtaining the position of leadership. It has placed the industrial and trade monopolies under its complete control. It made the state, as a monopoly, (especially the nation-state) thoroughly dependent on itself. It also took total control of the fundamental layers of the economy, such as usage (that is, the consumer), production, and exchange platforms. The means used to accomplish this is a comprehensive list of instruments such as the IMF, World Bank, the World Trade Organization; all the central banks of the world, global banks, various credit bonds, markets, and the stock exchanges, bonds and notes, consumer cards, interest rates, and exchange rates. Because of these institutions, money has acquired ghostly presence. Put differently: money has instated itself in the position of the old hierarchical ruler of the patriarchal family. These institutions play the role of its offspring. Hence, all these institutions have money as their forefather.

These institutions form a terrible network amongst themselves. They are extremely organized. They know each other's every detail. They influence one another. They move money on the basis of short, medium, and long terms. The respective financial instruments for these are fashionably called "hot money," "bonds and notes," and "long term bonds", but the names and terms may change. They are the fastest realized societal construction. The most important means of payment is the US dollar and the Euro. Although the system is still being improved, it can be considered complete.

How, then, is profit (the main goal), realized in this new system?

All the relations and conflicts of the economic, social, and political worlds were transferred to this new virtual system. Even the ideological, academic, and other cultural areas became its prey. A closer look at this truth may increase our ability to make sense of it.

What does it mean to have the dollar (while the Euro is held in reserve) as the fundamental unit of book keeping? What relationships and conflicts—and hence alliances and wars—are reflected by the areas in which the dollar is accumulated, the exchange rates between currencies, activities in the bonds, notes, and equity markets, and by the changes in interest rates and prices? Could it not be that the Third World War, which is so often talked about, is taking place within this unreal, virtual world? Is it not possible that the wars fought in the actual world are simply their manifestations?

It is widely accepted that after the Second World War the United States became the hegemonic power. The global influence of the dollar as monetary unit is the consequence of this hegemony. Interestingly enough, the dollar threw off its dependency on gold just as this hegemony had reached its peak. This clearly reflects its status as world hegemon: responsible and accountable to no one. It is widely known that the United States has released billions of dollars in the world which have no value since the 1980's. This is terrible and means that the United States has made billions of dollars each year just by letting the mint work. Never before, in no other age or location, has money been able to advance itself this much. Has there ever been any other tool than this phenomenon that explains how money itself is the hegemon? If we keep in mind that all the nation-states are in debt (the most heavily indebted, interestingly enough, is the United States itself), we can increase our understanding of why money is the absolute hegemon. The agitation caused around the world by the money speculations orchestrated by the US Central Bank (by manipulation of the interest rate, and price reductions and escalations) also explains how well the financial system has adapted. There is an abundance of facts proving the power of money.

The connection between crises and the system is even more striking. Crises resulting from chain reactions in Asia, Russia, and Latin America are purely monetary occurrences that are reflected in the real economy only much later. In the past, a crisis would start in the real world and then spread to the monetary world; the crisis of the financial age is just the reverse. When the crisis finally appears in the real world, the hegemons of the finance world end it, not allowing it to worsen, but not before pulling the relevant countries into line! The example of Russia is enlightening. The USSR officially broke up in 1991 and the financial crisis it was put into gradually worsened. The crisis was made to peak in 1998.

I was in Moscow at the time, due to developments following my departure from Damascus. The Russian officials told me to leave the country urgently and that they would do anything to ensure that this happened. Even the Chief of Intelligence told me, "If it were six months later, everything would have been much easier and we would not have treated you this way." Yes, the 1998 crisis had taken control of Russia as was admitted first hand by the competent authorities. I remember it all very well: this operation was executed by the then Foreign Affairs Minister of Israel, Ariel Sharon, and the United States Secretary of State, Madeleine Albright. They came to Moscow in a hurry and managed to get me thrown out of Russia in return for ten billion dollars. An agreement with the IMF was signed to this end. There was also the Blue Stream agreement signed between Russia and Turkey in return for my deportation. This agreement was another condition put forward by Russia despite opposition from the USA. As Russia was drawn deeper into the neoliberal policies of the system's hegemon, it was able to gradually recover from its paralyzed state and to be integrated into the system. This was how a counterrevolution took place in the age of virtual and financial counterrevolutions!

Analyzing how the age of finance rules the real world will be highly instructive. We have often emphasized that money's ability to rule the real economic world is linked to its rise to command power. Those projects that serve the hegemon's main policies are given top priority. How should the world economy be designed with respect to the age of finance? What region should focus on which goods? What would its share be? How should the fundamental policies of the countries be arranged; their economic and social structuring be renewed? How should they pay their debts and use their resources? Moreover, how can what the system calls "rebellious" or "mobster" countries and economies be brought into line? How can the former USSR block (the Warsaw Pact countries), China, and the so-called Third World countries be integrated into the hegemonic system? How should relations with Israel be arranged?

On the whole, a project that is put before a country, firm, state, or individual will fall within the parameters of what the party concerned can adapt to, so that they will fall in line with the general criteria of the new financial age and its neoliberal policies. Investments related to these projects are bound to many political and military conditions. Only after such an agreement is reached will the necessary finance or monetary instruments be provided. Those who do not comply are brought to the point of bankruptcy as a result of the imposed crisis. In fact, the age of finance is in essence the age of conditional lending.

This is how the system works. Even these short descriptions show that capitalism is *not* economy in the age of finance. Not only are these paper games *not* economy, they themselves provide the proof that they are non-economic impositions. The monopoly in fact attains its maximum profits through these paper instruments. What clearer evidence can there be that this system is anti-economy? The profits attained in the financial system and age have been obtained for almost free of charge when compared with the trade and industrial age. In return for small coupons everyone is drawn into being involved in profit, and thus is made a partner in crime; the system survives, it is even stronger than before. The age of finance is even more non-economy than industrialism. It is a form of society and its culture.

It is clear that we face a highly monopolized monetary system. This is such a super-monopolization phase that where even states (including the United States as a state) are being dissolved into it. This system has attained a position of power where it controls, develops, breaks-down, and reinstates all the processes of power. This is the essence of the new globalization. The age of communication does not, as may be thought, characterize globalization. Its essence is the entwinement of economy and politics—or political monopoly—to an unprecedented level. This denotes all local, national, political, and economic willpowers coming under the control of the global powers of the super-monopolies. This is a new situation and it requires our focused attention.

The effect of money on the societal reality is purely for the purpose of conquering. The goal is to create a monetary and virtual society. Capitalization of society can most effectively be obtained by allowing it to participate in profits through instruments such as bonds, repurchase agreements, debentures, and shares. As a result, society, but especially the middle class, is integrated with the financial world. In return for a small profit they are turned into a force to defend the system. Their reflexes against the system are significantly weakened. Through the creation of consumerist society, consumer credit, microcredit, and many other varieties of project credits there is an attempt to seize tight control of society. The method is simple. First of all, by imposing a crisis, a new unemployed world is added to the already existing world of unemployed. The collapse of the middle class is engineered and they are forced to ask for mercy, once again. Hunger and poverty are imposed to the point of starvation. Turmoil and chaos deepen and, later, in return for the acceptance of some conditions, credit is given to reconstruct the society.

In the past, efforts were made to transform societies through revolutions and enlightening cultural movements. Present-day financial methods will (or try to) attain any desired result through a more complete, minutely planned, no-risk approach. There are endless renewed efforts to construct homogenization on a global scale and to create a mass-like, herd-like society so that not the slightest objection will be raised against the system. In a way, these social projects are substitutions for the old revolutions and utopias; there is no longer a need for revolutions and utopias. Everything can be pinned down to a project and, besides, the prospective financiers will be ready and willing. This must be what they call the counter-society, simulacrum society, virtual society, or a single-minded society. Are the things imposed on us not part of a project for the realization of fascism on a global scale, but with a new mask? There is thus a need to define and recognize all aspects of the society of the financial age.

The political and state policies of the financial age are partly contradictory to that of the Industrial Age. Industrialism mainly focused on policies of nationalism and the nation-state, and endeavored to create the required monopolies. However, in view of its need to become global, the age of finance sees these monopolies as obstacles. Capitalism that has become a world-system cannot support the nation-state monopoly to the end of time. The nation-state monopolies that have a tendency to keep to themselves become obstacles to the monopolies, which wish to move on a global scale. The financial age can only increase its profits if it is able to use its tools on a global scale. The nation-state poses a serious obstacle to this. It will either adjust to this new situation or be destroyed. North Korea, Libya, Syria, Iran, and Iraq were able to protect their existence only after they accepted such a modification. When Iraq later declined to accept it, it incurred the wrath of the financial age. A new country must then be constructed: it cannot be destroyed completely. Countries such as Brazil, Turkey, Argentine, China, India, and Russia are profound in their commitment to nation-statism. Hence, they are at the top of the list of countries that must be disciplined by the imposition of crises and subsequently be re-integrated into the system.

More importantly, the nation-state prevents the development of exhaustive globalization. Globalization requires states that will make do with a smaller scale, with limited and subordinate power instead of local political units of the nation-state type. It attempts to transform medium size states with the help of local units. The paradox between the nation-state and the globalization of the financial age may continue for a while, also because the limited anti-capitalist elements within them necessitate this. Rectifying the profound failures caused especially by the nation-state, but by the classical state in general, is attempted with a buffer system that is called civil society but one that does not fully represent civil society in its essence. Relieving the predicament of liberalism's nation-state is attempted by draining civil society of its democratic content. Civil society is the political arena over which the classical and the democratic civilizations have quarreled over most often. The democratization of civil society is a question of principle and hence it falls under democratic politics. It is one of our fundamental duties to analyze how it can be done and to work towards its achievement.

Ideologically, some main issues and questions arising from the financial age include: the clash of civilizations, radicalism, terrorism, the reconstruction of the state, globalism, and the elevation of religion. The thesis on the clash of civilizations is important from two aspects. It may be expected that the system will impose on the entire world the civilization to which its hegemonic power belongs. But, contrary to what is believed and is projected, there is no white, Anglo-Saxon, Christian civilization. The fact that the socialist civilization attempted to be created by real socialism could not display qualities that surpassed capitalist modernity caused its re-integration into the system. This allowed the world to overcome an apparent civilization crisis. Hence, the clash between the two blocks is now seen not as a clash between two civilizations but between the two hegemonic powers (representing the same modernity), especially after the disintegration of the USSR and China's capitalist development.

On the other hand, the Islamic world is an area of an ancient civilization, and also represents a kind of regional nationalism. If we add the conflict with Israel to this, we can see how the problem of civilizations is brought to a head. During all three stages of the Age of Capitalism, the Middle East could not be integrated into the system. The nation-state brought the civilization question to an impasse instead of resolving it. The escalation of religious nationalism in Saudi Arabia and Shi'ite Iran together with the intense use of violence and the ongoing consequences of the Israeli-Palestinian question has increased the parameters of the debate on civilization. This is the intra-civilizational dimension of the problem. Another dimension is the desire of the people of the region, the mosaic societies, to protect their existence and defend their cultural identity, and to rid themselves of the fascist state, which is a mixture of the despotic and the nation-state. In a way, it reflects the clash between the democratic civilization, which is potentially very strong, and the classical despotic civilization on a regional scale. Clearly, with additional issues such as petrol and water, we can talk about serious civilizational clashes in the Middle East.

Radicalism is, in its essence, a nation-statist reaction to the globalism of the financial age. It comes to the fore as ideological and political movements with religious and racist traits aiming to further introvert the nation-state. Many such examples can be found in every region. There are those with a religious color, be it Islamic, Christian, Hindu, or African animist, and those with right-wing nationalist and racist elements, present in every nation-state. Often they overlap. They represent a more reactionary form of localism against globalism. On the other hand, local, democratic, cultural, feminist movements and the New Left come together (albeit insufficiently so) at platforms such as the World Social Forum demonstrating the strength to discuss democratic civilization. Terrorism is most probably a provocative movement of the system itself. There are strong indications that this is an instrument deliberately used to legitimize the rule of the financial age. Al-Qaida, for example, is still a mystery.

Indeed, the age of finance itself has strong terroristic qualities. The social relationships that have been damaged by money are themselves a question of terrorism. There is no terror that can be as effective as the hegemony of money that alienates society from its most profound ties. Most of the activities undertaken by the system to construct and sustain its existence in all economic, societal, and political areas form a part of unprecedented terror. It tries to disguise this huge terror it inflicts with the help of provocative elements. The realization of making money out of money on a large scale and outside of the boundaries of the real economy is in fact the strong and crafty man establishing himself as a system to rule society. The robberies of the forty thieves are nothing compared to the robberies of the financial age monopoly. Robberies on such a huge scale can only occur in a system of total terror. Therefore, the phenomenon called the communication age can only be required to disguise the terror of finance. Maybe the concept of media terror will be more meaningful in this context. In short, the system itself is the biggest terrorist of all times.

The elevation—or boost—of religion only makes sense in relation to covering and concealing things. The system's way of exploitation requires a supreme legitimization power, such as that of religion. The process of excluding society from production, initiated to meet the needs of society, has reached its peak with the age of finance, ensuing mass unemployment. Periods that cannot be explained scientifically can only be cushioned with the help of religion: this is exactly what has happened. It is not the religious culture that is suppressed but the renewed religionization. When an age becomes conservative it plunges into such ideological reality. Thus, rentier economy, the herd-like mentality, clash of civilizations, terror and religious conservatism ensure that society is tightly bound. The system of iron cage, of mass surveillance: when it cannot totally control society, such new ideological factors are articulated and implemented.

At first, the age of finance seems to be capitalism's strongest era, but all its characteristics really represent a collapse. This indicates that the system has exhausted its ability to perpetuate itself. The more devoid of meaning an age becomes, the greater is its need to become conservative. This need is not due to its strengths but to its weaknesses. Production is a fundamental activity that a human being and society cannot do without. However, the age of finance is the admission that this cannot be provided. A system that cannot realize production is a system with no work. This is exactly what has happened. The system, which is so much in conflict with work and production, has only one chance for survival, and that is terror. Indeed, this is what is really happening, accompanied by propaganda, distortions, and provocations.

In the 1980s, a wave of terror was initiated by Reagan and Thatcher, the heads of state of the two hegemonic powers, the United States and Great Britain, by their respective attacks on Nicaragua and the Argentine forces in the Falkland Islands. Those who came to power in Pakistan and Turkey through coups d'état were their closest supporters. Latin America was totally terrorized. The arms race that continued in the form of the so-called "Star Wars" deterred Russia from attempting to become a hegemonic power. The Deng Xiaoping reforms in China were nothing but concessions to the system. The result was the end of the concessions attained by the national liberation struggles and welfare states. Instead, everywhere the winds of terror of the financial age began to blow. Clinton continued this implementation through effective, albeit mild, policies.

The Middle East was the only place that was not completely conquered. Instead, it was turned into an area where the problems stemming from civilization, radicalism, terror, and religion have become a Gordian knot. If the system does not wish to deteriorate it has to complete its conquest in one way or another. In addition, there is the vital question of oil. Oil is the sector from which the age of finance has derived the most value, and it is generally believed that the dire need for oil will continue for another century. The conflict between Israel and the Arabs has been hanging over the system like the sword of Damocles. Shi'ite Iran continues to pose a great danger to the system.

The Middle East is a web of problems inherited from England and France. In fact, in this region the First World War has not yet been brought to conclusion. Coups, rebellions, civil and guerrilla wars are all indications of this unconcluded stage. Borders drawn with a ruler just to increase the problems. One could have expected that because of these problems the United States would work on a project for the region. If it wasn't for the Cold War, the USSR, Latin America, and problems with Europe, it would have indeed been compelled to intervene in the region long ago. With the onset of 1990s, the problem areas mentioned above were partly solved in accordance with the system. But the problems associated with Middle East became more intense. Either the USA had to give up totally or had to intervene. If it were to give up, the oil and Israel would be lost and Iran would have the opportunity to become a hegemonic power. And then, of course, there was the threat of Saddam Hussein's ambition to become the Bismarck of the Arabs.

The Age of Trade was accompanied by terrible wars of plunder of the colonies. The Industrial Age brought two big world wars, internal class struggles, and national liberation struggles. The financial capital, on the other hand, has turned into a power battle of the society against society. This very last representative of the civilizational monopolies may wind up at the bottom of this structural chaos if the Middle East is totally lost. Indeed, this is nearly the case. The chances of the system for success now to a large extent lie with developments in the region. That is why a Third World War, with its unique characteristics, goes on in this region. Later developments will confirm this.

I believe the critical and strategic relationship of this period with what happened to me will be understood more clearly later. Indeed, the issue is already gradually becoming more clear. Apparently, during the two meetings between the most influential leader of Syria, Hafez Al-Assad, and the most influential leader of the United States, Bill Clinton, half the time was spent talking about me. I clearly brought the situation to a standstill. A long term strategic role in the Greater Middle East Project was given to the Kurds. The Kurds and Kurdistan would be used as battering rams in the resolution of the problems experienced by the financial capital in the region. At different times, Armenians and others (Helens, Assyrians, and even Jews, Arabs, and Palestinians) have been used to the same end. The Kurdish stick may have a resolving effect when dealing with those powers that are pro status quo and excessively pro nation-state, that are foiling attempts at solving problems originating with the system, and do not stop dreaming of becoming the regional hegemon.

It is now clear that such a plan has been in preparation since the 1970s. It seems that I got involved in it as an unforeseen element that has brought things to a standstill. I was either going to do as I was told and become their soldier or I would be disposed of. My character was not suitable for being a soldier of the system. Understandably, I was seen to be the first and the easiest element to get rid of. The First World War started when the Austrian heir to the throne was killed by a Serbian militant. But the war went on in the Middle East and it would continue more intensely, but now as a Third World War. This time, quite contrary to the occurrences of the past, I would be the victim—the outcome of a plan devised by all the organized forces of the system. Here the similarities and repetition of history through renewal are quite striking. In my defense during my court case in the Athens Court of Appeals, I said "Just as Prometheus was chained to a rock in the Caucasus with the help of the gods Athena, Hades, and Ares, I have been chained to the rocks of İmralı Island by their human descendants." It seems, though, that my statement was not quite complete.

With this analysis of mine it will be better understood that I have been chained by a real god. This small offspring of god, that grew strong in the secrecy of the cloisters of history and later came into money, emerged in the Capitalist Age to stand openly before society. It has achieved such a level of acceptance that all the other gods of former ages have vanished. The kings were dragged to the floor and their heads cut off. It has imposed the bloodiest times and the most profound exploitation on the humanity. It has polluted under and above ground. It has really destroyed the human race and, even worse, uncountable varieties and numbers of living beings.

The divinity ascribed to money has given birth to a phenomenon more dreadful than a "real" god. If I have been able to describe, at least partly, the system it rests upon and what it entails, the happiness I will get out of this may be my exclusive reward. Spinoza said, "To understand is to be free." I, too, believe that there is no freedom other than this. To become as free as I can understand is my strength in life. The main god of the age of finance united with all its supporters and accomplices to chain me to the rocks of İmralı. But in return, it has found those that have lit the torch of freedom opposing itself. They are located at the Zagros and Taurus mountains where all the sacred gods and goddesses of history have had their thrones, and their torch of freedom shall never be extinguished.

Apollo is the god of light and defense. I quite like him. Dionysus is the mountain god of wine, love, and joy. I also like the culture he embodies. They are both versions of more ancient gods with Zagros and Taurus roots that have spilled over to Anatolia. They clearly represent the identity of peoples that have been filtered over thousands of years. Light and joy are the most beautiful expressions of life. I am also trying to understand the two ancient gods of our region, Gudea and El-Lāh.[2] I would really like to know why they have consented to leave our peoples in pain with no light and defense against Money-Lāh—the Money God. As a lovestruck child of the region, I am happy to have not abandoned our peoples to the mercy of the devious, crooked, and barren Money God. I believe that my friends and the communities they belong to shall always be happy with me.

Conclusion

Is a compromise between the statist civilization and the democratic civilization possible? I would like to briefly outline this volume of my defense with several short conclusions:

First: Without an analysis of the emergence of power throughout the course of history we cannot achieve a sound sociology. The social sciences that have developed within the theoretical framework (or paradigm) of positivist science have come to a total dead-end. If this were not the case, how would we explain the extreme level of exploitation and incidence of war in our time? A scientist's responsibility towards society is no less than that of a cleric or an ethicist. If scientific reasoning is indeed superior to mythology, religion, and philosophy in the quest for meaningfulness (and it had its revolution and attained its victory in the seventeenth century), then how could science not show its superiority over such unprecedented incidences of war and exploitation? It just may be that science's integration with power is behind these atrocities. A science that has itself become the power loses its freedom.

If science is defined as the most advanced interpretation of meaning, then its quick integration with power either indicates a defeat of science, or there is a serious discrepancy between science and how it is defined. I attempted to show how this problem is linked to positivism. Although positivism criticizes metaphysics and religion quite a lot, it is itself metaphysics and religion intertwined with the most vulgar materialism. Thus, it even falls behind religion and metaphysics. This is apparent from the irresponsible approach of the disciplines referred to as positivist sciences: They did not do anything against exploitation and wars. They do not even regard these as their problem. Subsequently, they became the science of those in power. An important conclusion that can be drawn from this is the urgent need for science to develop a renewed interpretation of meaning. Science needs another paradigmatic revolution. In this work, I tested my ability to interpret things by understanding their meaning. The results I arrived at correlate with this attempt.

Second: Power should be thought of as a tradition, a very ancient one at that. Power is not the sum of actions that emerge daily and enforce its authority upon societies. Moreover, we have to understand that power is not limited only to the state. Reducing the concept of power to the state and different state forms is the basis of the previous mistakes, as has often been the case. To say that power is the combination of war acts and other obvious features will be nothing but the most opportunistic way in which power can be defined. I have often used the phrase "crafty and strong man" as an illustrative metaphor like the much used "invisible hand of the market." I think it can be highly instructive in our understanding of the basis of power. Those that regulate power, each relation and those involved in such relations, at times openly but most often secretly are the ones that construct power.

Power is a social phenomenon with the utmost ability for continuity and concentration. The man, who has domesticated the woman, is probably the first and the biggest shareholder in this. First by establishing a monopoly over the power of meaning, and later by establishing themselves as priests—thus gaining a religious identity—the shamans' role in the sanctification and mystification of the naked strength of power was significant. We can link the mythology of power and all the concepts of divinization to this group. Mythological and religious rhetoric is highly effective in the construction and legitimizing of power. The group that did the most to further society's acceptance of power is the trinity of the priest, ruler, and commander of the hierarchic and patriarchal regime. They were the creators of traditions such as the use of the throne to symbolize power. Deification and exaltation, the throne, the disunity between god and human, the discrediting of goddesses, and servitude are all strong symbols of power that are remnants of this period.

Third: State power is a more permanent and concrete form of power that comes into existence because of the presence of hierarchy, the domestication of women, servitude, and slavery. It refers to the regulation of power relations that have become quite widespread in the society, and clarifies and designates everyone's responsibility, as well as making more effective and sparing use of such relations. Power embodies the state but it is much more than just the state. States are monopolist institutions that mark the beginning of history. In the final analysis, the increasing economic strength of society ceases to be the subject of democratic politics and becomes an area over which a monopoly of the ruling power is established. This is how surplus production and values are seized. All other elements related to state—mythology, philosophy, religion, science, war, and the various policies—are connected to this main aim. This remains the case even in a communist state. Power becomes official within a society through the state and enhances its legitimacy.

Activities, wars, and discourses that society may find meaningful are matters of the most interest to those representing the state. Judicially, the state is a set of rules. Another way to define the state may be as the tradition that is reinforced with power and bound to rules. Within this framework it may also be called the aggregate of the most advanced abstract relations. Although categories such as theocratic, despotic, monarchic, imperialist, republican, absolutist, nation-, class-based, ethnic, secular, democratic, and social state may all appear to be different, in essence they are all the regulation of power—relations made tangible. As they became socially more complex and class divisions formed, towns played a leading role in the development of state and power. Nevertheless, towns cannot be identified only with the state.

Fourth: Civilization is the overarching definition for the state's attainment of social control based predominately in its concentration within the town. The state's rule of the town was the first serious venture of the civilization. Civilization has some characteristics that go beyond being the state. It is closely linked to time and location. It harbors many ethnicities, peoples, nations, religions, and schools of thought. State is the nucleus of civilization, but it is not everything. Similarly, the town is a fundamental location for the state, but the town is not only the state or even only power. Civilizations may multiply in different locations and times as with the Egyptian, Sumerian, Median, Persian, Greco-Roman, Christian, Islamic, Indian, Chinese, Aztec, and European civilizations. In all of them urbaneness, class division, and the existence of towns are common factors. The relationship within and amongst civilizations may be peaceful or hostile depending on the substance of its economic and political monopoly. Peace will follow if the offered share is acceptable: it will be called a "fair split." But if it is unacceptable, the civilizations'— and hence the states'—tool of choice for attaining "justice" is war. There is a close relationship between war, violence, civilization, state, justice, and law. Essentially they all indicate whether the activities (economic, political, and ideological) of social groups and individuals are protected by themselves or appropriated by some other groups or persons. Civilization is the sum of the relationships between these traditions, institutions and rules. A civilization may sometimes be expressed in terms of the formation of class and surplus product, such as a slave-owning, feudal, or capitalist civilization. Domesticated woman, hierarchic patriarchy, state, and civilization are the layers that form the entirety of power. This formulates how comprehensive this aggregate of power relations is.

Fifth: Democratic civilization is a social category separate from state civilization. I use it with the aim to conceptualize the social forms prior to the formation of state and civilization, as well as the structures that later existed outside the state. Throughout history, states were always careful to equate themselves with the society. The cornerstone of their ideological rhetoric has always been the impossibility of having a sociality that is distinct from the state. The representatives of the state react strongest when told that state and society are different entities and that there are fundamental contradictions between them. Nevertheless, I must emphasize that the state is essentially nothing but a very small interest monopoly whose fundamental aim is not dealing with public affairs in the interests of society, but using these affairs as a cover to gain legitimacy.

Undoubtedly, society has become more complex since the primitive communal era and there are many common social affairs that need to be taken care of. Whilst the state excludes society by putting these affairs under its own jurisdiction and, therefore, they become the justification for state's legitimacy, democratic society on the other hand proposes or ensures that these common affairs are taken care of by society as a whole. The difference between state civilization and democratic civilization is based precisely on this. This is of critical importance. When communities are able to represent themselves and act on their own behalves concerning all their affairs, *then* they can be said to be democratic. But if most of their own affairs are seen to by the state or other groups, then they incur a loss of skills, freedom, equality, and conscience. Individuals and groups who cannot represent themselves or see to their own affairs cannot become conscious and acquire skills, and they cannot live freely and equally. As can be seen, a difference in facts can lead to such important results.

A fundamental fact relating to society that needs to be pointed out is the communal order according to which primitive clans and tribes have lived for millions of years. In this communal order, we can detect the most primitive form of democracy. Just as the state represents the nucleus of the state civilization, the primitive communal order is the nucleus of the democratic civilization. This alone shows us how strong the democratic roots are. The subject of written history is state civilizations. The fact that societies have lived in communal orders for millions of years, taking care of their own affairs, does not fall within the scope of this history. But this is what historiography should reflect because, due to its long duration and wide occurrence, the communal life of the human species defines society itself. This is the true society. State and civilization have arrived much later and are artificial. They are indeed a dead weight mounted on society. Without them society would have continued its development. Indeed, development does continue but it is a development condemned to be distorted, bloody, and exploited. When we look at societies that use writing and have a state we see that in their language and history they use a terminology of lies, deceptions, tyranny and oppression. The established world of symbols imposes the feeling that a life without oppression and exploitation and without the oppressed, subjects, and slaves is not possible for societies. From mere symbols this was turned into reality and communities, in terms of their democratic potential, were caught and chained in the childhood-stage of their lives. This is what is *not* normal—a civilization with chains. This is the civilization that has used the atom bomb; the civilization that, apart from three hundred years of peace, has been at war for all of its five thousand year old life. It is responsible for the uninhabitable conditions of the environment and the deadlock in all social problems.

These are the strong justifications for a democratic move. What is not natural is the excessive growth of the state civilization as opposed to the dwindling of the democratic civilization. This is the main paradox of all societies. It constitutes the civilizational disease of not being able to develop in the presence of democracy. The society full of joy and love should be considered no less normal than the sorrowful, painful, and loveless society. Indeed, *democratic civilization is the society that is advancing towards a civilization full of joy and love.* This is more than just an option: it is the difference made by free life, which is the natural way of life and the one suitable to human nature, the one in which emotional and analytical intelligence can be unified.

Sixth: The order of capital is not the product of four hundred years of capitalism but a product of the five thousand year old state civilization. The surplus product that initially appeared in agriculture is the material basis of capital. Its early organization took place in the temple grounds where the top floor was that of the god (or top ruler); the middle floor was that of the priest (the deputy of the top ruler—an envoy in relation to the community and rules) who upheld the legitimacy of power; the ground floor belonged to the slaves who worked to get fed. This system has been propagated to the present: multiplying, dissociating, and becoming more layered. Urbanization, class division, and state-formation are really products of the surplus product. Society has continuously been subjected to the division of labor, separated into ranks, habituated to power and forced to either defend or attack: all this describes the phenomenon called civilization. These positions also clearly reveal civilization's connection with capital. Although capital is in a narrow sense economically defined as multiplying itself over the short term, in a broader sense multiplying itself over a long term is essentially the same. Just as the daily surplus of the merchant can be described as capital, the yearly surplus product of the land-monopoly could also be described as capital.

History indicates that the age of trade began before civilization, starting at Uruk at 4,000 BCE and continuing into the present. It is in fact six thousand years old. The merchant civilization, which has always been secondary to the agricultural civilization, has at times resulted in magnificent city civilizations, but in general it has not been welcomed by the communities. The exploitative way in which it made its acquisitions has played an important role in this. On the whole, it has settled in the darkened corridors and secluded corners of social history. Its development has escalated during every civilization era. The commercial sector became the hegemonic power in the Italian towns for the first time in history between the thirteenth and the sixteenth century, and later in all of European towns from the fifteenth to the eighteenth century. It thus played a fundamental role in the birth of European civilization. It not only rose to become the new actor in society, it also established its influence over the political platform. The big trade monopolies and colonial plunders played a decisive role in the increase of capital. It even managed to establish its hegemony over movements such as the Renaissance, Reformation, and Enlightenment.

Industrialization, with the help of the nineteenth century Industrial Revolution, has become the real area of profit for capital. The peak of the European civilization was reached when production, circulation, and consumption fell into the hands of industrial monopolies. This resulted in class struggles internally and national liberation struggles externally. The hegemonic ideology of the system neutralized both of these resistance struggles in return for compromises allowed by the system. By the end of twentieth century the crises caused by industrialism, especially the urban and environmental problems, became structural in character. This resulted in the age of finance. This period signifies the liberation of capital from its dependence on production and the liberation of money from gold reserves. They became totally irresponsible and this period turned into a full-scale crisis of civilization. The social potential of capital has been exhausted, but it tries to maintain its existence by renewing and sustaining itself as virtual systems. The capital-profit order, which has become reliant on rolls of paper, is trying to render society unable to act through continuous crises. The third global move of the capitalist system is in fact the third and final stage of the structural crisis phase of civilization.

I found it appropriate to refer to the Age of Capitalism as a social crisis. I postulated as a fundamental thesis the fact that, although generally seen as the civilization most concerned with the economy, capitalism is not economy at all but an external power monopoly that imposes itself on economy and, therefore, cannot be seen as legitimate. The establishment of the domination of capitalism, which is the most selfish, self-seeking, and belligerent force, over society can only represent an "extraordinary" situation in history, that is, the situation of crisis. The age of finance is indeed all aspects of this reality surfacing in all the different parts of society. There are many indicators signaling the system's depletion, such as the system itself breeding continuous terror, leaving a large portion of society unemployed, even degrading employment to a sort of unemployment, resulting in the masses and a herd-like society; the industrialization of arts, sex, and sports; and, the infiltration of power into the tiniest veins of society. Thus is the assumption created that the entire history and entire future can only exist if it is based on the order of capital. The main role of the sector called "the media" lies in its ability to present this virtual and simulacrum society as real. On the other hand, the society that we should realize and live in is continuously presented as infertile, unrealistic, utopian and, therefore, left out of discussion. Capital, contrary to popular belief, is a power monopoly and regime of violence that has wedded itself to the economy from the start, distorting it profoundly. And instead of producing the necessities, it plunges into areas where it can attain a cancer-like growth of profits.

Seventh: In contrast to the order of capital, economy is the area where society's material needs are attained. The reason for its remaining within the domain of use value for such a long time is the communal order. Social cohesion can only be governed on the principle that everyone's life should be guaranteed. Human nature requires this. The purpose of production has never been perceived as making profit. Although the gift economy was essential, after long periods of hesitation and as result of increasing labor division, the exchange economy found a place in society. As in the case of the use value, the formation of the exchange value was not profit-oriented. It entailed satisfying needs through increased variety and interdependence. Initially the relationship between commodification, market, and money was not profit-motivated: it developed to satisfy the required diversity and interdependency. Market economy is not a capital-profit economy but an economy in which exchange extensively steps in. Trade is a beneficial and necessary economic activity only if it is remunerated with a corresponding value for the effort made for circulation. The market where prices are determined through non-monopolist competition becomes an area where the economy pulsates. Money is just a tool to ease exchange. All circles, including small tradespeople and professionals, can be elements beneficial to the economy if they do not tend towards exploitation in the marketplace. The division of needs into sectors such as food, clothing, shelter, transport, and entertainment is an indication that the economy has developed. Efforts concerning these sectors can be meaningful if they are truly economic activities. In the eyes of society all such efforts are understandable, valuable, and ethical.

The strong reactions and objections are aimed at the monopolist enforcements imposed upon the economy externally through the methods using coercion, force, or refined deception (such as famine, stock, prices, and speculation on the value of money). Throughout history this monopolist imposition has been understood to be bad, ugly, tyrannical, cruel, unjust, and something that should not exist. This order for establishing monopolies is also called the order of capital and profit. Its main principle is to enable some to make a fortune while the majority is left unemployed, poor, and at the threshold of hunger so that they will continuously be in need of the order of capital. The justification is that competition will take off when the opportunity arises to make a fortune, which then will further the economy. This is nothing but a big lie as can be seen from the fact that those at the top of the financial order have nothing to do with economy (apart from speculative matters such as the stock exchange, interest rates, and exchange rates). The relationship they establish with the economy is synonymous with the crisis. Aside from profit nothing concerns them.

Thanks to the distortive scientific discipline called political economy, the real economic activities have been driven out of the economic arena while activities that are *not* economic have been presented as the indispensable and sacred elements (speculative matters such as stock exchange, interest rates, and exchange rates) of the economy: it is proffered as "high economy." The power monopoly is successfully presenting us things that are *not* economy as economy, and what is not economy—indeed the opposite of economy—as high economy or the sacred of economy. Our reply when asked what we see as the fundamental economic issue must be: "Above all, to rid ourselves of this monopoly through which we are robbed." In order to have a real economy we need to get rid of that which is *not* economy, anti-economy, and is externally imposed by the monopoly of power. We need to rid ourselves of the speculators' games of interest rate, stock exchange, and exchange rate. Real economy is the production, division, and consumption of produce that fulfill real needs, that are accessible, and produced according to environmentally friendly investment techniques. In order to build such an economy, the necessary first step is a planned, structured, and organized action to liberate ourselves from this non-economy.

Eight: The first opposition to the barbarity of the Capitalist Age came from the tribes and clans who resisted and rebelled against attempts to colonize or semi-colonize them. The Native American tribes of the north, as well as the Aztec civilization of South America resisted to the end. The Asian and African civilizations, tribes, and peoples (the Chinese, Indian, and Ethiopian civilizations, along with thousands of tribes) also continued their resistance and rebellion. As the national liberation movements of the twentieth century they achieved many important successes (albeit with many shortcomings and errors). Internally, the major stimulant was the proletarianization process itself. Contrary to widespread belief, being able to sell one's labor freely at the market is not a way out of being a serf or partial slavery. On the contrary, it is being condemned to the cruelest slavery where you have no way out but to obtain a wage. That the nature of the new despotic regime is worse than anything before can be seen in people's inability to find work and the continued insufficiency of the wage.

All major rebellions against capitalism were waged so as *not* to become such workers. They were not rebellions aiming to become workers, but *not* to become workers. If, mislead by false representation, we proclaim, "Long live the struggle of the workers," this amounts to saying, "Long live slavery." What is right and is indeed supported by life itself is to reject being condemned to wages. These half-peasant and half-salesclerk rebellions that developed on their own are continuously intertwined with the history of capitalism. On the other hand, the intellectuals who were not optimistic about the feudal order and could not tell how the new order would develop were constantly searching for the "City of the Sun."[1] The initial utopists never endorsed capitalism. On the contrary, against this nightmare they always presented their own utopian projects for a future full of hope. The period of transition to capitalism was also the period when the struggle for the age of communal order, equality, and freedom was waged by a broad group of heroic utopists such as Erasmus, Tommaso Campanella, Saint-Simon, and Charles Fourier.

Under the leadership of Marx and Engels the first scientifically based struggle began against capitalism. Although it contained important shortcomings and errors, this very first movement to oppose the system, acting in the name of scientific socialism, became the nightmare of capitalism for one hundred and fifty years. There was much heroism and many important victories were attained. It became the official ideology of the USSR for seventy years. It raised Mainland China to its feet. It became the source of inspiration for national liberation struggles. The misfortune of this anti-systemic movement was its inability to analyze capitalist modernity and to make a radical break from it. The scientific framework it was embedded in was positivist. They understood very little of the continuity of the state civilization and tradition of power within the capitalist civilization. Nevertheless, they deserve to become the cornerstone of the democratic civilization.

Furthermore, we should not belittle the anti-capitalism of the anarchists. Proudhon, Bakunin, and Kropotkin especially but many other anarchists were masterful revolutionaries who were able to integrate their critique of the system with the principles of democratic communalism. Freedom and commune movement are in indebted to them. The fundamental failing and shortcoming of this movement was seeing capitalism as a purely economic system and not fully understanding its civilizational and power roots, as well as their inability to break the molds of modernity.

The intellectual and students' movement that reached their peak in 1968 were the biggest protest movements at the onset of the age of finance. Although its utopic aspect overrode most other, it became the torch of freedom and light against the dirtiest and darkest order of all times. The subsequent development of cultural, feminist, environmental and ecologic movements with their anti-modernist perspectives marked this era. They extended the struggle for equality, freedom, and democracy by not basing it on power. They become the voice of global society against global capitalism. These opponents of the system are strengthened through their self-criticism regarding past practice and a more comprehensive understanding of history and society. For the first time, they may completely break away from capitalist civilization, unite with the democratic civilization, and advance on the path of freedom, equality, and communalism.

Ninth: Behind the failure of the nineteenth and twentieth century revolutionaries lie their errors in relation to power and its modern embodiment: the nation-state. They anticipated that the resolution of the social problems would be achieved when they came to power. The main goal of their program was to take power into their own hands. All forms of struggle were formulated from this perspective. However, power itself is lack of freedom, lack of equality, anti-democracy. The traditional character of this tool is so strong that it will tamper with even the strongest revolutionaries involving themselves with it. Worse, they do not even have an historical and sociological analysis of power which they consider to be the tool of liberation. Not much has been put forward with regard to how power was formed over the course of history, the phases it passed through, its relationship with economy and state, the role it has played within the civilizations, and its position within society. It was as if it fell into the hands of the revolutionaries, like a magical wand it would simply turn everywhere into heaven. Its touch would immediately resolve any issue. The dictatorial style became so appealing that the dictatorship of the proletariat was declared against the dictatorship of the bourgeoisie. This was nothing but falling into a trap. A hundred and fifty years of heroic struggle was overwhelmed by the gulf of power. Finally, though, it has become clear that the tool at hand is the most backward, anti-egalitarian, anti-freedom, and anti-democratic mechanism of capitalism. But much was lost. A similar disease of power experienced during the early history of Christianity struck again.

The freedom movements' approach to the nation-state was even more of a disaster. This Leviathan of the modernity, molded into form with nationalism, sexism, religionism, and scientism, was accepted as the fundamental and proper framework within which to wage the struggle. The centralized nation-state was portrayed as more progressive and a tool (or rather a goal) to resolve problems in comparison to democratic confederalism. There was in fact no accurate analysis of the nation-state revealing how it created the most abnormal citizen by using the nationalism, sexist society and fanatic religiousness of the power monopoly, as well as the positivism of scientism: there was no analysis exposing the nation-state as the structure that allowed for the absorption of society into the state and resulted in fascism. When scientific socialism came to prefer this tool, which extended power to all layers of society, the fate of socialism became clear from the start. The official declaration of its disintegration in 1989 was but a formality. As the democratic quality of the Soviets had been lost in the beginning of the October Revolution, it should have been clear that what it would give birth to would not be socialism but capitalism. The inability of the national liberation struggles to deliver the expected results is also closely related to this form of power. How can one construct freedom and equality by using a tool that forms the basis for the oppression of freedom, equality, and democracy? Democracy, since it was seen as a tool that would loosen power, was removed right at the start.

The nation-state, as proto-fascism, bulldozed not only the wealth that societies had obtained through the ages but also destroyed their hope for the future. Thus, the only thing left is the nation-state, which is protected by the positivist religion of nationalism that is nothing but the idolatry of objects, which has constructed itself as the only truth, and is known by its brutality which has culminated in genocide, and has itself become divine. For the first time in capital's five thousand year history this power monopoly which was obtained through the fusion of economy, politics, society, and ideology was the source of all these problems. Clearly, unless and until the nation-state is surpassed both as a theoretical ideal and as an actual state form the socialist struggle will amount to nothing but self-deception.

If industrialism is not recognized and analyzed as nation-state's twin, then the canceration of cities and environmental destruction cannot be prevented. Industrialism, which is upheld as a revolutionary goal, is nothing but state monopolism's way of making maximum profits. This may, at best, be interpreted as *Pharaoh socialism*. The USSR until its disintegration, and currently Chinese socialism, became the strongest reinforcing agent of the capitalist system by being the most vulgar operators of industrialism. The fact that they became the strictest proponents of a nation-statist and industrialist modernity was a victory for liberal capitalism.

A more instructive approach may be reached if we understand that a system (like the one enforced in the age of finance) which presents itself as the most economic is in reality the exact opposite of what it claims to be. If it talks about finance, then we should think of power that has been extended to all layers of society. If it talks about economy, then we should see it as being non-economic and even counter-economic. If its talks about neoliberalism, then we should really understand it as rigid conservatism. Only such an approach will allow us to arrive at more accurate interpretations.

The nation-state, industrialism, and financial monopoly are instruments that not only prevent the disintegration of capitalist modernity, they also prevent the disintegration of the five thousand year old structure of civilization. Until they are able to re-structure themselves to become more permanent, they will cling onto these instruments. These will also be used as weapons to rush any of the alternatives, forcing them into the open whilst still incomplete and imperfect, or to tame and neutralize them.

Tenth: Throughout history the democratic and the poor sections of society have been backing the wrong horse. They have believed they would beat their enemies solely by using the weapons of the enemy. They have not been able to develop weaponry suitable for their libertarian, egalitarian, and democratic character. In cases where they did develop them, they gave those up too soon, whether the weapons were successful or not: it was just easier to use the more advanced weaponry of their rivals. They did not just take over their enemies' military equipment and instruments, but everything from the construction of their gods to their clothing, their architecture, their ideologies, forms of exploitation, power constructions—every single pre-constructed element of the civilizational mentality and institutions. Or, they were just absorbed by them and became like them. This is what is meant by backing the same horse as your rivals.

The Semite and Aryan tribal chiefs attacked the Sumerian civilization from all directions. But they subsequently embraced the Sumerian mindset and institutions for what they were and either became their representatives or servants. There the thousands of years of tribal resistance and the melodies of their epic heroism that still touch our hearts went down the drain.

Of the Apiru that attacked the Egyptian civilization the majority were turned into slaves.[2] From the small number that was not enslaved, no one advanced further than the level of palatial bureaucrat. We know of a Hebrew tribe that descends from both the Sumerian-Babylonian and Egyptian civilization. They not only created problems for themselves but for the whole world: they were neither completely enslaved nor did they manage to be completely free.

The Median and Scythian tribes withstood and attacked the Assyrian Empire for three hundred years. In the end, though, they only served as harbingers of the Urartu and Persian Empires—exact copies of the Assyrian Empire! Some from the Median and Scythian tribes could not escape from becoming their military chiefs and most from becoming their subjects.

Resistance to the Greco-Roman civilization continued ceaselessly for about five hundred years. Externally, there was the resistance and incursions of Celtic, Nordic, Gothic, and Hunnic tribes; internally, there were slave rebellions and resistance from Christianity, the party of the poor with various different ethnic roots. What did centuries of resistance achieve? Nothing but an insignificant copy of the Roman crown that ornamented the Holy See and some tribal chiefs. The memory of the innumerable resistance fighters who were fed to the lions, burnt, and crucified has been frozen into the ice-cold chronicles of the civilization.

The Arabic, Turkish, Kurdish, Armenian, Assyrian, Circassian, and Hellenic tribes that resisted and assailed the Sassanid and Byzantine civilizations (and their heirs) left behind them only the crowns of sultans, poor tribes, subjects of Aghas, and slaves; in short, nothing but an insignificant copy of these ancient civilizations.

The heritage of the great revolutionary society of the Neolithic Age, a society adhering to the communal order and receptive to the sanctity of life, has not yet been depleted even though so much of it, both materially and morally, has been consumed by all the civilizations. This touches my heart and saddens me. We have to embrace as our own the history of those who so heroically resisted and attacked: let us embrace this as our own history—the history of democratic civilization. Of course, we have to scrutinize this history, which has been forgotten and appropriated, and then write and claim it as our own. We should never claim the history of the puny holders of crowns and palaces, and palatial subjects who were seduced by the trimmings of civilizational crowns and betrayed the labor of the tribal poor, their resistance and rebellion, their achievements and wisdom. Without this differentiation, the history of the democratic civilization cannot be written. And if this history is not written we cannot wage a successful struggle for democracy, freedom, and equality. History is our roots. Just as a tree cannot continue its existence without its roots, the human species cannot choose a free and honorable way of living if it doesn't base itself on its social history.

The prevailing civilizational history proclaims that there is only one history and no other. Unless we can break free from this reductionist and dogmatic notion of history, a democratic and socially conscious history cannot be developed. It should not be presumed that the history of the democratic civilization is lacking or void of events, alliances, and institutions. On the contrary, this history abounds with the richest materials. It has a wealth equal to that of the history of the civilization: it has its own mythology, religion, philosophy, science, and arts; it has its own authors, sages, and poets. All we need to do is to acquire the skills to evaluate, select, differentiate, and write it according to our own paradigm! I am not saying that we cannot make use of the weapons, institutions, and mentalities of the enemies and rivals. But I am saying that, in addition, we have to develop our own mentality, institutions, and weapons, and that we should base ourselves on them. If not, we can never escape being the victims of their mentality, institutions, and weapons, and becoming like them.

Eleventh: Of course, what cannot be deduced from my analysis is that civilizations will inevitably fight each other until one is eliminated and the other can claim victory, without the possibility of compromise. Notions such as these arise from an understanding of dialectics where thesis and antitheses destroy each other. As I tried to explain when I discussed my philosophical approach to the dialectics of universal development, I consider this interpretation unsuitable. Although there may well be destructive extremes, things mainly develop interconnectedly and nurturing one another like in a symbiotic relationship. This is the dialectical essence that mostly functions within the nature of society. The main state of societies is coexistence based on compromise and on not destroying but nurturing one another. There are many present and past examples illustrating this quality of societies. What is exceptional are the relationships that are destructive and excessively attuned to differences, much like the rarity of predators such as lions in the animal kingdom.

It is possible for the state civilization and democratic civilization to coexist through compromise and without destroying each other. But for this to happen they first have to recognize and respect each other's identities. To impose one's own identity upon the other through coercion, the abuse of various advantages, or manipulation is not a method of compromise but of elimination. It is the method of power and war which has infiltrated all layers of society, past and present. Europe, and to a degree the United States, has learned the necessary lessons from the power-and-war method they have so frequently used in the past four hundred years, to try to reconstruct the nation-state as federal union without completely destroying the nation-state. Because the main reason for internal and external wars are nation-state type of power organization. This is accomplished by blending arguments for human rights, civil society, democratization, etc. Clearly, they are attempting to give the old, rigid nation-state a more flexible form so that it can be turned into a tool that resolves problems. There are similar developments in Russia and China. North Korea, Iraq, Syria, Turkey, and Iran, which insist on being inflexible nation-states, are pressured more harshly than others. Iraq was chosen to be an example to all. The West wishes to emerge from the crisis, which has become chaotic, with as few losses and injuries as possible.

It has been asked whether the system constitutes a Roman-type empire. Undoubtedly, it constitutes a more effective global rule than that of Rome. Whether we call it a hegemonic power or an empire, the significance of this power's will is indisputable. It will attempt sustaining its system through continuous restoration. EU-type continental arrangements are now on the agenda for Asia, Africa, and the Americas as well, as they are trying to develop the Greater Middle East Project, and are thinking about reforming the UN. There are constant economic, cultural, and social reorganizations. Although the present civilizational system, in which we are being herded by, is going through its most chaotic period of its final age it clearly does not remain idle.

Does the system have a compromise reflex? I would say yes; this method is never omitted either. Indeed, this is the method it has most often tried and from which it has derived the most favorable results. If its opponents' awareness, organization, and desire for freedom remain weak, the system will always be the one emerging from the negotiation processes successfully. For example, this was the method used to neutralize real socialism, as we observed in the case of the USSR and China. It has used their weaknesses of modernism (the nation-state, industrialism, and positivism) to attain this victory. Assimilating and neutralizing the national liberationists and social democrats was much easier. It has also succeeded in marginalizing the anarchist, feminist, ecologic, and some other radical movements.

Despite all these indicators of its strength, the power of the system is not all there is to it. Moreover, I believe it is experiencing its weakest period yet. If the democratic civilization front is still unable to gain the desired, necessary, and rightfully earned achievements, the fundamental reason is that it has not completed the paradigm shift: it has not realized the necessary revolution in its basic scientific framework. Furthermore, it has not yet acquired a sufficient program, organization, and practical strength. These goals are not unattainable. The democratic civilizational movement can claim its own essential identity: freedom, equality, and democracy; it can attain a profound historical and social evaluation; it can construct its program, organization, and forms of action globally, regionally, and locally. The World Democratic Confederacy, and regional democratic confederacies for Asia, Africa, Europe, and Australia can be put on the agenda. Especially the Middle East Democratic Confederacy project would be a meaningful endeavor, considering the present chaotic situation in this region.

We should not repeat the tactics of the all-or-nothing approach. Neither this approach, that is either revolution or war, nor its reverse of peace to the end as propagated by Jesus, can be successful and effective against the complicated traditional notion of power. Resistance, rebellion, and constructing the new must become our way of life. Not losing the initiative in our struggle for freedom while making compromises with all the forces of the system at the right time and place: this is a more constructive method and will allow for making gains. However, I must reiterate that our identity is democratic civilization. It may enter into rapprochement with the forces of the system *on the condition* that we should never allow ourselves to be absorbed and lost in the state civilization, and we should construct and protect democratic civilization!

Twelfth: I would like to end this conclusion with a final note on my style of writing. As I began writing my defense, I mentioned that as a method I aimed to use and interweave mythological, religious, philosophical, and scientific categories of meaning. I believe I was partially successful in this.

We cannot abandon mythological discourse. Especially as the prehistorical period, Neolithic Age, Antiquity, and the history of democratic civilization are predominantly mythological in character. These societies expressed themselves strongest through legends and the dialogues of sages.

If successful sociological analysis of these are made, the historical narrative shall definitely be strengthened and become more colorful.

The religious view, not as it is but after being subjected to sociological interpretation, is also an indispensable element in the narrative of history. History, to a significant degree, is hidden in religious dogmas. There are many reasons as to why. Moreover, social developments appear in religious narrative, albeit mostly expressed in its unique style. If approached from sociological and historical perspectives, we will find religion an incredibly informative source.

It is clear that without philosophy history cannot be written. Although positivism is itself the most vulgar metaphysics, it makes the absurd claim that history should be based solely on perceived phenomena. Positivism, which is the official line and religion of capitalism, behaves as if there was never any capital in history, as if everything just suddenly descended on Europe from the heavens above. In truth, these are mythological approaches! When they turn into a religion, they become the modern age idolatry. Therefore, we should put philosophy to regular and profound use because it is an indispensable source for any historical and social narrative.

With the *scientific approach*, I do not mean overly objective or subjective forms of narration. I am aware of the similarities between perception and fact. The scientific method I use may be described as "interpretive" since I use all the sources I mentioned above in an interwoven fashion. It will be clear from the approach that I have used in my analysis that I do not rely too heavily on objectivity. Those familiar with the issues I have dealt with would also have noticed that I have not slipped into subjectivism either.

In order to constantly advance my ability to interpret, I tried to overcome the subject-object dichotomy without denying it. I hope that you will forgive my mistakes and shortcomings. If I have helped strengthen the understanding abilities of everyone who has an interest in society, then I shall be most happy.

Abdullah Öcalan visiting the ruins of the ancient city of Palmyra in Syria in the mid-1990s.

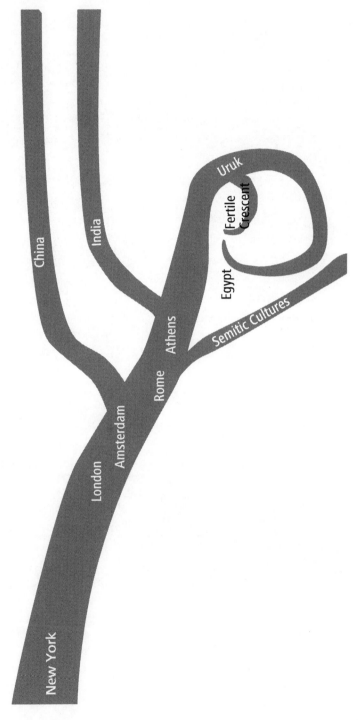

The Main Currents of Civilization
According to Abdullah Öcalan

China

India

Uruk

Fertile Crescent

Egypt

Semitic Cultures

Athens

Rome

Amsterdam

London

New York

Introduction

1. This book was originally a submission made to the European Court of Human Rights in 2008.

2. René Descartes (1596-1650) was the father of methodological skepticism and a key figure in the Scientific Revolution. Detailed discussions on this topic can be found in Section 1, Volume I of *Manifesto for a Democratic Civilization*.

3. Göbeklitepe is described by the excavator Klaus Schmidt as early Neolithic sanctuaries dating back to the tenth to eighth millennium BCE. It is 12 km to the northeast of the city of Urfa.

4. Criticism of Marxism has come from various ideologies and has included economical, ethical and empirical criticisms. Democratic socialists, anarchists, and social ecologists have criticized the notion that socialism can only be achieved through class conflict, the need for a transitional state phase, and the labor theory of value.

5. *Ana 'l-Haqq* ("I am the truth") refers to the teachings of Mansur Al-Hallaj.

Section 1

1. Expanding on a remark by Cicero, Bookchin distinguishes between first nature and second nature. The second nature, society, emerges from within the first, biological nature. See, for example, Murray Bookchin, *Remaking Society: Pathways to a Green Future* (Montreal: Black Rose Books, 1989).

2. Both the British and the Dutch East India Company, for instance, were state chartered trading companies who had been granted law-making and military powers.

3. A classic example comes from 1607, when Isaac le Maire dumped his stock in the Dutch East India Company, forcing the price down; he then bought it back at a lower price. See Murray Sale, "Japan goes Dutch," *London Review of Books*, 23:7 (April 2001).

4. The expression "Koyun kurt ile gezerdi//Fikir başka başka olmasa" is from a song called "Güzelliğin On Par Etmez" by Aşık Veysel—one of the most prominent representatives of the Anatolian ashik tradition in the 20th century.

5. *Homo homini lupus*; a variation of the proverb first coined by Plautus in the play *Asinaria*; later Thomas Hobbes drew upon the proverb in *De Cive* (*On the Citizen*).

6. Arguably, Western sociology was born when Auguste Comte in his 1848 work, *A General View of Positivism*, claimed that society operated according to absolute laws,

just like the physical world. Compte held that all societies underwent a social evolution according to a general "law of three stages." The immensely popular and influential early sociologist Herbert Spencer (1820–1903) held that evolution, which took place through natural selection and "survival of the fittest," affected social as well as biological phenomena. Like Comte, Spencer argued that all societies progressed over time and by stages; this progress is accomplished through competition. Influenced by Spencer and Darwin, Lewis H. Morgan (1818–1881) postulated three developmental stages for all societies, wherein technological progress was the force behind social progress. Morgan's significant influence on Marx and Friedrich Engels can be seen in their theory of sociocultural evolution in which the internal contradictions in a society create a series of escalating stages that will culminate in a socialist society.

7. See William Roseberry, "Marx and Anthropology," *Annual Review of Anthropology*, 26 (1997), 25-46.

8. Fernand Braudel, on the other hand, bases his interpretation of the birth of capitalism on broad observations and comparisons. Moreover, as he places his interpretation within the integrity of history, society, power, civilization-culture, and spatial development, he clarifies the problems associated with the question of method. Braudel is cautious about positivist approaches. [A.Ö.]

9. Archaeological excavations indicate that this way of life existed all over Upper Mesopotamia, especially in the inner arcs of the Zagros-Taurus Mountains (Bradostiyan, Garzan, Amanos (Nur) and Nevali Çori, Çayönü, Çemê Hallan at the inner skirts of Middle Taurus). [A.Ö.]

10. See for instance James Mellaart, *Catal Huyuk: A Neolithic Town in Anatolia* (New York: McGraw-Hill, 1967). For a different interpretation, see the work of Ian Hodder; for instance his "Çatalhöyük 2005 Archive Report" (Available at http://www.catalhoyuk.com).

11. *The Wheels of Commerce* was the second volume of Fernand Braudel's *Civilization and Capitalism: 15th-18th Century* (Palo Alto: University of California Press, 1992).

12. *Iltizam* was a form of taxation in the Ottoman Empire. Iltizams were sold off by the government to wealthy notables, who would then reap up to five times the amount they had paid by taxing the peasants and extracting agricultural production.

13. An example of this is the 1953 coup in Iran, orchestrated by the USA and Britain.

14. Examples of the former is the 1976 coup in Argentine; an example of the latter is the slaughter in 1965—of up to a million alleged communist sympathizers—carried out by General Suharto, who ousted Megawati's father, President Sukarno, to become Indonesia's

military dictator. What is less well known is that the British and American governments did not just cover up the massacre; they had a direct hand in bringing it about. Even less widely known is that the supposed pro-communist coup that triggered the crisis was almost certainly also the work of the CIA.

15. The 1323-1328 Peasant revolt in Flanders, the 1378 Revolt of the Ciompi by the Florentine textile workers, the 1381 Peasant's revolt in England, and the 1524 Stühlingen Peasants' rebellion are but a few examples of such uprisings that were brutally repressed.

16. The Diadochi were the direct successors to Alexander the Great: The dynasties of Antigonus, Lysimachus, Cassander, Ptolemy, and Seleucus divided the territories conquered by Alexander into Hellenistic empires.

17. See Asghar Ali Engineer for an insightful analysis of the role of trade and commerce in the birth and expansion of Islam. Asghar Ali Engineer, "Origin and Development of Islam," *Social Scientist*, 3:9 (April 1975), 22-44.

18. "If we are to look for an economic change correlated with the origin of Islam, then it is here that we must look," states Montgomery Watt: "In the rise of Mecca to wealth and power we have a movement from nomadic economy to a mercantile and capitalist economy." Montgomery Watt, *Mohammad at Mecca* (London, Oxford University Press, 1953).

19. The Code of Ur-Nammu, ca. 2050 BC, the Code of Hammurabi, ca. 1790 BC and the Law of the Twelve Tables, 451 BC.

20. In his 1609 treatise *Mare Liberum* ("The free sea"), Grotius argued that the sea was international territory and thus all nations were free to use it for maritime trade, thus providing ideological justification for the Dutch to use their naval power to break up the Portuguese trade monopoly in the East—and then to establish their own.

21. Following in the vein of the French jurist-philosopher Jean Bodin (1530–1596), Hobbes argued in his *Leviathan* (1651) that the sovereign should have all civil, military, judicial, and ecclesiastical powers.

22. Like Thomas More, Tommaso Campanella, Henri de Saint-Simon, and Charles Fourier.

23. The concept of the crafty man is a reference to Enki, the "the crafty God" in Sumerian mythology. Samuel Noah Cramer, *Myths of Enki, The Crafty God* (New York: Oxford University Press, 1989).

24. Indeed, through treaties enforced by her navy, Carthage long succeeded in preventing the young Roman Republic from trading in the West Mediterranean and establishing an empire that would threaten her hold over her own dominions. But at the end of the first Punic War (264 to 241 BCE), Rome incorporated Sicily into its republic and became the

dominant naval power of the Mediterranean.

25. The female presence in Rome has always enchanted me, but I think I discovered its secret when I came to understand the story of Zenobia. Rome was not just the city where all roads led to—all talented and powerful kings and queens were led to Rome as well. Interestingly enough—or rather, half-comical and half tragically—I also ended up in a latter-day Rome. May this be a result of lessons the present hegemony learned from history? Had I understood Spartacus, Saint Paul, and Giordano Bruno better I would have taken more care. If only I had read Gramsci better. Ah, the socialists! [A.Ö.]

26. In the early periods of Sumer, Egypt, and Ancient India, divinity is expressed by the feminine prefix—the masculine qualities of the deities arise only at a later stage. All known great goddesses, such as Ishtar, Inanna, Isis, Demeter, and Kybele, come form this age. [A.Ö.] See also Öcalan's *Prison Writings I: The Roots of Civilization*, particularly Section 2, Chapter 1.

27. "The farming way of life originated in the Near East some 11,000 years ago and had reached most of the European continent 5000 years later." Pontus Skoglund et al., "Origins and Genetic Legacy of Neolithic Farmers and Hunter-Gatherers in Europe," *Science*, 336:6080 (April 2012), 466-469.

28. The only region not sufficiently occupied by the old civilizational culture to prevent a radical cultural transformation was the inner regions of the Arabian Peninsula. Isolated by the vast desert, this geographical vacuum shaped the social geography of Islam. If not for this geographical feature, there would have been no rise of Islam. [A.Ö.]

29. When analyzing the reciprocal role of the capitalist sector in terms of its act to shape society, I will approach the question of social formats more concretely. [A.Ö.]

30. The establishment of wealth and private property gave rise to patriarchal societies. Instead of being passed on to the next generation of children, property and wealth were passed down through the line of the patriarch, or father. In order to ensure a rightful heir, a woman's sexuality had to be controlled.

31. A *hadith* is a saying that is attributed to Mohammad and a part of Muslim tradition.

32. "According to the Greek historian Herodotus, Cambyses misinterpreted a dream as meaning that his brother Smerdis was plotting against him, and had Smerdis secretly murdered. To Cambyses's horror, though, a priest—who happened to be named Smerdis too, and happened to look exactly like the dead Smerdis—now seized the throne, pretending to be the real Smerdis. Cambyses jumped onto his horse to rush home and reveal the fraud (and the fact that he had murdered his own brother) but accidentally stabbed himself in the thigh and died. Meanwhile, Fake Smerdis was exposed when one of his wives discovered that

he had no ears (Fake Smerdis's ears having been cut off as punishment sometime earlier). Seven noblemen then murdered Fake Smerdis and held a contest for the throne: each plotter brought his horse to a chosen place, the plan being that whoever's horse neighed first when the sun rose would become king. Darius won (he cheated). Most historians suspect that Darius actually murdered the genuine Smerdis and overthrew a priestly clique around him." Ian Morris, *Why the West Rules—for Now: The Patterns of History and What They Reveal About the Future* (London: Profile Books, 2010), 249.

33. The Reign of Terror, which was marked by mass executions of the "enemies of the revolution," span from 5 September 1793 to 28 July 1794.

34. During the Terror, Robespierre, Louis de Saint-Just, and Couthon were alleged to have formed an unofficial triumvirate (a political regime dominated by three powerful individuals) which was used against them in the coup of 9 Thermidor.

35. *Soviet* literally means "council," a body of elected representatives. During the early twentieth century, soviet became synonymous with the socialist-leaning councils of workers, peasants and soldiers during the 1905 revolution.

36. Anthony Giddens, *The Consequences of Modernity* (Palo Alto: Stanford University Press, 1990), 4-10.

37. Fernand Braudel, *Civilization and Capitalism: 15th-18th century*, vol. 1 (New York: Harper & Row, 1982), 229-230.

Section 2

1. The *Ilmihal* is a concise manual of Islamic faith, worship, and ethics.

2. Immanuel Wallerstein, *Historical Capitalism and Capitalist Civilization* (London: Verso, 1995), 98.

3. Theodor W. Adorno, *Minima Moralia*; in Dennis Redmond's 2005 translation (Available at http://www.marxists.org). Another translation is "Wrong life cannot be lived rightly."

4. In sociology, the iron cage is Max Weber's term for the increased rationalization of social life, particularly in Western capitalist societies. The "iron cage" thus traps individuals in systems based purely on teleological efficiency, rational calculation, and control.

5. This period is also referred to as the Palaeolithic Period, or Old Stone Age (from the Greek *palaios*, "old," and *lithos*, "stone," referring to the knapped stone tools that characterize the period) and the period of primitive savagery. However, the sociological term is *Era of primitive communism*. [A.Ö.]

6. The Tell Halaf period occurred from about 6,100 to 5,500 BCE in what is today called

7. There is a general agreement that the Ubaid culture has begun before 5,000 BCE and ended with the beginning of Uruk period around 3,800 BCE.

8. I discuss the profound influence of these civilizations in more detail in Part 1 of my *Prison Writings I: The Roots of Civilization*. [A.Ö.]

9. As seen, for instance, in the seven tablets known as *Enuma Elish*.

10. This is modern-day Niffer, or Nuffar, in south-eastern Iraq. Nippur was one of the world's longest-lived sites: from the prehistoric Ubaid period 5000 BCE until about 800 CE.

11. The Weidner tablet suggests that the Akkadian Empire fell as divine retribution because Sargon transferred the holy city status from Nippur to Babylon.

12. There are lots of discussions and research into this. One such example is Eva Cancik-Kirschbaum, Nicole Brisch and Jesper Eidem, eds., *Constituent, Confederate, and Conquered Space in Upper Mesopotamia: The Emergence of the Mittani State* (Berlin: De Gruyter, 2014).

13. According to *The Online Etymology Dictionary*, Islam literally means "submission" (to the will of God), from the root *aslama* "he resigned, he surrendered, he submitted," causative conjunction of *salima* "he was safe" and related to salam "peace."

14. Öcalan here refers to the Turkish word for republic, *cumhuriyet*, which comes from an Arabic root that means *coming together* or *forming a community*.

15. In response to the plea by Pope Sixtus IV, a Christian army (consisting mainly of Neapolitan and Hungarian troops) besieged Otranto in May 1481 to take back the city and to prevent Rome from suffering the same fate as Constantinople. Two days after the siege began, Mehmed II died, and the resulting succession crisis prevented the Turks from sending reinforcements, and the Turkish garrison in Otranto surrendered.

Section 3

1. The Napoleonic Code was a French civil law code introduced in March 1804, which came to influence the entire European continent following the Napoleonic wars (1803–1815).

2. Adorno's quote is from *Kulturkritik und Gesellschaft* (1951); it is more famously known as the statement that "There can be no poetry after Auschwitz."

3. "The dialectic of Hegel was placed upon its head; or rather, turned off its head, on which it was standing, and placed upon its feet." Friedrich Engels, "Ludwig Feuerbach and the End of Classical German Philosophy," *Die Neue Zeit*, Nos. 4 and 5 (1886).

4. Öcalan detailed his thoughts on this topic in the fourth and fifth volumes of *Manifesto for*

a Democratic Civilization. These volumes were published as *Ortadoğu'da Uygarlık Krizi ve Demokratik Uygarlık Çözümü* (2010) and *Kürt Sorunu ve Demokratik Ulus Çözümü* (2012); both to be translated.

5. Abraham is widely accepted as the father of Abrahamic religions, but information about his identity is all disguised as mythology, just as is the case with the prophets Moses and Jesus. There is a need for comprehensive sociological research, so that the facts may become more clear; but, like many researchers, Öcalan assumes that Abraham came from Urfa. Harran, mentioned several times in the book of *Genesis*, is located only a few miles from Urfa.

6. Spinoza's most widely read book, *Ethics*, was published after his death in 1677. Here, he wrote that "the highest activity a human being can attain is learning for understanding, because to understand is to be free."

7. The Jews fleeing from the Reconquista to the Ottoman Empire had been settled in Salonica (modern day Thessaloniki). The city became the center of Jewish life in the Ottoman Empire.

8. Leviathan is a sea monster referenced in the Tanakh, or the Old Testament. *Leviathan* is also the title of the book Thomas Hobbes published in 1651, whose name derives from this biblical Leviathan. The work concerns the structure of society and legitimate government, and is regarded as one of the earliest and most influential examples of social contract theory. Here, Leviathan is used as a synonym for the state.

Section 4

1. In *Anti-Dühring*, Engels describes the modern state like this: "The modern state, no matter what its form, is essentially a capitalist machine, the state of the capitalists, the ideal personification of the total national capital."

2. In Arabic, El-Lāh (*allah*) actually means the-God. *Lāh* is related to the Hebrew word *El*, God.

Conclusion

1. *City of the Sun (La città del Sole)* is a utopian work by Tommaso Campanella (1602).

2. The "Habiru" or "Apiru" was the name given by various Sumerian, Egyptian, Akkadian, Hittite, Mitanni, and Ugaritic sources (dated, roughly, between 1800 BC and 1100 BC) to a group of people living as nomadic invaders in areas of the Fertile Crescent from Northeastern Mesopotamia and Iran to the borders of Egypt in Canaan. Often, the Habiru are considered to be the early Hebrews.

Index